The Governance
of Common Property
in the Pacific Region

The Governance
of Common Property
in the Pacific Region

edited by Peter Larmour

Australian
National
University

E PRESS

Published by ANU E Press
The Australian National University
Canberra ACT 0200, Australia
Email: anuepress@anu.edu.au
This title is also available online at http://epress.anu.edu.au

National Library of Australia Cataloguing-in-Publication entry

Title: The governance of common property in the Pacific region / edited by Peter Larmour.

ISBN: 9781922144744 (pbk.) 9781922144751 (ebook)

Subjects: Commons--Pacific Area.
          Natural resources, Communal--Pacific Area.
          Land tenure--Pacific Area.
          Right of property--Pacific Area.

Other Authors/Contributors:
          Larmour, Peter

Dewey Number: 333.2

First published by National Centre for Development Studies, 1997.

This edition © 2013 ANU E Press

Contents

Figures and tables

Symbols used in tables

n.a.	not applicable
..	not available

Abbreviations

ANU	The Australian National University
BQCMB	Beverly-Qamanirjuaq Caribou Management Board
CPR	common pool resources
DFAT	Department of Foreign Affairs and Trade, Australia
EEZ	Exclusive Economic Zones
ESCAP	Economic and Social Commission for Asia and the Pacific
FFA	Forum Fisheries Agency
FFC	Forum Fisheries Committee
FSM	Federated States of Micronesia
GDP	gross domesic product
IFA	Inuvialuit Final Agreement
ILG	Incorporated Land Group
LMP	Land Mobilisation Program
MARPOL	International Convention on the Prevention of Pollution from Ships
MTC	minimum terms and conditions
NLTB	Native Land Trust Board
NWMB	Nunavut Wildlife Management Board
NWT	Northwest Territories (Canada)
OPA	Office of Pacific Island Affairs
PNG	Papua New Guinea
SPC	South Pacific Commission
UNCLOS	United Nations Convention on the Law of the Sea
UNDP	United Nations Development Programme

Contributors

Chris Ballard is a Research Fellow in the Resource Management in Asia-Pacific project at the Research School of Pacific and Asian Studies, ANU.

Satish Chand is a Postdoctoral Fellow at the Economics Division, Research School of Pacific and Asian Studies, ANU.

Rod Duncan is a PhD student, Economics Department, Stanford University.

Ron Duncan is the Executive Director of the National Centre for Development Studies, ANU.

Colin Hunt lectures at the National Centre for Development Studies, ANU and specialises in ecological and resource economies.

Kilyali Kalit coordinates activities for the World Wildlife Fund in Port Moresby, Papua New Guinea.

Sir Hugh Kawharu is the Foundation Professor of Anthropology and Maori Studies, The University of Auckland.

Andrew A.L. Lakau is Executive Director of the Pacific Land Tenure and Policy Centre in Lae, Papua New Guinea.

Peter Larmour is the Director of Graduate Studies in Development Administration at the National Centre for Development Studies, ANU.

Janaline Oh works in the Office of Pacific Island Affairs, Department of Foreign Affairs and Trade, Canberra, on regional resources issues.

Henry Reynolds is an Australia Research Council Senior Research Fellow, James Cook University.

Deborah Bird Rose is a Senior Fellow of the North Australia Research Unit, ANU, and has worked with Aboriginal claimants on land claims and in land disputes, and with the Aboriginal Land Commissioner.

R. Gerard Ward is Professor of Human Geography, Research School of Pacific and Asian Studies, ANU.

Peter J. Usher is Chairman of the Wildlife Management Advisory Council, Northwest Territory, one of the co-management bodies established under the Inuvialuit Final Agreement in the Canadian Western Arctic.

Elspeth Young is a geographer and Director, Graduate Studies in Environmental Management and Development, National Centre for Development Studies, ANU.

Foreword

With the inevitable lessening of the importance of traditional forms of management of land and water resources in Pacific island countries accompanying the development of the state and the internationalisation of these economies, common property problems have arisen in many natural resource areas. This publication covers many of the problem areas which have arisen and discusses various approaches to better management.

The papers in the volume were initially presented at a conference organised by the National Centre for Development Studies and held at The Australian National University on 19–20 September 1996. The conference was generously financed by AusAID and the Resource Management in Asia-Pacific project of the Research School of Pacific and Asian Studies. The Centre is grateful for their support.

The Centre also extends its appreciation to Dayaneetha De Silva and other publications staff of NCDS for their fine editorial and pagemaking efforts in bringing the publication to fruition as well as Centre staff led by Jennie Colman for organising the conference. It also thanks the ANU Cartography Unit for their help in preparing the maps for publication.

Ron Duncan
Executive Director
NCDS

Introduction

Peter Larmour

Common property has often been regarded as an obstacle to development and best—or inevitably—replaced by private or state ownership.
However, there are now many well-documented examples of
successful management of open-access resources, and experiments in
'co-management' by users, owners, and government officials. The idea
that the government should intervene to remedy the defects of
common property, perhaps by registration, is now contested by a
celebration of indigenous systems of self-management (Bromley 1989,
Bromley and Cernea 1989). Government intervention may sometimes
make things worse. Common property claims are also part of
indigenous peoples' defence and reaffirmation of political sovereignty.

The following chapters offer perspectives on common property
from different academic disciplines, and from different islands and
regions within and around the Pacific ocean. The disciplines include
Geography, Economics, Anthropology, Law, History, and Political
Science. The Pacific region includes settler societies like Australia,
New Zealand and Canada, where indigenous systems were margina-
lised, and islands like Papua New Guinea and Fiji, where they were
conserved, and even strengthened during and after colonial rule. The
word 'governance' in the title recognises the political context of
property rights, and refers to the idea that order, including systems of

property, is the outcome of interactions between governments, markets and communities (Larmour 1996a, 1996b).

What is common property?

Bromley defines property in terms of rights and duties towards a stream of benefits flowing from the resource. He notes that rights to use private property may be qualified, for example, by zoning legislation. He goes on to define common property as follows

> The management group (the owners) have a right to exclude non-members, and non-members have a duty to abide by this exclusion. Individual members of the management group (the co-owners) have both rights and duties with respect to usage rates and maintenance of the thing owned (Bromley 1989:872).

By contrast, in non-property there is

> ...no defined group of users or owners and so the benefit stream is available to anyone. Individuals have both privilege and no right with respect to usage rates and maintenance of the asset. The asset is an open access resource (Bromley 1989:872).

The same resource may be treated in some circumstances as common property and in others as open access, or something in between. Common property regimes may dissolve into the free-for-all of open access. Equally, property regimes (common, private, or state) may be established over formerly open-access regimes—the creation of Exclusive Economic Zones would be a good example.

The distinction between common and open-access regimes can be explained in terms of the characteristics of the resource, particularly excludability and rivalry.

In Table 1, excludability refers to the technical difficulty and expense of excluding people from using the resource. Rivalry refers to the degree to which one person's consumption eats into another's. Roads, for example, are mostly excludable. Users can be charged a toll, and non-payers excluded. They are also mostly non-rivalrous, except when they become congested. Public goods are famously non-rivalrous and non-excludable, but there are few examples beyond clean air or even, perhaps, gravity (Keohane and Ostrom 1994:416). Common pool resources, however, are both rivalrous and non-excludable.

Excludability and rivalry are matters of degree, and excludability is a technical and economic matter. Exclusion is often technically possible, but not worth the cost, for example fencing a farm. Changes in technology may also make exclusion cheaper—electronic sensing makes it easier to charge vehicles entering crowded town centres. In Table 1, the offshore fishery is to some extent rivalrous: if I catch a fish, you cannot, but many fish escape us both and die naturally. Exclusion is technically possible, but at the cost of maritime surveillance, patrol boats and so on. It may be managed as common property or left to open access.

While the characteristics of any particular resource may limit the possible ways it may be managed, property regimes are also determined by other historical and political factors, such as colonisation or democratisation.

Table 1 Excludability and rivalry

	non-rivalrous	rivalrous
excludable	toll goods *e.g. uncongested roads*	private goods *e.g. ice cream*
non-excludable	public goods *e.g. clean air*	common pool resources *e.g. offshore fisheries*

Hardin's powerful image of the 'tragedy of the commons' is often blamed for obscuring the distinction between common property and open access resources (McCay and Acheson 1990:6–10, Feeny, Hanna and McEvoy 1996). Ostrom is particularly scathing about the policy conclusions typically drawn from Hardin's model: privatisation, or state ownership as 'the only way' (1990:8–15), and she goes on to identify conditions for long running self-management of what she calls CPRs (common pool, or open access, resources). She defines a 'common pool resource' as

> a natural or man-made resource system that is sufficiently large to make it costly (but not impossible) to exclude potential beneficiaries from obtaining benefits from its use (Ostrom 1990:30).

The conditions for self-management of such a resource are
1. clearly defined boundaries
2. congruence between appropriation and provision rules and local conditions
3. collective choice arrangements

4. monitoring
5. graduated sanctions
6. conflict resolution mechanisms
7. minimal recognition of rights to organise
8. (For CPRs that are part of larger systems) nested enterprises (Ostrom 1990:90).

Taken together, these are quite a demanding set of conditions, explaining why common property regimes may easily dissolve into open access.

Arguments against common property

David Hume classically put the arguments against common property in the form of a parable about 'draining the meadow.'

> Two neighbours may agree to drain a meadow, which they possess in common: because it is easy for them to know each others' mind; and each must perceive that the immediate consequence of his failing in his part is the abandoning the whole project. But it is very difficult, and indeed impossible, that a thousand persons should agree in any such action; it being difficult for them to concert so complicated a design, and still more difficult for them to execute it; while each seeks a pretext to free himself of the trouble and expense, and would lay the whole burden on others (1911[1740]:239).

Hume raised two issues, which are now called 'transaction costs', which are the costs of making and keeping agreements, and the problem of the 'free rider', who benefits from the activity, but shirks from participation. The idea of transaction costs has allowed New Institutional Economists to explain the existence, and persistence, of non-market institutions which (they argue) arise in order to reduce transaction costs. The existence of firms, private property, and the state itself have been explained in this way (Williamson 1975, Demsetz 1967, North 1990).

The common property of indigenous people is often used as an example. Demsetz (1967) refers to an historical study of the fur trade in Labrador, noting how the local Indians began marking off and excluding other families from defined hunting areas as the trade developed. More empirically, Trosper (1978) investigated the relative efficiency of American Indians ranching on land leased from tribes through the Bureau of Indian Affairs. Trosper finds these American Indians as financially and technically efficient as their non-Indian neighbours, but investing less, perhaps because of uncertainty over lease renewal (a transaction cost), or because of knowledge of large coal deposits under the land, and the likelihood of eventual strip-mining. In any case he is cautious in recommending privatisation, recognising the political, historical and ethical point that

> the federal government has created a connection between individual land ownership and eradication of tribal existence (Trosper 1978: 514).

Clearly, there are transaction costs in making and keeping agreements about the use of common property, and institutions such as cooperatives, trusteeship, and majority voting rules may be created to reduce those costs—for example, the lengthy negotiations over the law of the sea and the institution of Exclusive Economic Zones, or the Forum Fisheries Agency in the South Pacific.

Michael Taylor and Sara Singleton (1993) use ideas about transaction costs to extend Ostrom's 'design rules'. They praise Ostrom for isolating the features of successful common pool resource management, but fault her for failing to provide an explanation for 'why the successful groups are able to monitor themselves and why endogenous sanctioning alone suffices' (Taylor and Singleton 1993:207).

They argue that the successful groups have characteristics 'in virtue of which the transaction costs of an endogenous solution are relatively low' (Taylor and Singleton 1993:199). These are

- stability of relations among members: they expect to be dealing with each other for a long time, over a number of interactions
- multiplex relations: they deal with each other in different contexts
- direct relations: they deal with each other face to face, unmediated by officials
- shared beliefs and preferences.

They summarise these characteristics as 'community', arguing that it reduces the search, bargaining and monitoring and enforcement costs of managing common pool resources. There is less uncertainty about what each other wants. Tradeoffs are easier to identify and implement. Monitoring and informal enforcement are less costly. Equally, 'economic inequality, and ethnic, linguistic, religious or other forms of cultural heterogeneity', weaken community, and increase transaction costs (Taylor and Singleton 1993:200).

The politics of distribution of property rights

While clear property rights may enhance efficiency, the allocation of clear rights has political implications. A good illustration is Bates' (1995) discussion of Coase's famous example of the railway that pollutes the farmland through which it travels. The example originally came from Pigou, who saw the 'uncompensated damage done to surrounding woods by sparks from railway engines' as a case for regulation (quoted in Coase 1960:31). Coase's criticism was that the harm was in a sense reciprocal, and the economic issue was the optimal mix of trains and woods, not the extinction of one or the other. The case gets more interesting if the railway cuts through customary land in a colony. Issues of 'who was there first', and whether governments create or merely recognise rights, would be important.

Coase argued that a system of property rights, rather than government regulation, could force the railway to take into account these externalities. But the distribution of property rights would not matter: either the farmers' right to be free of pollution would force the railway to compensate them, or reduce train traffic. Or the railway company's right to pollute would force the farmers to pay the company to reduce its traffic in order to protect their farm income. Either way, if it is easy to reach agreements, the traffic is reduced to a level that takes into account the pollution it causes, and to an economically optimal mix of trains and farms.

Bates (1995) notices the political point: the relative ability of farmers and railway companies to put pressure on the government to allocate the property rights to one, or the other. Farmers, for example, may be better, or worse, organised than railway owners. Authoritarian regimes may be more sympathetic to concentrated interests, like railway owners, than to diffuse interests, like farmers. In democratic systems, however, farmers' votes may count. In developing countries the government may favour the interests of exporters, or domestic rather than foreign firms. The railway may run through a government's political support base, or through that of its opponents.

Clear (and hence efficient) property rights in the Pacific region are often very unevenly distributed between different ethnic groups, between foreigners and locals, between income groups, and between genders. Freehold tends to be owned by non-indigenous, higher-income, men. Customary land tends to be owned by indigenous, lower-income men and women. Foreigners are generally excluded from both. These categories of people differ in their political rights, and in their ability to organise themselves in order to influence government policy.

Nor are transaction costs evenly distributed. Atwood (1990:666) argues that clarification may reduce transaction costs for some people (for instance, outsiders) but increase them for others (such as insiders, who now have to pay survey and registration fees whereas previously they could rely on the cheaper, but secure, informal methods they were familiar with). The cost of lawyers often weighs disproportionately on the poor. For example, the recent Land Commission in Cook Islands found a strong popular opinion that transaction costs biased outcomes in favour of the rich and well-educated, both within families, and in the courts. The Commission found that ambiguity about voting rules within families 'has allowed the cunning and shrewd among us to abuse the system' (*Cook Islands Press*, Sunday 7–14 April 1996). Once in court

> The procedural rules and courtroom environment have become more formal and legalistic, causing great dissatisfaction, discomfort, distrust and added expense to our people (*Cook Islands Press* 1996:2).

The Commission recommended reducing such transaction costs by specifying voting rules more clearly, relying more on written genealogies, excluding lawyers, and registering landholdings (presumably increasing the tax burden, which might also fall unevenly).

Papua New Guinea's 'land mobilisation' program, though often obscure about its intentions, seems to be particularly aimed at reducing the transaction costs for outsiders. This reduction might be at the cost of increasing them for insiders who 'knew their way around' the informal system, or became insiders before they transacted—for example, by marriage.

The role of the government in self-managed common property resources

To talk of the role of government in self-management may sound contradictory, but all common property resources are now embedded in states, and the reach of states is extending into Exclusive Economic Zones, Antarctica, and space (though some of these states, such as Somalia or Liberia, have collapsed from within). Particular government agencies are often appropriators, as well as regulators, of CPRs, in what Ostrom calls the 'rich mix' (1990:184) of public and private agencies, such as those involved in the governance of the California water table. Local governments and local courts are often involved, or competitive with, the institutions of self-management. Indeed, it is hard to tell where 'the government' stops and 'non-government' or 'self-government' begins.

The structures of government seem to matter. Federal, or semi-federal systems, such as those in Micronesia and Melanesia allow for the nesting of locally variable property systems within a supportive national framework, as in Papua New Guinea's experiments with different provincial land registration systems. Parliamentary politics puts a brake on centrally initiated changes in land legislation. Explaining the absence of much land reform in the South Pacific, Crocombe argued

> political leaders considered almost any modification of tenure too sensitive for the voting public, and too vulnerable to misrepresentation by any political opposition (1987: 394).

An independent national judiciary, however, is not necessarily one which would be supportive of local common pool resources. It may be able to provide local 'conflict resolution mechanisms' (Ostrom's rule 6), but at the cost of creating opportunities to appeal that may undermine the legitimacy of local regimes. Similarly, court support for individual human rights, such as freedom of movement, or freedom not to participate in commons-maintaining activities, may also undermine common pool resources.

Government strategies towards common pool resources

Government approaches towards common pool resource managers will depend on the constitutional and political situation, as well as the technical character of the resource. In colonial situations, or where indigenous people are a minority, the government may simply marginalise them.

> If the state disregards the interests of those segments of the population largely dependent upon common property resources—then external threats to common property will not receive the same governmental response as would a threat to private property (Bromley and Cernea 1989:19).

In postcolonial situations, the government may find common pool resource regimes politically suspect, or an obstacle to their programs of nationalist modernisation, as Anderson observed in Malaysia

> the government choked off all efforts by the fishermen to help them-
> selves or adapt to their situation. It replaced grassroots democracy in
> the cooperatives and elsewhere with appointed party men; it abolished
> the one political party that spoke to and for the fishermen; it stopped
> the conflict over capturing the commons; it tried to regulate fishing
> effort (Anderson 1990:334).

Often it seems the best that a government can do is keep out. Thus
Wade concludes from his study of the management of common
property within 'village republics' in India,

> the less the state can, or wishes to, undermine locally based
> authorities, and the less the state can enforce private property rights
> effectively, the better the chances of success (Wade 1988:216).

But the state may have a more positive role, too.

> If a political regime does not provide arenas in which low cost,
> enforceable agreements can be reached, it is very difficult to meet the
> potentially high costs of self-organisation (Ostrom 1990:146).

Several of Ostrom's design rules for long running common pool
resources point to more specific conditions. First, individuals affected
by the rules must be able to participate in modify them (rule 3). Some
minimum political rights of participation must be recognised,
including participation by women, who are often users of common
pool resources. The central government has to recognise the local
users' rights to organise themselves (rule 7).

> If external governmental officials presume that only they have the
> authority to set the rules, then it will be very difficult for local
> appropriators to sustain a rule governed CPR over the long run
> (Ostrom 1990:101).

Even rights to get around the common pool resource regime, and
appeal to some external authority, may undermine it. Such appeals
might be to courts, as mentioned above, but also to political authorities
called in to protect their supporters or constituents. More generally,
Ostrom's rule implies that central governments should not feel politically
threatened by local organisations, undermine or seek to incorporate
them into the ruling party.

Ostrom concludes that common pool resource regimes should be
nested: organised by levels, with the smaller fitting within the larger.
Rules at one level, without the support of appropriate rules at the level
above, or below, may not work. This rule implies, at least, some

dialogue between levels, and might be threatened, for example, by different parties or ethnic groups being in power at different levels.

At first sight these design rules seem unexceptionably benign, and consistent with devolved, democratic systems like those in place in most of the Pacific region. But the prohibition on appeals, and Ostrom's endorsement of self enforcement, rather than using the police, in rule 5 already challenge some conceptions of the 'rule of law', and modern states' claims to what Max Weber famously called 'the monopoly of the legitimate use of violence'.

The chapters

Next, I want summarise each chapter, and then discuss how they conceptualise common property, and what they have to say about governance.

The first two chapters deal generally with the Pacific islands. Ward's is concerned with changes taking place to customary land tenure in the islands. He finds a spontaneous tendency towards individualisation, in spite of government declarations of support for traditional, communal ownership. In some cases what now counts as traditional was a product of colonial rule, or, in Tonga, nineteenth century land reform. Everywhere, the pragmatic, adaptive character of 'custom' is stifled by codification, and people seek ways around the law to achieve their purposes.

Chand and Duncan's chapter finds the Pacific island nations unable to support their growing populations in a condition of 'subsistence affluence', but is optimistic about their prospects for growth through trade and specialisation. Customary tenure, which is appropriate for subsistence agriculture, must therefore give way to freehold or long leases that allow for trade and investment in land. They identify sources of supply and demand for changes in land tenure: opportunities for emigration, for example, may reduce the demand for change in tenure, while entrenched traditional institutions may be reluctant to supply it. They go on to propose a formal model of the factors that determine changes in land values.

The next three chapters focus on mining in Papua New Guinea, where practically all the land is under customary ownership. Ballard and Lakau are particularly concerned with the moral consequences of large-scale mining, and the differences it opens up between what Ballard calls the 'resource élite' and the 'downstream majority'.

Ballard shows how land tenure is deeply embedded in wider political relationships, and is not easily reduced to a code that everyone can agree on. He finds landowners gaining steadily increasing shares of mining revenues, while mining companies provide the local services that the state cannot afford.

Lakau finds that custom provides an equivocal guide to the ownership of minerals. On the one hand, valuable mineral resources like clay and salt might be regarded as belonging to the group that owned the land. On the other hand, landowners might be regarded as trustees for a wider, public or common interest, in looking after rivers and gravel. The law in Papua New Guinea, however, now vests mineral rights in the state.

Duncan and Duncan address the insecurity of the contracts that have been drawn up, and often broken, between mining companies and landowners. Using a model of strikes in labour negotiations, they notice that very different information is available to each side; that each side's interests change during the time of the contract; that contracts cannot cover all contingencies; and that the government is not a disinterested arbiter between mining companies and landowners. They go on to propose a set of recommendations that might provide more stability.

The next four chapters deal with the very different circumstances of New Zealand, Canada and Australia where indigenous minorities are reclaiming rights to land and natural resources lost to trappers, settlers, pastoralists and governments.

Kawharu's chapter deals with two institutional consequences of the recovery of the Treaty of Waitangi as the foundation of New Zealand's constitution. The first, which began in 1982, was the link between existing Maori land law and the Treaty. Kawharu describes how the New Zealand Maori Council sought to reverse a long process of individualisation of Maori title, by linking the law to the protection of kinship values expressed in the treaty. The second, which followed the New Zealand government's attempt to put a 'fiscal envelope' around future compensation claims, concerned Maori representation at national level. Kawharu describes the difficulties in reconciling the need for a peak body, with the more local and tribal basis of traditional Maori politics, and the non-tribal basis in which many Maori now live their day-to-day lives.

Usher's chapter also deals with constitutional changes and the renegotiation of relationships with Canada's indigenous people. His main concern is with institutions for the co-management of particular resources that have been set up, sometimes *ad hoc*, and sometimes in permanent settlement of indigenous claims. Though formally advisory, these boards or committees include equal numbers of government officials and indigenous representatives. Usher finds several conditions for success: that the structures are negotiated, rather than invitations being issued to join existing structures; that aboriginal members are accountable representatives; that only claims-based boards are permanent. Usher finds co-management particularly useful in dealing with migratory species that cross boundaries, and in negotiating access for outsiders.

Reynold's chapter points to a paradox in the Australian High Court's famous Mabo judgment that found, in some circumstances, 'native title' had survived in Australia. While overthrowing the idea that Australia was *terra nullius* in terms of land tenure, by allowing that native title had existed, and might have survived, the Court preserved the idea that the country was *terra nullius* in terms of sovereignty. It accepted the idea the Crown was the first and only sovereign, and that this sovereignty was established instantly, absolutely, and throughout the country (and so able to extinguish native title, by law, if it wished). Instead, Reynolds proposes a doctrine of aboriginal sovereignties, surviving until extinguished piecemeal by settlement, but persisting in a more plural vision of Australia.

Rose's chapter also reflects on the Mabo decision, but in a way that, following the literature on common property, links management to ownership. The Aboriginal rights belatedly uncovered by the Australian High Court are related to responsibilities for environmental management, by means that included fire-stick farming, and protecting the places where kangaroos foraged during droughts. Totems, she argues, provide the link between rights and responsibilities. Having traced the intellectual history of anthropological theory of totemism, which typically used Australian data, Rose proposes an ecological explanation: totems are associated with duties towards the management of particular plants and animals.

Thus Rose finds governance of resources to be a matter of differentiated but complementary responsibilities often exercised at a regional scale. Restraint is as important as activity. Self-interest is not necessarily opposed to the interests of others, the interests of the collectivity, and the continuity of other species. Governance is achieved through common property institutions like totemism.

The chapters by Hunt and Oh deal with the management of fisheries in the South Pacific on two levels. Hunt's paper shifts between the intergovernmental level, and the subgovernmental level, at which inshore resources are managed by coastal communities (with some government support, perhaps through council by-laws). Hunt shows how these two management regimes may interact, for example when tuna boats collect bait from inshore fisheries. Oh's paper looks in greater detail at the level at which governments have negotiated to manage highly migratory species within 200 nautical mile Exclusive Economic Zones. In this game, the small states are nominally equal players with much larger countries. Oh shows how this form of management imposes duties as well as rights on the claimants.

Finally, Kalit and Young's paper brings the regions and some of the themes together in a comparison of Papua New Guinean and Australian aboriginal ideas about the management of common property, and recommends the creation of intermediate institutions to help landowners manage and exploit their resources in a sustainable way.

Ideas about common property

Several of the chapters adopt Bromley's definition of common property, as distinct from private property, and an open-access free-for-all. But they introduce important elaborations, qualifications and quite different conceptualisations as well.

Ward raises the question of equality among members of the group managing the resource. He notices that common property might involve great inequality within a group. He also is careful to distinguish the legal concept of 'customary land' from the implication that customary ownership is necessarily communal. He finds historical precedents for individual customary ownership, and alienability of customary land, and suggests that in some cases the idea of communal ownership may be a colonial construction, perhaps no longer relevant to the needs of independent citizens.

Chand and Duncan take the traditional negative view of common property, noting the problem of free riders, and the disincentives that common property may pose for investment. They note that self-management may work only for small groups, with effective norms, and see a global tendency towards clear, individualised, transferable titles.

Ballard recognises the 'insistence' with which people in Melanesia identify with land, and so suggests a more reciprocal relationship between owners and land. Individuals and groups constitute themselves, as individuals and as groups, by referring to land. They do not exist before, or separately from it.

Lakau's chapter makes the important distinction between group or clan interests, and broader 'societal' or 'public' interests. The common interests of a group may be just as 'selfish' as that of an individual, while groups may have common interests that they can only satisfy by acting together as members of a wider society (and face similar disincentives to act together, as Oh and Hunt's discussions of the two levels of management of fisheries suggest). Lakau then goes on to raise doubts about whether the state, as presently constituted, can plausibly act in the societal or public interest—particularly if, as in mining, it is a player as well as a referee. Landowning groups, he suggests, may 'free ride' on society. Duncan and Duncan also discuss the conflicts of interest faced by the state using mining revenues to fund its budget, and a similar suspicion of the state underlies Kalit and Young's argument for intermediate bodies (though these may be in conflict too). Similar issues about the role of peak bodies representing the interests of tribes are raised by Kawharu.

Governance

In almost all of the chapters, issues of resource management slide quickly into questions of governance, just as questions of land tenure become quickly questions of sovereignty. Ward noticed the overlapping claims to sovereignty that underlay competing and confusing systems of tenure. He also saw the legitimacy of politicians, and of islands states generally, tied up in sometimes unrealistic claims about tradition. Chand and Duncan explicitly recognises the intertwining of ownership and governance in traditional systems, such as Tonga. They see central governments as one of the causes for the breakdown of village level self-management, while government institutions that entrench custom (such as Fiji's Native Land Trust Board) limit the supply of change.

For Ballard, land provides a 'foothold' from which local people may gain attention from the state. But the state turns out to be a figment ('only a concept'), franchising out the delivery of services, and unable to command any moral authority at local level. Lakau confronts these questions more directly, questioning the private interests and competence of state officials. For Duncan and Duncan, the lack of neutrality of the government is one source of contract instability, while one function of an ideal state (if it could be conjured up) would be to provide the stable framework which long-term, sustainable investment requires.

The chapters on New Zealand, Canada and Australia deal with questions of sovereignty more subtly and more directly. In Kawharu's reading of the Treaty of Waitangi, Maori and Europeans exchanged sovereignty for *rangatiratanga* (trusteeship or, more broadly, 'good government') that protected and maintained Maori institutions and way of life (a part of the deal that had lapsed until the recovery of the Treaty). Usher questions the possibility of sovereignty at subnational level in an era in which nation–states are in decline in the face of globalisation. The co-management arrangements he commends are explicitly not to do with self government. Indeed the idea that the boards are advisory to ministers goes back to very traditional concepts of the 'sovereignty of parliament'. Reynolds floats the idea of pluralistic, divisible, and graded, sovereignties, against the absolute claims to sovereignty embodied in Australian executive, parliamentary and judicial institutions.

Sovereignty and governance are also in the foreground in Oh and Hunt's discussions of fisheries. Sovereign power is invoked to support local management regimes in Hunt's recommendations for conservation by-laws. For Oh, sovereign governments are themselves players in an international management regime (which might, therefore, be unprofitably excluding non-government actors). The United Nations' Law of the Sea Convention however, grants them 'sovereign rights' rather than absolute sovereignty over the Exclusive Economic Zones.

The government is more in the background in Kalit and Young's bottom-up approach, but they note the importance of a benign political climate for self-management, and the contradictions that Ward's first chapter noted between the government's role as custodian of custom and promoter of development. Decentralised or intermediate institutions may embody these contradictions by turning them into intergovernmental relations.

References

Anderson, E., 1990. 'A Malaysian tragedy of the commons', in B. McCay and J. Acheson (eds), *The Question of the Commons: the culture and ecology of communal resources*, University of Arizona, Tuscon:327–43.

Atwood, D., 1990. 'Land registration in Africa: the impact on agricultural production', *World Development* 18:659–71.

Bates, R., 1995. 'Social dilemmas and rational individuals: an assessment of the new institutionalism', in J. Hariss, J. Hunter and C. Lewis (eds), *The New Institutional Economics and Third World Development*, Routledge, London and New York:27–48.

Bromley, D., 1989. 'Property relations and economic development: the other land reform', *World Development* 17:867–77.

Bromley, D., and Chapagain, D., 1984. 'The village against the center: resource depletion in South Asia', *American Journal of Agricultural Economics* 66:868–73.

Bromley, D. and Cernea, M., 1989. *'The Management of Common Property Natural Resources: some conceptual and operational fallacies'*, World Bank Discussion Paper 57, The World Bank, Washington DC.

Coase, R., 1960. 'The problem of social cost', *The Journal of Law and Economics* 3:1–44.

Cook Islands Press, Sunday 7–14, April 1996.

Cramb, R., and Wills, I., 1990. 'The role of traditional institutions in rural development: community based land tenure and government land policy in Sarawak, Malaysia', *World Development* 18(3):347–60.

Crocombe, R., 1987. 'Land reform: prospects for prosperity', in R. Crocombe (ed.), *Land Tenure in the Pacific*, University of the South Pacific, Suva:368–98.

Demsetz, H., 1967. 'Towards a theory of property rights', *The American Economic Review* 57(2):347–59.

Feeny, D., Hanna, S. and McEvoy, A., 1996. 'Questioning the assumptions of the Tragedy of the Commons model of fisheries', *Land Economics* 72(2):187–205.

Hume, D., 1911[1740], *A Treatise of Human Nature*, Dent, London.

Keohane, R., and Ostrom, E., 1994. 'Introduction', Special Issue on Local Commons and Global Interdependence, *Journal of Theoretical Politics* 6(4):403–28.

Larmour, P., 1996a. *Research on Governance in Weak States in Melanesia,* State, Society and Governance in Melanesia Discussion Paper 96/1, Research School of Pacific and Asian Studies, The Australian National University, Canberra.

———, 1996b. *Models of Governance and Development Adminstration,* Society and Governance in Melanesia Discussion Paper 96/2, Research School of Pacific and Asian Studies, The Australian National University, Canberra.

McCay, B. and Acheson, J., 1990. 'Human ecology of the commons', in B. McCay and J. Acheson (eds), *The Question of the Commons: the culture and ecology of communal resources,* University of Arizona, Tuscon:1–34.

North, D., 1990. *Institutions, Institutional Change and Economic Performance,* Cambridge University Press, Cambridge.

Ostrom, E., 1990. *Governing the Commons: the evolution of institutions of collective action,* Cambridge University Press, Cambridge.

Simpson, S.R., 1976. *Land, Law and Registration,* Cambridge University Press, Cambridge.

Taylor, M., 1992. 'The economics and politics of property rights and common pool resources', *Natural Resources Journal* 32(3):633–48.

———, and Singleton, S., 1993. 'The Communal Resource: transaction costs and the solution of collective action problems', *Politics and Society* 21(2):195–214.

Trosper, R., 1978. 'American Indian relative ranching efficiency', *The American Economic Review* 68(4):503–16.

Wade, R., 1988. *Village Republics,* Cambridge University Press, Cambridge.

Ward, G. and Kingdon, E., (eds), 1995. *Land Custom and Practice in the South Pacific,* Cambridge University Press, Cambridge.

Williamson, O., 1975. *Markets and Hierarchies,* Free Press, New York.

1

Changing forms of communal tenure

R. Gerard Ward

Practices in relation to customary land are changing in the Pacific islands. The changes include a tendency for people to want to privatise, or individualise, control of holdings within the realm of customary land; for current practice to diverge from what is stated to be custom; and for practice to diverge from the law where tenure has been codified.

It is also necessary to question whether we are dealing with common property at all in Pacific island land tenure. We might also consider whether customary land tenure, especially as often practised, is necessarily the inhibiting factor for development which it often is said to be.

Does any one individual or entity, anywhere, really own land in the sense of having full personal control over its use and its disposal? There are few if any places or polities within which landholders have absolute and exclusive rights over the control, use, or assignment of land. Unencumbered ownership of land is extremely rare. Crocombe has pointed out that it may not be 'sufficiently recognised that human beings do not own land: what they own is rights to land, that is, rights *vis-à-vis* other human beings' (1972:220). And different people may hold overlapping rights over the same land. This is true for developed as well as developing countries. Even if we take the case of freehold land within the general realm of British-derived law, which might be considered to provide a particularly strong form of control or ownership, it may still be subject to possible resumption by the state (the Crown in the British case). Other parties, such as the neighbours over the back fence, or agencies such as electricity or sewerage authorities, may have easements over it. Its use may be constrained by planning regulations. The extent to which the subsoil (and what it contains) is included in ownership rights may vary. Its disposal may be constrained by laws which limit the right to own land to members of specific groups.

It is often argued that some form of transferable landholding such as freehold tenure, or long-term transferable leasehold, is a requirement for successful development. Much of this argument hangs on the belief that land is the only, or the best, security for raising capital through loans, and that its transferability in the event of default is essential for successful development. But other mechanisms have been used successfully as the basis for credit, at least for smallholder farmers. Security and transferability of rights are certainly key features, but these can be provided under a variety of tenures. The extent to which these exist under customary tenure is often overlooked.

Some of the land problems in the Pacific islands arise because different groups or agencies may assert the power to confer legitimacy on rights which may be claimed over land, and do so on the basis of quite different ideologies, legal or cultural concepts. Such groups include customary landholders, governments, and land management instrumentalities. One has only to compare the different premises which have been used by colonial administrations, independent governments, and rural clans or kinship groups to see the scope for confusion. Given the weakness of state institutions in a number of Pacific island countries, and the limited understanding or acceptance of ideas of national sovereignty, it is unrealistic to assume that ideas and laws imposed at a national level on a matter as sensitive, as culturally loaded, and as variable as land tenure will be uniformly accepted or observed by claimants to customary land.

Thus great complexity of tenure arrangements may exist, even within the one state, and even where a codified version of traditional or customary tenure has been adopted. It is also necessary to recognise that 'customary tenure' changes over time, and at differing rates in different places, as custom itself changes in some uncertain relationship with technological, economic, social and political change.

Furthermore, practice in the allocation, holding and use of land may change long before it is given the imprimatur of 'custom'. Within most Pacific island countries it is probably misleading to speak of *the* customary system of tenure because of the differences between what different communities might accept as customary in their own case. Under a generally accepted framework of certain general principles, a great deal of pragmatic divergence occurs. Until the authority of the state is much stronger than it is in most Pacific island countries, it may be necessary for those who seek to foster specific development projects requiring long-term use and exploitation of land for agricultural, mining, industrial or other uses, to take heed of local attitudes and claims to rights over land.

Common property or common land?

Most land in the Pacific islands is not common property in either the sense of open access to all people, or equal access to all members of a particular community which claims ownership. The same is usually true of reef and lagoon fishing grounds as well (see, for instance, Carrier 1987). Johannes and MacFarlane point to the contrast between Europe and European concepts in which marine resources were thought of as a common good, and the Pacific islands where fishing grounds were explicitly the property of individuals or specific groups (1991:73). It is generally true in the Pacific islands that amongst groups which occupy an area, all the core members will have some rights to exploit the products of the area, to reside within it, and to occupy parts of it under some form of usufruct. But it would be unusual for all to have equal rights within the whole area. Most groups will also include residents who are not core members but have been given some more limited, conditional rights which fall far short of equality of access.

A generalised example, drawn largely from Fiji, but in its essential features common to other areas may illustrate this point (Figure 1.1). A community of several clans may claim an area of land as its territory. In places the boundaries may not be clearly defined. Within that territory, each clan is acknowledged or, where the system is codified, recorded as the controllers or owners of particular areas. The whole is not the common property of the community for more intensive uses, despite the fact that, by custom, all residents may be free to gather forest products from most of the uncultivated parts of the territory.

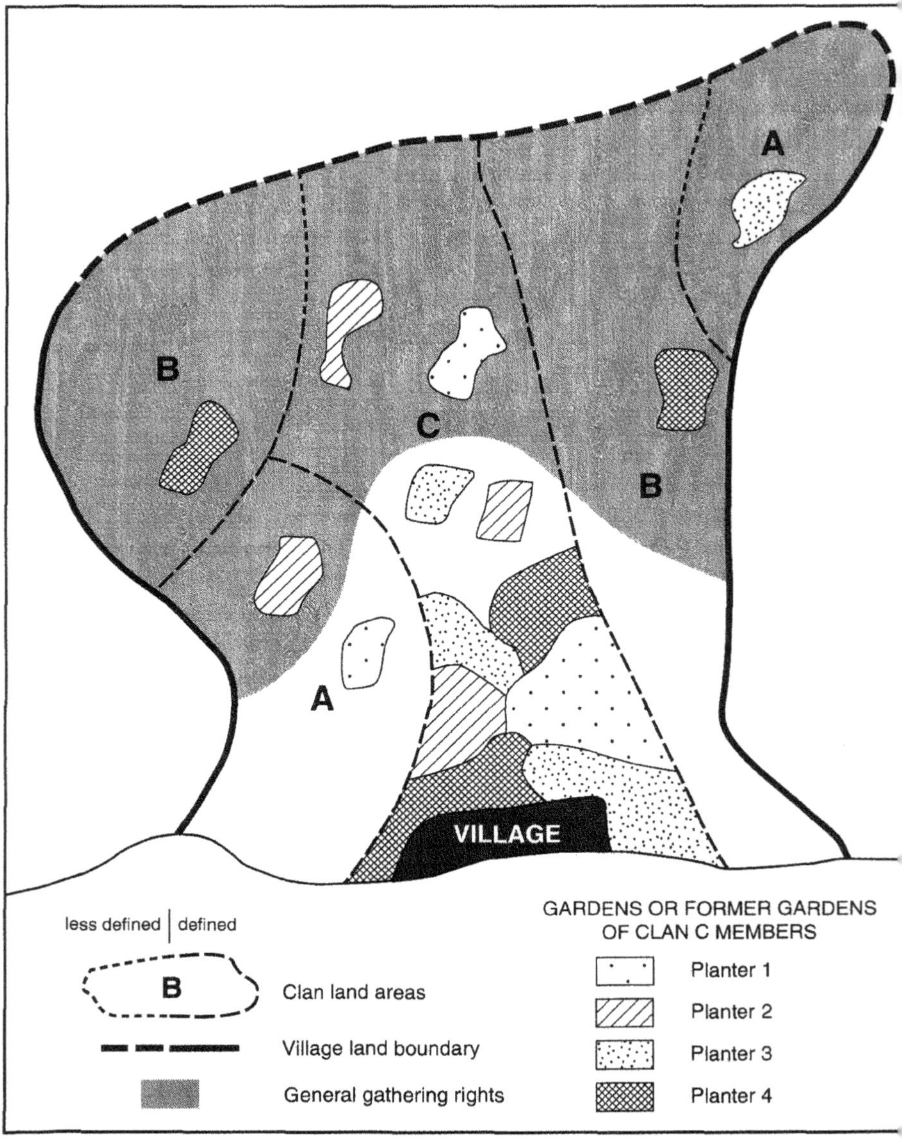

Figure 1.1 Landholdings in a hypothetical village. Drawn by J. Sheehan, Cartography Unit, Research School of Pacific and Asian Studies.

Although some limited rights may approach commonality within this forest or uncultivated land, individual trees or products may be recognised as the property of individuals and control of hunting and gathering may rest with particular people or sub-groups. Within the land of one clan, members may not all have equal rights to clear and cultivate any part because specific individuals, or families (in Figure 1.1, planters 1–4) may hold residual and relatively exclusive rights to occupy, which stem from the last period of cultivation of the particular piece. The land of a house site may be very specifically under the control of a particular nuclear or extended family. Specific resource sites, such as a spring or a source of clay, although within the boundaries of a clan's land, may be controlled by specific members of that or another clan, with relatively free access being allowed to almost all, but under 'grace and favour'.

A superficial examination of this type of system, perhaps influenced by a framework of ideas stemming from nineteenth century sociology, may note that all members appear to be able to hunt, gather, or collect water from any area or site within the community's broader territory, and that many people cultivate gardens scattered throughout the territory, and not only on the land of their own clan, and then jump to the conclusion that land is common property. Few Pacific islanders would accept such an interpretation. The situation is not one of free and equal access for all. It is not directly comparable to the forms of access found on, say, English common land, and even there, commoner's rights are not held by all.

Neither is it generally true that those members of the community who use specific pieces of land are insecure in their continued use of that land. Indeed the very security of that right to continued occupation under customary tenure is what many now use as validation in a process of privatisation currently taking place in a number of island countries. If security of occupation or usufruct is a feature of land tenure systems which is considered desirable for development purposes, then most Pacific island customary tenure systems have this. What may not be possible is the transfer of those occupation rights to others who are not community members, but in practice one finds many instances where such transfers have occurred in both former and recent times.

Communal tenure or 'customary' tenure?

Communal land may be considered to be a variant of the category 'common property' with the assumption that all within the 'commune' or the 'community' have rights of access. To apply this title to customary land in the Pacific islands also overemphasises the degree of shared access. True, ultimate control over land may be vested in a group but, as suggested above, that group may be a specific sub-set of the whole community so that, as O'Meara (1995) has suggested for Samoa, the phrase 'corporate family ownership' may give a clearer impression of the reality of some forms of customary tenure, with the role of the family head somewhat analogous to that of the managing director of a company or corporation. Therefore I think it best to avoid the term 'communal land', preferring the vaguer term 'customary' land. The crucial point is that customs change, and so does customary land tenure.

Older variations in customary tenure

The discourse of the post-independence Pacific island nations, and particularly the political rhetoric, tends to imply that traditional ways were and are unchanging, handed down from time immemorial. That this is patently not so is obvious from the way Christianity has been incorporated into tradition. An example in the case of land tenure is the way the current land tenure system of Tonga, based on inheritable leaseholds from Crown or nobles' estates, is now thought of as 'traditional' when in fact it is a late nineteenth century product. The 1875 constitution abolished customary land rights as the Crown took control of all land, allocated much of it to nobles' estates, and gave all adult men the right to inheritable usufruct over holdings allocated from those estates. In effect these were perpetual, heritable, individual, but inalienable leases. It was a land reform which, in its sweeping nature, was almost without equal outside the old Soviet bloc. This recent, rather individualistic system, with European feudal overtones, is now Tonga's 'traditional' system.

In Fiji the current codified system, widely accepted as traditional, is also a colonial creation under which the variety of pre-1874 tenure arrangements was reduced. The plea of a number of leading chiefs for individual allotments was ignored as it did not fit current anthropological theories. Ownership groupings were simplified to aid recording and the scope for modification in the face of demographic or other change was virtually eliminated (see France 1969, Ward 1995).

Furthermore, the doctrine of inalienability of Native Land, which is a major plank of current Fijian tradition, is itself a product of colonial codification under an ordinance of 1912, rather than a true reflection of older practice (Ward 1995:206–8). As France noted 'permanent alienation of land is a common feature of Fijian culture and the concept can be easily and unambiguously expressed in the Fijian language' (1969:52).

As in Tonga and Fiji, many of the changes in customary tenure in other countries in the late nineteenth and early twentieth century were colonial government initiatives. The Land Court in the Cook Islands, 'owing to its misunderstanding of the significance of lineage affiliation in determining ownership of and succession to land rights...awards title in common to all children of a previous owner, thus creating excessive fragmentation of ownership' (Crocombe 1987a:60). In this case the problems of 'common property' which arose, and which a number of attempts have been made to solve, are not so much a result of customary tenure, but of colonial intervention. In French Polynesia major changes were imposed by the French administration (Tetiarahi 1987) often 'based on misinterpretations of how the land tenure system worked' (Joralemon 1983:97). In New Caledonia (as in Fiji) ownership was registered by relatively large groups when in fact cultivated land was held by relatively small family groups (A. Ward 1982:3–4). Other examples can be cited from around the region, many of which illustrate that what is now considered 'customary' is of relatively recent origin. What they also tell us is that, if political conditions are right, or a government is strong, major changes can be made, and accepted, in customary land tenure systems, and that many of the current problems attributed to customary tenure stem from European misinterpretations of the tenure forms which existed in the late nineteenth and early twentieth centuries. More thorough understanding might well have avoided many current difficulties, particularly if the variability and scope for change had been recognised.

Current changes in custom

Custom, as accepted behaviour, usually contains a large component of pragmatism. Close examination of pre-colonial events in the region shows that this pragmatism was reflected in many changes in land tenure arrangements, due to warfare, changing population or other pressures, migration, obligations, and even acts of grace and favour. Mobility was common and when people claim to have occupied an area from 'time immemorial' their own traditions often describe movement from some other place. One result of the codification of land tenure systems, as in Fiji, Tonga or the Cook Islands, has been to impose a much more static situation, at least in legal terms. Because holdings were surveyed, and owning groups specified and their members recorded, the processes which formerly allowed land to be reallocated as needs changed ceased to operate (officially at least). Greater rigidity has also occurred or is likely, where the 'traditional' land tenure system has been given status in national constitutions without precise codification or survey. Western Samoa and Vanuatu are examples. Cases which come before the Western Samoa Land and Titles Court have tended to be settled on the basis of arguments which draw on older conditions rather than current practice and for many years it was the case that the Court could be 'regarded as a mechanism integral to the maintenance of chiefship' (Powles 1986:206). This is less true today and there are signs of a more pragmatic approach but, as O'Meara (1995) shows, the decisions of the Court still draw on custom which lags a long way behind practice.

In Vanuatu, where the independence constitution vested the ownership of all land in the 'custom owners' there is an implicit assumption that such ownership is identifiable, generally accepted, and relatively unchanging over time. Rodman (1995:92–102) has shown that this is not necessarily the case. On the island of Ambae, for example, major changes occurred in the nature of customary holdings in the early twentieth century in response to the reduction of warfare and the adoption of copra production as a road to power and as a role for big men. Such men established relatively large and permanent holdings, in contrast to the smaller and less permanent holdings of previous times. Therefore a basic question remains for Vanuatu if recording of landholdings is to proceed. What is to be the date for which the landholdings are to be formally recognised by the state? Should it be the time of contact, the beginning of the present century or the establishment of the Anglo-French Condominium, the date of independence or the date of survey? Each could be justified. Each would give a different pattern of ownership. And will there be mechanisms for transfer of ownership which might stand in lieu of older and no longer acceptable mechanisms such as force? An issue under political consideration in 1995 was how to adapt the customary land system to the needs of expanding urban areas. Should leaseholds be allowed and if so, on what conditions? Elections and political turmoil have left the matter open in Vanuatu in 1996 but the same questions may also be asked in other countries and also remain unanswered.

Fiji is one country where such questions were answered in the late 1930s and the Native Land Trust Board (NLTB) was set up explicitly to regularise the leasing of Native Land, to protect Fijian interests, and to make unused land available for use by non-owners amongst both Fijian and other ethnic groups. A system of sanctioned leases was introduced and is controlled by the NLTB. The Board and the recorded owners receive specified shares of the rents. Some other countries have considered introducing comparable systems. Niue is a current example. But there is little uniformity within the region, except that in a number of countries outright alienation is not permitted and leasehold arrangements may be complex and difficult to establish.

Despite the rigidity which has been introduced into codified or constitutionally sanctioned customary systems, extra-legal change has occurred in many areas. Pragmatism has often outweighed legality. The NLTB system worked relatively well in Fiji for some decades but is now under strain for several reasons. On the owners' side many feel that the system is too rigid, the rents they receive are too low in relation to the land's productivity, the chiefs receive too large a share of the rents, and the leases lock up the land in the hands of lessees for too long. Some have also voiced concern that the relevant act removes ultimate control of Native Land from the hands of the owning groups themselves. Lessees or would-be lessees have concerns about the difficulty of obtaining land, the security of leases and particularly the chances of renewal as large numbers of leases expire within the next few years. As a result, a whole range of extra-legal arrangements are now found. They include tenancies arranged directly between land-owners and farmers outside the NLTB system, with much higher rents and much shorter terms. Sharecropping is common though its legality may be questionable. Native Reserve land, which cannot be leased legally to non-Fijians, is rented and occupied by non-Fijians with the informal consent of the owners. And Fijians from outside the land-owning group may be allowed, under pseudo-traditional conventions, to reside on land over which they have no traditional rights. This last is a modern version of the old customary right of owners to accept outsiders as members of their community, but today the relationship may be basically commercial.

Within areas held under customary tenure and used by members of the owning group, change in practice has also occurred in several countries. The details vary but there are some relatively common features. Most reflect changing technological, economic and social needs and are related to the changing context for individuals and groups who are involved in commercial rather than subsistence agriculture; who wish to employ wage labour rather than rely on the mechanism of reciprocity; who need land for urban housing; who seek to migrate to areas where they have no immediate kin; who wish to take advantage of the monetary value of land near urban areas; or who wish to ensure adequate land is available and inheritable by their immediate family.

One of the most common changes is what may be described as a process of privatising the customary land. This is usually based on the common traditional custom that if people have cleared and planted land, they may continue to control it as long as they continue to have it planted or in use, or intend to re-use it after a current fallow period. The adoption of long-term tree crops such as coconuts, cocoa, or coffee for commercial agriculture, or of pastoralism, placed an entirely new time span on this convention. Where a family's coconut requirements in a subsistence economy could be met from a few palms, the convention of separation of ownership of the palms and that of the land on which they grew created few problems. Others might plant food gardens under the scattered individually-owned palms. But once large areas were closely planted in a monocrop, say of coconuts, which might continue to be harvested for 50 years or more, the process of return to fallow and the possibility of reallocation was interrupted.

An old Chinese proverb states that 'long tenancy becomes property' (Elvin 1970:107) and this is what has been happening in a number of places in the Pacific islands. The usufruct of land now remains in the same family for decades, and as agricultural activities are increasingly carried out within the nuclear family, or with paid labour independent of the wider kin or residential group, holdings are increasingly seen as being under the long-term control of individuals or nuclear families. As Macpherson (1988) has said in the title of a paper on Western Samoa, 'the road to power is a chainsaw', and some use a chainsaw to clear a large area which is then put under pasture in order to gain personal, secure, family tenure. In effect traditional features of customary tenure are being used to produce non-traditional results, namely the establishment of long-term individual holdings. The process is not new in the region. Keesing (1934:280–281) noted such tendencies in Samoa in the 1930s and they were more clearly evident in the 1950s (Ward 1962); Chatterton (1974:15) reported such trends in Papua in the 1970s; they were evident in some forms in

Fiji in the late 1950s (Ward 1960); and I have already referred to the emergence of such forms in Vanuatu early this century (Rodman 1995). Elsewhere the process may be less clearly developed but shows signs of emerging, as in Solomon islands where Larmour (1984:8) suggests that 'trustees' named of behalf of their owning group may 'in time appropriate rights of ownership to themselves', as some have done in Papua New Guinea.

In the rather different case of Tonga, practice has also diverged from the post-constitutional 'custom' (James 1995). An extra-legal land market has developed. A number of older customary practices have been exploited to control and channel the succession to allotments. Informal leasing of parts of allotments is common. To counter problems of the inalienable nature of allotments in relation to provision of credit against the security of land, arrangements have been made for lending institutions to take control over of the management of enterprises or allotments in cases of default, but only until the loan involved has been worked off.

These evolutionary changes within customary systems provide a dilemma for governments. The individualisation of holdings of customary land may be extra-legal or illegal, but may reflect what more and more people want, and may be more in accord with the concepts of those fostering 'development'. But it carries the risk that a few will attain control of the majority of the land, and leave some community members virtually landless. Allied to customary ways of transferring control of land to others, such processes could well meet many of the supposed requirements for effective development. But few Pacific island governments seem to have the will to accept that customary tenure practices change, or to give some validation to such processes.

Having limited the extent to which customary land could be alienated, usually for the good paternalistic reason of protecting indigenous people from the socioeconomic effects of losing their land, colonial and independent governments have subsequently faced the need to make land available for enterprises which were not previously envisaged under customary tenure. Because of the rigidity installed into customary tenures it has usually been assumed that such land requirements had to be met outside the customary systems. Hence the use of the power, taken to itself by the state, to alienate customary land for state purposes and arrangements, such as those of the NLTB in Fiji, to regularise leases. In a number of countries it has proved difficult for governments to manage the dual tenure systems and provide land for urban expansion or other non-customary activities. Vanuatu, Western Samoa and Niue have all been considering the problems at a political level in recent years but at present only Niue is endeavouring to introduce a new system.

One factor which tends to hold the official view of customary tenure in a backward-looking posture is the extent to which its maintenance has become an integral part of both the process of creating national or ethnic identity, and the maintenance of the status and power of élites, including political leaders. Politicians use customary land and the associated tenure arrangements as markers differentiating their own people from others, and as important components of custom and national identity. Land and tenure systems are seen and trumpeted as key elements in the 'Fijian way of life', *kastom, fa'a Samoa,* and custom which has been followed 'from time immemorial'. In arguing the need to maintain traditional ways, barriers are erected to official acknowledgment of the existence of, and the need for, change.

There are political risks in advocating changes in customary land tenure. There may also be advantage in maintaining the rather fluid *status quo* if one is able to use traditional mechanisms for personal benefit. How long the current divergences between custom, law and practice can be tolerated is an open question. Official recognition of the *de facto* changes, and their acceptance into a new widely accepted version of customary land arrangements, may be slow. Yet the fact that they are occurring shows how adaptable customary tenure can be in the face of new needs. Perhaps more scope exists to build on this flexibility, to examine current practice and try to give it recognition, rather than to try and replace customary systems on the false assumption that they allow open access and hence are likely to have damaging or inhibiting consequences. As McCay and Acheson (1987:34) say, 'by equating common property [or, I would add, customary tenure] with open access, the tragedy-of-the-commons approach ignores important social institutions and their roles in managing the commons. Moreover, its policy solutions—government intervention or privatisation—can weaken or demolish existing institutions and worsen or even create 'tragedies of the commons [or of customary land]'.

References

Carrier, J.G., 1987.'Marine tenure and conservation in Papua New Guinea', in McCay and Acheson (eds), *The Question of the Commons: the culture and ecology of communal resources*, University of Arizona Press, Tucson:142–67.

Chatterton, P., 1974.'The historical dimension', in P. Sack (ed.), *Problem of Choice: land in Papua New Guinea's future*, The Australian National University Press, Canberra:8–15,.

Crocombe, R.G., 1972.'Land tenure in the South Pacific', in R.G. Ward (ed.), *Man in the Pacific Islands*, Clarendon Press, Oxford:219–51.

——, 1987a.'The Cook Islands: fragmentation and emigration', in R.G. Crocombe (ed.), *Land Tenure in the Pacific*, University of the South Pacific, Suva:59–73.

——, (ed.), 1987b. *Land Tenure in the Pacific*, University of the South Pacific, Suva.

Elvin, J.M., 1970. 'The last thousand years of Chinese history: changing patterns in land tenure', *Modern Asian Studies* 4(20):97–114.

J.W. Fox and K.B. Cumberland (eds), 1962. *Western Samoa: land, life and agriculture in tropical Polynesia*, Whitcombe and Tombs, Christchurch.

France, P., 1969. *The Charter of the Land: custom and colonization in Fiji*, Oxford University Press, Melbourne.

James, K., 1995. 'Right and privilege in Tongan land tenure', in Ward and Kingdon (eds), *Land, Custom and Practice in the South Pacific*, Cambridge University Press, Cambridge:157–97.

Johannes, R.E. and MacFarlane, J.W., 1991. *Traditional Fishing in the Torres Strait Islands*, CSIRO Division of Fisheries, Hobart.

Joralemon, V.L., 1983. 'Collective land tenure and agricultural development: a Polynesian case', *Human Organization*, 42(2):95–105.

Keesing, F.M., 1934. *Modern Samoa: its government and changing life*, Allen and Unwin, London.

Larmour, P., 1984. 'Alienated land and independence in Melanesia', *Pacific Studies* 8(1):1–47.

McCay, B.J. and Acheson, J.M., 1987. 'Human ecology of the commons' in McCay and Acheson (eds), *The Question of the Commons: the culture and ecology of communal resources*, University of Arizona Press, Tucson:1–34.

———, (eds),1987. *The Question of the Commons: the culture and ecology of communal resources*, University of Arizona Press, Tucson.

Macpherson, C., 1988. 'The road to power is a chainsaw: villages and innovation in Western Samoa', *Pacific Studies* 11(2):1–24.

O'Meara, J.T., 1995. 'From corporate to individual land tenure in Western Samoa', in G. Ward and E. Kingdon (eds), *Land, Custom and Practice in the South Pacific*, Cambridge University Press, Cambridge:109–56.

Powles, C.G., 1986. 'Legal systems and political cultures: competition for dominance in Western Samoa', in P.G. Sack, and E. Minchin (eds), *Legal Pluralism: proceedings of the Canberra Law Workshop 7*, Research School of Social Sciences, The Australian National University, Canberra:191–214.

Rodman, M., 1995. 'Breathing spaces: customary land tenure in Vanuatu' in G. Ward and E. Kingdon (eds), *Land, Custom and Practice in the South Pacific*, Cambridge University Press, Cambridge:65–108.

Sack, P.G. and Minchin, E. (eds), 1986. *Legal Pluralism: proceedings of the Canberra Law Workshop 7*, Research School of Social Sciences, The Australian National University, Canberra.

Tetiarahi, G., 1987. 'The Society Islands: squeezing out the Polynesians', in R. Crocombe (ed.), *Land Tenure in the Pacific*, University of the South Pacific, Suva:45–58.

Ward, A., 1982. *Land and Politics in New Caledonia*, Political and Social Change Monograph, The Australian National University, Canberra.

Ward, R.G., 1960. 'Village Agriculture in Viti Levu, Fiji', *New Zealand Geographer* 16(1):33–56.

———, 1962. 'Agriculture outside the village and commercial systems' in J.W. Fox and K.B. Cumberland (eds), *Western Samoa: land, life and agriculture in tropical Polynesia*, Whitcombe and Tombs, Christchurch:266–89.

———, 1995. *Land, Law and Custom: diverging realities in Fiji*, in Ward and Kingdon (eds), *Land, Custom and Practice in the South Pacific*, Cambridge University Press, Cambridge:198–249.

——— and Kingdon, E. (eds), 1995. *Land, Custom and Practice in the South Pacific*, Cambridge University Press, Cambridge.

2

Resolving property issues as a precondition for growth: access to land in the Pacific islands

Satish Chand and Ron Duncan

The island states in the South Pacific are heavily reliant on their natural resources for output, employment and earnings of foreign exchange. While these countries have had poor growth performance over the past two decades, improvement in access to natural resources is one area where there is potential for significant economic gains. This paper argues that subsistence affluence is non-existent in these countries and that their future prosperity depends on engagement in international trade, including inflows of foreign investment capital. Promotion of land-based investments, such as in agriculture and infrastructure, is one of the preconditions for growth. It is imperative, therefore, that security of access to land currently under communal ownership be enhanced so as to encourage efficient use of this resource and enhance the inflow of technology and capital. A modelling framework is developed which captures the major factors believed to create pressures for change in land tenure.

All of the Pacific island countries are primary commodity dependent, with agriculture being the main source of output and exports. If this pattern of production and trade continues, there will be increasing pressure on land and land-based resources. Customary ownership of land and the role of land as a symbol of cultural heritage makes investigation of issues relating to land both complex and sensitive. Researchers may have shied away from working on land issues in the island countries because of this sensitivity. We are aware of these concerns and our parameters are drawn so as to confine the discussion to the economics of making more productive use of a factor of production that may be in abundant supply in some, but not all, of these nations.

From an econnomist's viewpoint, land is just another factor of production, with the peculiarity that it is relatively inelastic in supply. Customary ownership of land may give rise to the possibility of the 'free-rider' problem, an issue that traditional societies may manage via customary laws. However, the absence of individual rights to use of land creates uncertainties with respect to investment, particularly investments that have long gestation periods before providing returns. Such investment includes those involving infrastructure which has external benefits for aggregate output. Insecurity of access to land could reduce private investment in infrastructure which in turn is likely to retard the rate of long-run economic growth.

Globally, countries have moved away from customary ownership towards freehold title or to forms of leasehold which provide long-term security of access for use of the land. These forms of tenure resolve the free-rider problem and provide the security of tenure needed for long-term investment. Ensuring long-term access to land also provides the necessary incentive for sustainable use of the resource. What factors determine that such changes in tenure or access take place? When can we expect to see such changes in the Pacific island countries?

Each of the above issues and questions is treated in turn. Whilst our analysis may not cover all aspects of the land debate, we hope to have covered the salient features of the problem. This chapter first considers support for the view that the Pacific islands have 'subsistence affluence' and have it for the foreseeable future, making changes in land tenure of little importance. The evidence suggests the opposite. The next section reviews land tenure systems in some Pacific islands (the choice of countries discussed is entirely data driven), and subsequently presents a discussion of the factors which may lead to pressure for more secure access to use of land. The final part of this chapter develops a modelling framework which can be utilised to discern the contribution of various factors to increases in the value of land resources.

Is there 'subsistence affluence' in the Pacific islands?

Images of dancing youths in grass skirts, swaying coconut palms, and fish-filled lagoons that appear on tourist brochures support the view that the South Pacific island countries enjoy what has been described as 'subsistence affluence'. However, in recent decades there have been high population growth, rapidly-monetising economies, rural–urban migration, the trading off of future consumption for present consumption and the problems of land degradation. These developments are not at all consistent with economies being at stable but high living standards derived from their immediate environments. If we assume that populations were in equilibrium a century ago and use half of the current population growth rates to back-cast this sustainable subsistence level of population density, the numbers suggest that the current levels are far above a sustainable subsistence level. Under our conservative assumptions, the sustainable subsistence density in Kiribati is 38 people per square kilometre when the current density is two hundred and fifty per cent higher!

Table 2.1 Some basic indicators for the Forum island countries

Country	Per Capita GDP[a]	Agriculture in GDP (%)[b]	Pop. density[c]	Sustainable subsistence density[d]	Growth rate of GDP (%)[e]	Population growth[f]
Fiji	4007	19.6	39.7	17.1	2.6	1.7
Kiribati	..	24.3	100.0	38.3	-3.5	1.9
PNG	1425	27.0	8.2	2.5	2.1	2.4
Solomon Is.	..	44.3	10.6	2.1	6.8	3.3
Tonga	..	38.6	130.6	105.4	2.0	0.4
Vanuatu	1677	20.0	11.7	2.8	2.6	2.9
W. Samoa	2064	39.9	56.0	40.9	0.2	0.6

Notes: [a] Data are for 1990 and in 1985 US$ (Chain Index). [b] Data is from *Pacific Economic Bulletin* 10(1):104. [c] Density is per square kilometre. Data are for 1989. [d] Subsistence population density is computed as that of a century ago with the assumption that population then was at a steady state and grew on average at half the

reported annual rate, that is $S = \dfrac{D(1989)}{(1+\frac{g}{2})^{100}}$ where [d] is population density in 1989 and [g] is

the growth rate. [e] Calculated from data in [a]. [f] Annual average from 1970 to 1993 period.
Sources: [a]Summers, R. and Heston, A., 19'91, The Penn World Tables: an expanded set of international comparisons', *Quarterly Journal of Economics* CVI:1–45. [c,d, and e] World Bank, 1992. *World Bank World Tables*, World Bank, Washington DC.

Given that the days of subsistence affluence (if any) are past for most Pacific islanders, the feasible economic option for these nations is to grow on the basis of trade and specialisation in areas of their comparative advantage. There is little reason why the future could not be bright for the citizens of these nations. The link between population density and income can be broken via trade and productivity growth. Relative to some wealthy Asian nations such as Singapore, the Pacific island countries are well endowed with natural wealth. Furthermore, as the Pacific island countries lag behind in use of technology, they have strong potential for gains arising out of catch-up growth.

Landownership and use in the Pacific islands

Most Pacific island countries have a communal system of landowner-ship. Most of today's high-income societies began with similar land tenure systems. When communities are self-sufficient, with stable, low-density populations, customary land tenure arrangements are appropriate to their main pursuits—hunting/gathering or land-intensive shifting cultivation. A subsistence economy is basically in a static (no growth), autarkic (no trade) situation, with no surplus to trade and zero or low productivity growth. It appears rational to have communal landownership in a situation where the land requires protection from invasion. Furthermore, in traditional societies, land-ownership and governance are intertwined: there is little need for separation of landownership and political control over its use.

One problem with communal ownership is that title to a particular piece of land is often not clearly defined. Another is the potential for the free-rider problem associated with global commons. The free-rider problem is not unique to landownership. It appears in situations where there is access to some commonly held property. Consider the case of a fishing pond that belongs to a group of individuals. It is in the interest of the group as a whole to preserve the yield of fish from the pond, but for any individual the incentives are to exploit the resource so long as his/her actions are not detected. If every member of the group follows this strategy, the pond is depleted—an undesirable outcome for the group as a whole. One solution to this problem is cooperation amongst the members so as to maintain the extraction of fish at a sustainable level. Traditional societies typically had rules ('*tabus*') that ensured this cooperation. The clan head was charged with the responsibility of enforcing these rules, and encroachment of these *tabus* entailed severe punishment. Furthermore, the landowning groups were generally small, making the costs of cooperation low and the probability of being caught for violation of the *tabus* high. Non-traditional systems deviate from a number of the conditions that prevailed among such societies. For example, current technology poses fewer constraints on the size of farm plots and far more specialisation in production is possible now due to both international trade and formal types of employment.

The adoption of market-based institutions allows scope for more efficient use of land than under a cooperative system. In the former case, the individual who will use it most efficiently will be able to bid the highest price to gain access. Access to land may be gained either through freehold or leasehold title. However, in order for leasehold title to be as efficient as freehold, the length of lease must be sufficiently long and secure not to inhibit the titleholder to invest in the land. Security of tenure will be assessed in terms of the reliability of the state (in the case of freehold title) and the state or other owners (in the case of leasehold title) in guaranteeing continuation of tenure—what in economic terms is known as the 'reputation' effect.

All of the Pacific islands are now essentially market-based economies and democracy exists in all of them except Tonga. Individual freedom is entrenched within their constitutions. Modern technology is available, people are literate and aware of their rights, and per capita output has been on the increase, though at a pace that is much lower than in neighbouring East Asian economies. The creation of central forms of government has led to the breakdown or dilution of the traditional, village-level government together with its controls over use of natural resources. The landownership system in many of these states is still based on the traditional system though the extent of communal ownership of land varies.

Table 2.2 Categories of landownership in Fiji and Papua New Guinea (per cent)

	Freehold	State-owned	Communal title
Fiji	7	10	83
Papua New Guinea	–	3	97

Sources: Prasad, B. and C. Tisdell 1996. 'Getting property rights 'right': land tenure in Fiji', *Pacific Economic Bulletin* 11(1):31–46, for Fiji; and Moaina, R., 1997. 'Mining and petroleum', in Ila Temu (ed.), *Papua New Guinea: a 20/20 vision,* National Centre for Development Studies, Canberra and National Research Institute, Papua New Guinea:115–35, for Papua New Guinea.

There exist a number of impediments to gaining tenure in land by trade. For example, trade in traditional land title is barred by legislation in Fiji, Papua New Guinea and Tonga. Unclear titles to land is another impediment. The practice of 'handing-back' land to its traditional owners—which has taken place in Australia and Fiji within the past years—adds further insecurity to usage rights to land. These insecurities pose risks to investment in land. Hence an investor contemplating investing in land is going to factor these insecurities into the decision process. This may not only result in under-investment in land, but also could bias investment away from physical infrastructure, in turn, having a negative impact on long-run economic growth. We take this issue up in more detail in the next section.

Land as a factor of production

To an economist, land is a crucial factor of production with the main issue being to ensure efficient use of this resource. Unlike capital and labour, land has a low elasticity of supply. Changes such as terms of trade gains in favour of products that are intensive in land use would raise demand for land. This may bring into use previously marginal land (perhaps reclamation of mangroves) but ultimately the supply of land is finite. Thus, any payment for land can be considered as a pure economic rent and any increased demand for land will increase the rent. Land is a heterogenous factor, differing considerably in terms of fertility and access. For example, agricultural land near an urban centre will command a higher price than land of the same yield some distance away. The difference in land value in this case is pure economic rent resulting from difference in location.

Population growth may also raise demand for land. Population growth may take place as a result of essentially external causes. The introduction of clean water and improved sanitation has reduced infant mortality rates worldwide and led to sharp increases in fertility and population growth rates in most developing countries over the past 40 years. As Boserup (1965) argued, in traditional systems population growth and the resulting increase in population density can lead to higher agricultural productivity through farming becoming more labour-intensive with the fallow period in shifting-cultivation systems becoming shorter. But there has to be accompanying investment, either in the short-term, such as the

incorporation of organic fertiliser or in the longer-term, as in infrastructure to improve water or soil management. As a result, there is an
increased pressure for greater security of access to land.

But population growth stemming from such external causes is not
likely to be a primary source of growth in agricultural productivity.
Moreover, as Boserup argues, too great a population density can mean
that the necessary investment may not be forthcoming and the effect
on agricultural productivity may be adverse. Boserup's argument is
that only in some circumstances will the line of causation run from
increased population density to increased agricultural productivity to
increased pressure for greater security of access to the land. The line of
causation mostly runs in the opposite direction. Higher agricultural
productivity and higher incomes lead, in the shorter run, to better
health and increased fertility and life expectancy and therefore to
higher population growth rates. In the longer run, the fertility rates
adjust to the increased life expectancy and the population growth rate
falls. But it could be that in some situations increased population
density is an important trigger for traditional societies to seek changes
in land tenure.

Crocombe (1995) saw demand for land and land tenure changes as
being determined in part by the mobility of the population. For example,
if there is movement of population from rural to urban areas, there
will be increased demand for land to be made available for housing
and for non-agricultural productive purposes. Other forms of land
use, for mining projects, for electricity and telecommunications trans-
mission, and for airports, roads and ports, also create a demand for
better security of access.

A static-equilibrium, subsistence economy may also be disturbed
by becoming open to trade with other economies. Trade may result
from a lowering of transport costs, or of any other transactions costs,
which makes trade more profitable. Feeny (1988) argues that opening
a closed economy to trade breaks the link between population density
and the demand for land. As he sees it, in a closed economy, increasing
population density increases land rents relative to real wages but with
openness to trade, the relevant prices of commodities become those
determined on international markets and not those determined within
the closed economy. 'Real land rents are now linked to the endowments of land, labor, and capital, to production technology, and to the
external terms of trade' (Feeny 1988:276).

Introduction of new techniques of agricultural production can also lead to institutional changes in land tenure and security of access for use of the land. In the short run, the existing security of access will affect the kinds of technology which are adopted. If security of access is poor, or short term as with sharecropping, then farmers or other users will tend to adopt only those new technologies from which the benefits can be realised within the period of security of access. For example, improved fertilisers, pesticides, or crop varieties which yield their benefits over the crop production period will be favoured over investments needing greater security of access such as water or soil management infrastructure. Technologies requiring access to large areas of land, such as machinery, will not be adopted if land tenure and access does not allow amalgamation of contiguous land to form large farming areas.[1] In the long term, however, the prospects of productivity gains from adoption of new technologies can be expected to provide pressures for changes in land tenure and security of access. Significant gains in productivity from the 'green revolution' are attributed to use of chemical fertilisers, improved plant varieties, and irrigation. The last is an infrastructure investment, one that would be undertaken in a climate where security to access is assured.

Other factors may increase or decrease the pressures for institutional changes in land tenure and access arrangements in Pacific islands countries. The opportunities for earning income from other sources may lessen such pressures. For example, customary landowners who receive income from mining projects or timber harvesting, or remittances from relatives overseas, could presumably see less need to increase production from their land, and therefore generate less pressure to change land tenure arrangements. Conversely, loss of other income earning possibilities could increase the pressure. Since New Zealand reduced its aid transfers to Niue, resulting in the loss of employment by several hundred public servants, their demand for land to allow them to engage in agricultural activities (primarily, growing taro for the New Zealand market) has led to pressure to have local landowners and the many absentee landowners make their land more readily available for use by others.

It is also conceivable, therefore, that the large per capita aid transfers to Pacific islands countries are inhibiting institutional change in land tenure. This could happen due to the aid transfers leading to the appreciation of the exchange rate, thus making land-based export activities less desirable. Or the 'rents' available to the political élite from the aid transfers could have the impact of making them uninterested in pushing through institutional change in land tenure. Availability of other income-earning possibilities from land, such as mining and timber royalties, may alternatively increase the pressure for more secure title to the land—what is at issue is security over rents from the land, whatever the source. Increases in land disputes can therefore be seen as a sign of pressure for change in titling and security of access.

This discussion has concentrated on the possible demand-induced pressures for institutional change in land tenure/access. Supply-side factors—what Feeny has described as 'the willingness and capability of the fundamental institutions of government to provide new arrangements' (Feeny 1988:273)—may also be highly. With central governments only of recent origin and generally considered to be 'weak' in relation to the powers of clan leaders, governments may in fact face great difficulty in delivering change in land tenure arrangements. Some of the alienation of land from customary ownership under colonial rule in these countries was reversed upon gaining independence. In several cases, customary ownership was recognised in the new constitutions. Sutherland (1984) argues that the creation of the Native Lands Trust Board (NLTB) in Fiji, which controls all land use on behalf of communal landowners, was in fact a monopolisation of power over land use under traditional chiefs and has served to freeze institutional change in land tenure. Prasad and Tisdell (1996) agree that the formation of the Native Land Trust Board 'provides it with absolute monopoly power in the determination of the land rents and the allocation of leases' (1996:26). This is a sub-optimal position for efficient land use and, moreover, much of the rent collected from land leases 'is lost in terms of administrative costs of the NLTB and payments to heads of *mataqalis*' (Prasad and Tisdell 1996:25). The case for the NLTB is put by Ratu Mosese Volavola (1995), General Manager of the NLTB, who argues that the NLTB was an institutional response to the perceived 'chaos' of the 14,000 landowning units negotiating their lease rents with potential tenants, and that it is an arrangement which makes land more readily available under more secure arrangements for use by non-landowners. Within Papua New Guinea, there is an ongoing struggle between the state and the landowners over the rights to the rents from the land, particularly from mining projects but from timber as well.

Transaction costs of changing land tenure can be very large, as many writers have recognised (for instance, Binswanger et al. 1993). Land surveys and the resolution of the disputes over ownership are necessary before changes can be made. These procedures are usually very involved, time-consuming and costly. As Binswanger et al. also point out, customary landowners have every right to be suspicious of the results of institutional change in landownership as in most cases the better-informed and politically better-connected end up distorting the new system in their favour. The high costs of institutional change and resistance to change because of concern over the results could therefore provide strong reasons for the lack of change in land tenure in the Pacific islands countries.

Which of these several factors is more important in leading to changes in land tenure and/or in developing more secure access for land use?

Modelling pressures for more secure access

If the ownership of all land is given to a single institution, this institution will act as a monopolist. If we further assume that the markets of all the other factors of production are perfectly competitive, then the monopolist will extract all the rent from economic activities which use the land. The monopolist could either charge a rental that is equal to the net yield from the land (Y) or sell the land at price (V), the association between these two variables being given by equation (1) below

$$V = \frac{Y}{r} \tag{1}$$

where r is the sector-specific opportunity cost of capital. In this case r will include the nominal rate of interest, the rate of inflation and any sector-specific risks of investment, i.e.,

$$r = i - \pi + \rho \tag{2}$$

where i is the nominal rate of interest, π is the rate of inflation and ρ is the risk factor associated with investment in land. For simplicity, equation (2) assumes no country-specific risk.[2] Totally differentiating (1) lets us begin to see the possible sources of changes in land value.

$$dV = \frac{dY}{r} - \frac{Y}{r^2} dr \tag{3}$$

Yield, y, can be further decomposed as a product of price and quantity of output. Letting q and k represent per capita output and capital stock, respectively, and p the price of land-intensive products relative to other products, yield per worker is given by

$$y = pq = pAf(k) \qquad (4)^3$$

where A is an index of technology and f represents the standard neo-classical production function in intensive form. Differentiating (4) and substituting the result in (3) gives

$$dv = \frac{As_k}{r}\hat{k} + \frac{q}{r}\hat{A} + y\hat{p} - \frac{y}{r^2}dr \qquad (5)$$

where a circumflex denotes the growth of the respective variable and s_k denotes the share of capital in output. The identity in (5) tells us that the value of land increases with an increase in one or a combination of capital intensity, production technology, and the terms of trade in favour of land-intensive products and declines with an increase in r. We consider each of these components individually and discuss the potential role of policy in influencing these variables.

Taking account of $k = K/L$ where K and L are stocks of capital and labour, respectively, then

$$\hat{k} = \hat{K} - \hat{L} \qquad (6)$$

Substituting equation (6) into equation (5) and letting $a = As_k/r$, $b = q/r$, and n the population growth rate gives

$$dv = \alpha(sY - n) + \beta\hat{A} + y\hat{p} - \frac{y}{r^2}dr \qquad (7)$$

In the case of a completely open economy, the first right-hand side term in equation (7) has no role since complete mobility of either factor is going to be sufficient for factor price equalisation to hold even in the presence of non-tradeables. The other variables will determine changes in the value of land. The rate of technological growth will depend on technological growth in the rest of the world as well as indigenous technological progress. Sectoral terms of trade will be determined by world markets. The final right-hand side variable is a measure of country and sector-specific opportunity cost of capital.

In a completely closed economy, domestic savings and population growth together determine growth in capital intensity. In this economy, high population growth together with low savings will slow growth to the extent that it may be negative.

Realistically, countries will lie somewhere in between being either completely open or completely closed, although economies moving out of subsistence are likely to be nearer to the latter. Capital intensity can be related to scale in terms of land use, as larger farms make use of machines more economical. If the land tenure system does not permit efficient use of machines then adoption of such technology will be inhibited. However, the existence of such technology will create pressures for changes in land tenure.

Given that all of the Pacific island nations lag substantially in terms of the technological frontier, $\hat{A}$ can rise through catch-up via adoption and adaptation of international best-practice technology. Both the capital intensity and technology variables would be enhanced via freeing up of foreign direct investment and education leading to human capital deepening. The rate of technology growth will also be enhanced by research which adapts foreign technology to local conditions.

As for the terms-of-trade changes, the Pacific island countries have little influence on global prices. The removal of price distortions, including over-valued real exchange rates, against agriculture and other land-based products will provide gains over the transition period. Any economic rents, including foreign aid payments and overseas remittances, will also inflate the real exchange rate and hence constitute a bias against agriculture. Data on effective rates of protection for these countries is unavailable except for Fiji where it is shown that significant bias against agriculture exists (Chand 1996).

The last term in (5) can be influenced by changes in any component of r as reflected in equation (2) above. Freeing up of capital controls and removal of restrictions on foreign direct investment are both going to lower r. Other country-specific factors such as threats of nationalisation will raise r. Finally, sector-specific risks such as those relating to insecure property rights in the natural resource sector will add a sector-specific risk component. If the value of the resource is to be maximised, then r has to be kept as close as possible to the world price of capital.

Conclusion

Land has been an important resource in the Pacific islands and is likely to remain so for the foreseeable future. Given the relatively poor growth performance of these economies over the past two decades and the desire of the population to improve their living standards, strategies for more efficient use of available resources have to be adopted. This paper argues that one of the fronts that can be explored is raising the efficiency of land use. Lack of security to land has been an impediment to investment, providing incentives for under-utilisation of the resource. Given that land-based projects have long gestation periods but generate positive externalities for the rest of the economy, security of access to land is crucial for raising efficiency as well as the rate of economic growth. If these states are to attract foreign capital for development, then provision of such security is crucial for economic prosperity.

But providing such enhanced security of tenure does not necessarily imply that the Pacific island countries have to forego customary ownership. As Crocombe (1995) notes, it is the security of access which is crucial. For example, customary ownership with long-term leases would be sufficient for sustainable and efficient use of land.

The modelling framework developed here is amenable to empirical implementation for future research. The challenge is to find suitable proxies for the variables in the model. The estimates from the proposed empirical exercise give some idea of the relative importance of variables which affect the pressures for change in land tenure so as to permit greater investment and faster growth.

Notes

Helpful comments from Ross Garnaut and Neil Vousden on an earlier draft of this chapter are acknowledged.

1. Prasad and Tisdell (1996) point out that sugar farmers in Fiji have become reluctant to invest in long-term farming techniques because the leases to the land expire shortly, with no guarantee that leases will be renewed.
2. Incorporation of a country-specific risk will decompose r into two components, a sector-specific and a country-specific component.
3. Small letters are used to denote levels of the respective variable in per capita terms.

References

Bates, R.H. (ed.), 1988. *Toward a Political Economy of Development: a rational choice perspective*, UCLA, Berkeley.

Binswanger, H.P., Deininger, K. and Feder, G., 1993. *Power, distortions, revolt, and reform in agricultural land relations*, Policy Research WPS Working Paper Series 1164, World Bank, Washington DC.

Boserup, E., 1965. *Conditions of Agricultural Growth: the economics of agrarian change under population pressure*, Aldine, Chicago.

Chand, S., 1996. 'Fiji within the CER', *Pacific Economic Bulletin* 11(1): 63–72.

Crocombe, R., 1995. 'Overview,' in R.G. Crocombe (ed.), *Customary Land Tenure and Sustainable Development: complementarity or conflict*, The South Pacific Commission, Noumea and Institute of Pacific Studies, University of the South Pacific, Suva.

Feeny, D., 1988. 'The Development of Property Rights in Land: a comparative study', in R.H. Bates (ed.), *Toward a Political Economy of Development: a rational choice perspective*, UCLA, Berkeley: 272–99.

Garnaut, R. and Clunies Ross, A., 1983. *Taxation of Mineral Rents*, Clarendon Press, Oxford and New York.

Hamidan-Rad, P., 1997. 'Investment policy framework in PNG', in Ila Temu (ed.), *Papua New Guinea: a 20/20 vision*, National Centre for Development Studies, Canberra and National Research Institute, Papua New Guinea:47–64.

Moaina, R., 1997. 'Mining and petroleum', in Ila Temu (ed.), *Papua New Guinea: a 20/20 vision*, National Centre for Development Studies, Canberra and National Research Institute, Papua New Guinea:115–35.

Mulina, R., 1997. 'Growth with Stability: monetary and fiscal policy in Papua New Guinea', in Ila Temu (ed.), *Papua New Guinea: a 20/20 vision*, National Centre for Development Studies, Canberra and National Research Institute, Papua New Guinea:3–11.

Prasad, B. and C. Tisdell 1996. 'Getting property rights 'right': land tenure in Fiji', *Pacific Economic Bulletin* 11(1): 31–46.

Sutherland, W.M., 1984. The State and Capitalist Development in Fiji, PhD Thesis, University of Canterbury, Canterbury.

Temu, Ila (ed.), 1997. *Papua New Guinea: a 20/20 vision*, National Centre for Development Studies, Canberra and National Research Institute, Papua New Guinea.

Volavola, R.M., 1995. 'The Native Land Trust Board of Fiji' in R. Crocombe (ed.), *Customary Land Tenure and Sustainable Development: complementarity or conflict*, The South Pacific Commission, Noumea and Institute of Pacific Studies, University of the South Pacific, Suva.

3

It's the land, stupid! The moral economy of resource ownership in Papua New Guinea

Chris Ballard

The ties that bind

In her novel, *Postcards*, Annie Proulx sets about providing an identity for Loyal Blood, her rural American, Anglo-Saxon protagonist

> A sense of his place, his home, flooded him...His blood, urine, feces and semen, the tears, strands of hair, vomit, flakes of skin, his infant and childhood teeth, the clippings of finger and toenails, all the effluvia of his body were in that soil, part of that place. The work of his hands had changed the shape of the land, the weirs in the steep ditch beside the lane, the ditch itself, the smooth fields were echoes of himself in the landscape, for the laborer's vision and strength persists after the labor is done (1994:85–6).

For those of us for whom ties to land consist of casual contacts with small and often infrequently tended suburban gardens, one of the more difficult exercises in imagination is to conceive of the relationship between rural communities and the lands and the resources that they consider theirs. Yet what is doubly interesting about Proulx's attempt to situate Loyal Blood in the landscape is the shallow history and narrow social context of his location in place. There are no appeals to a past which extends beyond his own life, no sense of his embeddedness within a community and its history of engagement with the land, its 'language of memory'. Instead, his voice finds its ground in a personal stratigraphy, the sediment of his individual labour. For perhaps the majority of people commenting, legislating or advising on land issues in Papua New Guinea—the lettered élite, as it were—the construction of personal identity is at a double remove from that of rural Melanesians: both in its emphasis on the labour or performance of the individual, and in its excision of the latter's deeply sedimented ties, through a community, to a specific landscape.

To observe that rural communities in Melanesia enjoy some 'special' relationship with the land is now an almost dangerously common act of elision, as though rehearsing this well-worn phrase allows that relationship then to be put aside while the main thrust of analysis is pursued elsewhere. But because local communities at most resource projects in the region will stubbornly insist on making repeated reference to this 'special' relationship, I want to take up the question of the relationship between land and identity, and to consider specifically the way in which landownership confers 'voice'—the right to speak and the ability to influence the flow of benefits from the land and its resources.

'Land'—as a shorthand for ties to locality, whether terrestrial or marine—is the basis for membership and nationality for most Melanesians. A claim to land, rather than some abstract notion of citizenship, is how the majority of Melanesians secure a foothold on the political stage and gain the attention of the state. Land is both the prize in the process of resource development and the means of access to the contest between communities, who insist on their birthright and prior occupation, and the state, which asserts its sovereign and constitutional rights to certain elements of the land (Ballard 1996).

The terms for this debate hinge upon what Munro (1996) has described as the 'moral economy' of the state. How do states, and particularly new states such as those in Melanesia, go about identifying and establishing the extent of their authority? The transition from colonialism poses a number of problems for the sovereignty of the state, particularly in its role as 'the final arbiter of property rights…Where massive coercive capacity (or will) is absent and the transformation or regulation of social relations is the goal, the establishment of common ethico-political ground is essential' (Munro 1996:145). If communities constitute themselves through a 'language of memory', then the challenge for the state, as Munro describes it, is to 'insert the presuppositions of state authority into that language and remoralise the political forms of local authority so as to place the state's institutions at the centre of the community. In a sense, if the village is to be brought within the state, the state must be brought into the village' (Munro 1996:141). The capacity of newly independent states thus rests, to an important degree, on the extent to which the authority of the state is accorded recognition in the village.

What I try to suggest in this chapter is that the problems confronting Melanesian governments in the development of their natural resources have as much to do with issues of legitimacy and national identity as they do with the legal resolution of property issues or the appropriateness of economic models. Where the institutions of the state have little or no presence, material or symbolic, in the village, the ability of the state to insist upon its sovereignty—its voice—is open to challenge. Currently, state sovereignty comes to the fore most obviously in Melanesian societies in the debate over resource ownership and the competing claims founded upon relationships to land. If we are to understand the 'moral calculus of power' (Lonsdale cited in Munro 1996:119) of Melanesian states, we shall need first to describe the links between land and identity that are already present in rural communities and then to appreciate how those links are being refashioned and transformed in the encounter with the state and with resource developers. The chapter concludes with some observations on the practical difficulties of land mobilisation in an atmosphere of limited tolerance for state intervention, and a brief foray into the nature of the debate over the ecological sustainability of resource development in Papua New Guinea.

Land, identity, and land tenure in Papua New Guinea

One of the more widely cited statements about land in Papua New Guinea comes from three Bougainvillean students who wrote in 1974 that

> land is our physical life [and] our social life; it is marriage; it is status;
> it is security; it is politics; in fact, it is our only world...We have little
> or no experience of social survival detached from the land. For us to be
> completely landless is a nightmare which no dollar in the pocket or
> dollar in the bank will allay; we are a threatened people (Dove,
> Miriung and Togolo 1974:182).[1]

Like the presence of taro or sweet potato in a Highlands meal, no public statement by a Papua New Guinea leader on the issue of identity is complete without reference to land (Narokobi 1980, 1986; Samana 1988). The basis for this link between land and identity can be considered through reference to the Huli people, of the Haeapugua Basin in the Southern Highlands of Papua New Guinea, who have an identity as Huli only through kinship ties to other Huli, and collectively to the landscape of the basin (Ballard 1995).

A sense of the local landscape pervades every aspect of social life in Haeapugua, in clan and personal names, as a subject for speech and song, as the source of materials for clothing and decoration, and in the type and quality of foodstuffs. As elsewhere in Melanesia, this sense of identity-through-place finds expression in the common statement that water from the streams of one's own land is the sweetest—all other streams taste different and this taste is one of the markers of difference that establishes identity. If you were to take the Huli out of Haeapugua, as one group, they would no doubt thrive—as Huli do in all the metropolitan centres of Papua New Guinea. But without access and reference to their land, they would cease to be Huli. Urban Huli remain Huli largely through reference to other Huli, and particularly to those who remain 'in place'. Conceptions of what it is to be a social being are grounded in a specific territory, and the complete relocation of a community would offer no alternative means of reproducing that particular being. This is why it is difficult for rural communities to comprehend the notion of an outright and permanent sale or transfer of title to customary land—the only compelling arguments for such a case in the past have been those of overwhelming military force, or the threat of such force.

Across Papua New Guinea, people in public conversation will deny that wars were traditionally fought over land.[2] Instead, pigs, women, insults, and deaths are cited as proximate causes for conflicts in which land was temporarily or permanently seized. Yet it is quite obvious, over a longer span of time and with the benefit of hindsight, that many wars were fought precisely over land and resources, and with the specific intention of holding and occupying lands previously belonging to others. In the Haeapugua Basin, where I documented the oral history of ownership of some 3,000 garden blocks on the basin floor (Ballard 1995), what emerged clearly was that, while minor wars served to test and in some cases alter relationships with one's enemies and allies, the major wars periodically reconfigured the social landscape on a massive scale. The largest clan in the basin has systematically routed one neighbour after another, raising its holdings of the rich swampland margin areas from some 20 per cent in about 1820 to over 70 per cent today. But, in public contexts, people in the Haeapugua basin will vehemently deny that any war is ever fought for land. Thus the clan with the largest holdings at Haeapugua justifies its possession of new land on the grounds of failure to compensate for previous homicides (while refusing all attempts at compensation). If land appears sacrosanct in this way, it reflects a form of respect for one's neighbours, an acknowledgement of the universal nature of ties between land and identity. To covet someone else's land is to threaten to exterminate them, to assume or consume their identity.

Crucially, even where military conquest forces communities off their lands, their claims to that land are never entirely relinquished or extinguished. In about 1890, in one of the wars waged for territory in the Haeapugua basin, the Bogorali clan were dispersed, taking refuge with kin in the other Huli valleys. More than a century later, they still believe that they will ultimately return to their clan land. During the 1980s Bogorali clan members patiently orchestrated marriages in a coordinated attempt to insinuate themselves into the victorious clan, a strategy that was quickly overturned when it was discovered. Today, Bogorali children are still taught the names of streams and other features of a landscape that they have never seen at close quarters. One of their leaders, Hebe Gulugu, expresses the anguish of the dispossessed

> The roots [of our clan] are still there, as are some of the branches; I left them there, for some day I will go back. Hubi Ngoari mountain is mine. Padabi river springs from the heart of my fathers. Where the Dere river runs is mine…But now I am living under the arm of another clan and only my words go back there.

However one cares to phrase the nature of this 'special' relationship, there can be little doubt that it is manifest in a particularly resilient form of attachment to land, and that these ties are not seen to diminish swiftly over time. This is probably an accurate observation for most small-scale rural societies in Melanesia with at least some history of residential stability. For the purposes of this chapter, the relevant lesson is that the enduring nature of this form of connection must have significant implications for the long-term practical outcome of any attempt at land reform.

To what extent can traditional systems of land tenure be said to reflect the qualities of this special relationship? A critical observation to be made about rural Melanesian society is that, in an important sense, there are no discrete sets of principles or forms of behaviour that pertain exclusively to the issue of land tenure. Questions relating to land cannot be dissociated from a host of other social and political structures within a community. Principles of land tenure, carefully elicited and codified by legal anthropologists, can more accurately be described as rhetorical positions deployed in specific political contexts.[3] In appealing to different and often contradictory principles of land tenure, or indeed any other aspect of social life, orators in land disputes are simply drawing upon a wide range of cultural norms and precedents as these contribute to their position in a particular debate.

There is a sense of this processual nature of Melanesian land ownership that suffers considerably in the translation to legal code. Nowhere is this more evident than in the role played by recognition and acknowledgement in determining rights to land. Rather than clearcut distinctions between landowners and land users, there is an infinite series of shades of grey between the two. Claims to the ownership of land usually rest on descent from ancestors who are held to have been the first to use the land; but, as a precedent, the sense of rights created through ownership introduces the possibility of multiple claims, as users who are not owners also create rights for themselves and their descendants. Many land disputes revolve around just this form of conundrum; but it is not through the application of hard and fast rules that such disputes are resolved. Rather, those involved in the dispute arrive at solutions that are most likely to receive broad recognition within the community. Recognition derives from a negotiated consensus over the general observance of norms and principles in the dispute process, rather than a rigorous application of those norms in the form of a code.

The ownership of land is thus enmeshed in a web of other forms of relationship. Land cannot be 'just' land. It cannot be thought of as somehow free of its social and cultural contexts, its human load. The case is firming for Peter Sack's proposition that 'land in Papua New Guinea owns the people, instead of the people owning the land' (1974:200). In short, land cannot, under the present conditions of social life in rural Melanesia, be conceived of as a commodity. Much as Eric Wolf has observed, 'Land...is not a commodity in nature; it only becomes such when defined as such by a new cultural system intent on creating a new kind of economics' (1971:277). This is not to suggest that land in Melanesia cannot be commodified, but rather to make the obvious but no less important qualification that the social and cultural changes required to effect this transformation will have to be considerable.

The state and the uncaptured landowner

If, as others suggest in this volume (Duncan and Duncan, Chand and Duncan), commodification of land is the price of engaging with the larger world of capital, how is this transformation to be approached, and what are to be the respective roles of state and community in the process? How have colonial and independent states asserted their rights to land and resources, and what sort of recognition have these assertions received in rural communities? A common observation on the postcolonial state in Papua New Guinea is that it has experienced a series of challenges to its authority as its 'reach' and the supply of services, to the rural hinterland in particular, have declined (Narokobi 1986, Strathern 1993, Standish 1994).

In trying to comprehend the post-independence contraction of the state in Papua New Guinea, the role of state violence—or the threat of such violence—will require more attention than it has perhaps received. Certainly it was the monopoly on firearms that underwrote the success of the colonial administrations in the 'pacification' of the Highlands region from the 1920s on (Kituai 1993, Polier 1995:259). The significance of state coercion during the colonial period is more easily discerned from a post-independence perspective. Indeed, Hank Nelson (1995) has made it clear that anxiety about the deployment of force in an increasingly scrutinised environment was one of the key factors in the accelerated departure of Australian rule. There is no comprehensive overview of the state's internal use of force in Papua New Guinea since 1975, but my impression (gained through experience in the Highlands) is of a continuing but much less strategically guided legacy of state violence, particularly through the instrument of police raids. The colonial government may have been a military force to be negotiated with but, under the conditions of post-Independence Papua New Guinea, the legitimacy of the State's monopoly on the use of violence is very much in question. As Narokobi (1986:6) describes it, 'in very many respects, the number one enemy of the village or the clan is a thing called the Independent State of Papua New Guinea'. This is an attitude that extends to the ownership of land and resources, as Narokobi again makes clear: 'As a Minister of State and the Attorney-General, [I have to say] that the law [on State ownership of minerals] is correct, but as a "native" or as a villager, that [it] is not correct; I will never agree to it' (Ballard 1996:77).

In his 1969 discussion of land alienation during the colonial period, Peter Sack wrote, somewhat ambiguously, that 'the natives still believe their land is not really alienated' (1969:10–11). By the 1990s, any trace of this ambiguity has been extinguished, for the 'natives' now clearly know this for a fact. With just over 1 per cent of the total land area alienated, and the remainder recognised as customary land (Larmour 1991:1), the term 'landowner' in Papua New Guinea connotes an unusual degree of inclusion. Colin Filer (forthcoming) has recently documented the emergence of the 'landowner' as a cultural and political actor in Papua New Guinea. Tracking the incidence of use of the term 'landowner' in the *Post-Courier* newspaper, he proposes that the development of 'landowner' status as 'the principal vehicle of national populism…is a phenomenon which owes a good deal to the mineral prospecting boom of the early 1980s'. Papua New Guineans of the 1990s define themselves as 'landowners' in much the same way that Australians under a Coalition government now find themselves defined as (reluctant) 'taxpayers'. The agencies of definition may differ, but both imply a transformation in the fundamental orientation connoted by the term 'citizen' and a reduction in the role of the state.

The rise of the 'landowner' has been accompanied by a resurgence in references to that 'special' relationship with the land; from a series of 'landowner' letters to the *Post-Courier* daily newspaper which Filer quotes (Filer in press), the following extracts convey a sense of the terms in which this relationship is being expressed[4]

> Registration of customary land…will signal the loss of power which is usually derived from the special bond betweeen people and their land. It is this power that brought giant mining companies crawling into the courtroom; this same power legitimises our rights to demand compensation from unscrupulous transnational corporations…(*Post-Courier* 17 July 1995).

> We know we are blessed with resources. We are a rich people with what we have—people who know their true connection to the land will understand this (*Post-Courier* 1 August 1995).

Filer and others (Gerritsen 1996, Jackson 1992) have described in some detail the revolution in the relationship between the state and those landowner communities around mining projects during the current minerals boom. A process of political devolution has seen the state increasingly withdraw from its role in the redistribution of resource benefits to the broader nation, turning over ever larger proportions of those benefits to the resource landowner communities and simultaneously contracting out the provision of services to the resource developers. The most recent example of this form of 'franchise administration' is the decision to transfer responsibility, for those services funded by the Special Support Grant that is received from Ok Tedi Mining Ltd, from the provincial government of Western Province back to the company: a fiscal trajectory which Filer (1996b) neatly describes as 'taxation in reverse'.

Royalty agreements at different mining projects are a useful index of this process of state capitulation in the face of landowner communities unimpressed by claims of sovereign right to resources. The state maintains that it holds sovereign rights to all sub-surface resources, including minerals, and rights to surface access as an 'incident' of that ownership. Peter Donigi (1994) has published a sophisticated challenge to the constitutional basis for this claim, but rebuttals have come more frequently and more bluntly from landowner communities contesting the division of mining benefits. The list of major disputes at mineral projects is familiar to many. At each successive project, the terms have shifted steadily towards the benefit of immediate landowner communities, while eroding the policy resources of the state (Gerritsen 1996). The plans for Ok Tedi included payments to the project area landowners of 5 per cent of the 1.25 per cent royalty rate. At the Porgera, Misima and Kutubu projects, agreements yielding between 20 per cent and 30 per cent of the royalties were negotiated. The Ok Tedi rate was then renegotiated in 1991, settling at 30 per cent of royalties (Jackson 1993). Lihir, where the landowner association chairman, with some perspicuity, describes the State as 'only a concept' (Filer 1996:68), provides the high-water mark in this trend, with the landowners and their Development Authority due to receive up to 50 per cent of an augmented rate of 2 per cent of royalties, and 30 per cent of the Special Support Grant to the provincial government (Filer 1997)—an agreement that has had flow-on benefits for the landowners at other projects, who now also benefit from the 2 per cent rate.

Other critical watersheds in this history of erosion of public respect for the authority of the state in Papua New Guinea include: the rebellion on Bougainville following the closure of the Panguna mine, which continues to pose the most severe challenge to national sovereignty; the Placer share issue, which probably did more to destroy public confidence in the integrity of the national élite than any other single event (Jackson 1994); and the Mt Kare gold-rush, where

the inability of the state to secure either its own interests or those of
the resource developers in the face of landowner claims was played
out in public on a grand scale.

Largely by default and through an institutional incapacity to
enforce its own legislation or implement its own reforms, the state in
Papua New Guinea has created an élite resource interest group,
comprising the government of the day, resource companies and the
resource-rich or 'lucky strike' (Filer 1997) landowner communities.
Perhaps the distinction at Ok Tedi between the resource-landowning
Wopkaimin and the downstream Yonggom can be extended to
envisage a fundamental (but not impermeable) divide between a
national resource élite and a 'downstream' majority, where the latter
category includes all of those communities without significant or
accessible resources to offer. Of course almost all downstream
communities are also landowners and this is the basis on which they
then attempt to gain a hold on the development truck as it speeds
down their highway or river. The settlement of the Ok Tedi suit has
accorded a degree of formal recognition to this category of
relationship. It is now possible to suggest that the next series of
stakeholder clashes will be those entered into by the downstream
communities, such as the Duna of Lake Kopiago who perceive
pollution by tailings, dumped by the Porgera mine into the Strickland
river, to be entering their lakes and rivers through underground
channels (Nicole Haley pers. comm.), or the increasingly militant
landowners along the Okuk Highway that links the Porgera mine and
the Kutubu oilfields to the port of Lae.

Land mobilisation and state capacity

What are the implications of the fragility of this relationship between
community and state for the possible success of Papua New Guinea's
Land Mobilisation program? The mobilisation of customary land has
been a stated goal of successive governments since at least the 1973
report of the Commission of Inquiry into Land Matters (Ward 1983).
Two interim methods, Tenure Conversion and Lease-Leaseback, have
been implemented since then, with limited success. Significantly,
Hulme, reviewing the Lease-Leaseback program, observes mildly that
any attempt by the PNG Development Bank to assert its legal rights in
the event of non-repayment of loans would 'almost certainly result in
a civil disturbance. Most landowners believe that they retain their

customary rights...and they do not appreciate the legal implications of the lease-leaseback arrangements' (1983:98). But the recent Land Mobilisation Program (LMP), funded with a loan from the World Bank, has served to bring issues of land to the fore in an unprecedented way. Though the Program has initially only addressed issues relating to the administration of lands that were already alienated, it has been the focus of a heated public debate, culminating in widespread riots and even deaths (*Pacific News Bulletin*, August 1995, 10(8):7). Much of the argument about the current program has been conducted in a near-vacuum of reliable information and I do not intend to rehearse the debate here, or even to consider the social or economic merits of land mobilisation (but see Lakau, and Kalit and Young, this volume).

Here I want to focus on the extent to which the state's authority as the arbiter of social good is acknowledged, and on the practical question of the government's infrastructural capacity to actually implement this sort of reform. In a commentary on the mining sector which has much wider resonance, Richard Jackson has put the following question

> Does the government have the legal right, and the capacity to enforce the exercise of that right, to possess its territorial minerals? Only if the answer is yes is it worth answering questions of optimal mode and size of government investment in mineral projects, planning optimal benefits, integrating mining projects into national budgets and infrastructural planning. Clearly if the government's right and ability to hold mineral resources is in doubt, then all these (and many other) issues are academic (1996:107).

On both of the criteria nominated by Jackson—that of the government's right and of its ability to implement land reform—a centrally planned mobilisation program would currently appear to have little hope of success. Two major government pilot projects over the last decade have sought to tackle the issue of customary land registration: the East Sepik Provincial Government's Land Mobilisation Program (Fingleton 1991), and the more informal attempts at land mobilisation in East New Britain Province. For various reasons, neither program has met with much success. To be fair, land mobilisation is not going to be an overnight phenomenon, but the East Sepik initiative has not apparently resulted in the registration of a single block of customary land since the Customary Land Registration legislation came into force in 1987 (Haynes 1995:137), and the efforts of the East New Britain program, after a tentative beginning, were literally wiped out by the 1994 volcanic eruption (Michael Lowe, pers. comm.). The practical problems posed by a land registration program on a national scale seem insurmountable in the current climate of government/community relations. Kalit and Young (this volume) observe that Land Mobilisation on a national scale has effectively stalled in the aftermath of the 1995 riots, and propose in its stead a wide program of education on land tenure matters. A final irony is that what work is being done on the 'registration' of land claims by rural communities is being funded by the major minerals projects under the Infrastructure Taxation Credit Scheme (Filer 1997), inevitably with their own more limited goals in mind.

In this light, and reflecting my assertions about the embeddedness of land issues within other aspects of rural culture and society, the most attractive propositions for land reform in Papua New Guinea would appear to be those that emphasise a slower, negotiated and more organic process of transformation. Robert Cooter, the most articulate proponent of this position, places his faith in the 'common law process', arguing that the only legislation likely to achieve community recognition is that which emerges through engagement with a living, customary law (Cooter 1991).[5] The present form of legislative protection of customary ownership, inhibiting direct transactions over land, is inappropriate 'because limitations on customary land transaction should come from customary law itself, not from Parliament. Sales and leases of customary land should be enforceable in the land court to the extent that they conform to customary law, neither more nor less' (Cooter 1991:45). Resources would be most usefully directed not towards a centralised, 'top-down' campaign for land registration, but rather towards improving the capacity of existing village-level institutions, such as the land courts and magistrates. Further support for those institutions that have the most experience with customary law, through a program which facilitated the circulation and open discussion of court findings and accorded greater authority to those findings, would most effectively promote the development and codification of common law. This graduated approach, Cooter argues, would have the additional effect of according partial legal recognition to the daily reality of transactions over land amongst landowners, entirely unmediated by the state.

It would be surprising if this sort of view did not meet with some opposition from the Department of Lands and Physical Planning, but then the Department has only ever really addressed the tiny fraction of land that is alienated, and there are questions about its capacity to do even that. There does seem to be value in an approach which simultaneously recognises the practical difficulties for national programs of land registration posed by limited government capacity and an 'uncaptured peasantry', and identifies and strengthens those institutions that actually continue to function at a village level—those institutions, in Munro's terms, that have successfully been brought into the village. Though this approach constitutes effective recognition of the fact of village-level autonomy in contemporary Papua New Guinea, the state would retain an important role through guidance and supervision of the common law process on a national scale.

Landowners as an ecological nobility?

Given the emphasis in this chapter on the special relationship between rural communities and the land, it is necessary to conclude with some comments on the implications for resource sustainability of this moral contest between state and community. There seems to be a wilful slip in the logic of some commentators from a perception of rural communities in contest with resource developers and the state to the conclusion that these communities embody an ethic of environmental conservation—that they are somehow intrinsically 'ecologically noble' (Buege 1996). In a recent analysis of the Kutubu oil project, for example, we are told that 'the natural environment and spiritual landscape of the Foe, Fasu and Kikori, where they lived harmoniously for thousands of years, has been transformed without their prior informed consent' and told of 'cultures who have survived for thousands of years without jeopardising their own existence or that of everyone else' (Kennedy 1996:240, 248). Two principal objections can be made to assertions of this kind. As a general observation on rural Melanesian societies, this sense of ecological harmony is unlikely to hold true, either now or in the past (Dwyer 1994, Clarke 1995:58). More seriously, the discourse of ecological resistance fails to appreciate the aspirations and the internal politics of rural communities—the same author writes dismissively of what he describes as the 'fanciful wishes of the local people seeking to be developed' (Kennedy 1996:237).

The assertion of ecological harmony is at odds with the developing consensus that the sustainability of rural Melanesian subsistence systems appears to be a matter of scale, rather than of orientation. The recent work of ANU's Land Management Project has demonstrated fairly conclusively that many of the agricultural systems in practice have contributed significantly to environmental degradation in the past, and that in their present form and under current rates of population growth, they are inherently unsustainable (Allen 1996). It is a moot point whether land management systems in Papua New Guinea have ever achieved an ecological stability such as the harmony attributed to the relationship between the Foe and Fasu and their landscapes. Certainly, those communities that adopted sweet potato as a staple crop, following its introduction some 300 years ago, have yet to find a balance in their use of the land (Wood 1984, Ballard 1995).

A second objection to this nobilising impulse concerns the romantic tendency to invoke an image of exceptional communal solidarity, to 'sanitise the internal politics of the dominated' (Ortner 1995). This tendency has a number of unfortunate consequences. First, in describing community action in terms of resistance to encroachment, it fails to credit rural communities with the dynamism and capacity for transformation which they so evidently possess. A further consequence of this 'Rousseauian' portrait of ecological nobility is its contribution to the stragetic exoticisation and often deliberate ignorance of the political complexity of communities on the part of resource developers (Weiner 1991:72).

Second, the deliberate equation of social and ecological harmony, which incidentally guarantees the intervention of novel stakeholders professing claims to the land on global ecological grounds, has the effect of identifying the environment as the principal concern of rural communities. This then obscures any understanding of the motivation of individuals and communities, and would read the recent Ok Tedi court case, for example, largely in terms of the ecological impacts and not as a struggle to gain access to services and to economic opportunity.

Finally, the 'ecologically noble' perspective cannot anticipate the aspirations of individuals or communities in terms other than a fall from ecological grace. Alcida Ramos (1994) has described the cycle of adulation and then denigration experienced by representatives of Brazilian Indian communities as they first object to the lack of consultation about use of their land and then enter into negotiation with the forces of 'western seduction'.

This ignorance of the political complexity of rural communities, which in itself bespeaks a fundamental lack of will to hear their 'voice', to engage with their aspirations, is often shared in equal measure by agents of the state, environmental advocates and resource developers. What is required of each of these parties is closer attention to the ways in which land, and the identities it confers, are deployed as terms in the debate. There is no clear distinction between rhetoric and keenly held belief in references to land, which carry a weight in Melanesian discourse whose changing significance continues to elude an external or urban audience. The title of this chapter derives from the sign that James Cavill, Clinton's election campaign director, had up over his desk in an attempt to keep his eye on the main game, the economy. For anyone following the unfolding debate over the sustainability of resource exploitation in Melanesia, a similar tag suggests itself. For the issue at the heart of the debate over the ownership of resources and the division of resource benefits is—and always will be—the land, stupid.

Notes

The comments of Robin Hide, Janaline Oh, Brigid Ballard and John Clanchy are gratefully acknowledged in the revision of the original text. None of them bears responsibility for the result.

1. The transformative effects of large-scale mining projects on society in Papua New Guinea are witnessed by the contrasting fates of two of the authors: Mel Togolo, who is now Manager of Corporate Affairs for the mining company Placer Niugini, and Theodore Miriung, the Acting Premier of North Solomons Province, who was assassinated in October 1996, in the aftermath of the secessionist rebellion and the expulsion of CRA from the Panguna mine.
2. Thus that most public of statements, Bernard Narokobi's *The Melanesian Way*, must insist that 'Land was something permanent. No one could in those days remove the ground' (1980:112).
3. Merlan and Rumsey (1991) make this point more generally in reference to the rhetorical constitution of social groups amongst communities in the Nebilyer Valley.
4. In fact these letters to the papers are so intriguing, and lend support so readily to his arguments, that it is possible to imagine Filer actually writing many of them.
5. Cooter's position tallies closely with one of the principal conclusions drawn from another major foray into the morass of land issues in New Britain, the Kandrian–Gloucester Integrated Development Project. The conclusion here was that where government lacked the resources and political will to enforce its own provisions, policy on lands and resource issues should be negotiated and incremental (Simpson 1998:55).

References

Allen, Bryant, 1996. 'Land management: Papua New Guinea's dilemma,' *The Asia-Pacific Magazine* 1(1):36–42.

Ballard, Chris, 1995. The death of a great land: ritual, history and subsistence revolution in the Southern Highlands of Papua New Guinea, PhD thesis, The Australian National University, Canberra.

——, 1996. 'Citizens and landowners: the contest over land and mineral resources in Eastern Indonesia and Papua New Guinea,' in Donald Denoon, Chris Ballard, Glenn Banks and Peter Hancock (eds), *Mining and Mineral Resource Policy Issues in Asia-Pacific: prospects for the 21st century*, proceedings of the conference at the Australian National University, 1–3 November 1995, Division of Pacific and Asian History, Research School of Pacific and Asian Studies, The Australian National University, Canberra:76–81.

Buege, Douglas J., 1996. 'The ecologically noble savage revisited.' *Environmental Ethics* 18(1):71–88.

Clarke, William C., 1995. 'Lands rich in thought', *South Pacific Journal of Natural Science* 14:55–67.

Cooter, Robert, 1991. 'Kin groups and the common law process,' in Peter Larmour (ed.), *Customary Land Tenure: registration and decentralisation in Papua New Guinea*, Monograph 29, Institute of Applied Social and Economic Research, Boroko:33–49.

Denoon, Donald, Chris Ballard, Glenn Banks and Peter Hancock (eds), 1996. *Mining and Mineral Resource Policy Issues in Asia-Pacific: prospects for the 21st century*, proceedings of the conference at the Australian National University, 1–3 November 1995, Division of Pacific and Asian History, Research School of Pacific and Asian Studies, The Australian National University, Canberra.

Donigi, Peter, 1994. *Indigenous or Aboriginal Rights to Property: a Papua New Guinea perspective*, International Books, Utrecht.

Dove, J., T. Miriung and M. Togolo, 1974. 'Mining bitterness,' in Peter G. Sack (ed.), *Problem of Choice: land in Papua New Guinea's future*, Australian National University Press and Robert Brown and Associates, Canberra and Port Moresby:181–9.

Dwyer, Peter D., 1994. 'Modern conservation and indigenous peoples: in search of wisdom,' *Pacific Conservation Biology* 1:91–7.

Filer, Colin, 1996. 'Participation, governance and social impact: the planning of the Lihir gold mine,' in Donald Denoon, Chris Ballard, Glenn Banks and Peter Hancock (eds), *Mining and Mineral Resource Policy Issues in Asia-Pacific: prospects for the 21st century*, proceedings of the conference at the Australian National University, 1–3 November

1995, Division of Pacific and Asian History, Research School of Pacific and Asian Studies, The Australian National University, Canberra:67–75.

——, 1997. 'Resource rents' in Ila Temu (ed.), *Papua New Guinea: a 20/20 vision*, National Research Institute, Papua New Guinea, and National Centre for Development Studies, The Australian National University, Canberra:222–60.

——, forthcoming. 'Compensation, rent and power in Papua New Guinea,' in Susan Toft (ed.), *Compensation and Resource Development*, Law Reform Commission, Boroko, and National Centre for Development Studies, The Australian National University, Canberra.

Fingleton, Jim, 1991. 'The East Sepik land legislation,' in Peter Larmour (ed.) *Customary Land Tenure: registration and decentralisation in Papua New Guinea*, Monograph 29, Institute of Applied Social and Economic Research, Boroko:101–120.

Gerritsen, Rolf, 1996.'"Capital logic" and the erosion of public policy in Papua New Guinea,' in Donald Denoon, Chris Ballard, Glenn Banks and Peter Hancock (eds), *Mining and Mineral Resource Policy Issues in Asia-Pacific: prospects for the 21st century*, proceedings of the conference at the Australian National University, 1–3 November 1995, Division of Pacific and Asian History, Research School of Pacific and Asian Studies, The Australian National University, Canberra:82–90.

Haynes, C.E.P., 1995. 'The Land Mobilisation Program and customary land,' in Jonathan Aleck and Jackson Rannells (eds), *Custom at the Crossroads*, Faculty of Law, University of Papua New Guinea, Waigani:129–47.

Hulme, David, 1983. 'Credit, land registration and development: implications of the Lease-Leaseback system,' *Melanesian Law Journal* 11:91–8.

Jackson, Richard T., 1992. 'Undermining or determining the nature of the state?,' in Stephen Henningham and R.J. May with Lulu Turner (eds*), Resources, Development and Politics in the Pacific Islands*, Crawford House Press, Bathurst:79–89.

——, 1993. *Cracked Pot or Copper Bottomed Investment? The development of the Ok Tedi project, 1982–1991, a personal view*, Melanesian Studies Centre, James Cook University of North Queensland, Townsville.

——, 1994. 'One full circle: BCL to PJV,' *Taim Lain* 2(1):18–26.

——, 1996. Discussant, in Donald Denoon, Chris Ballard, Glenn Banks and Peter Hancock (eds), *Mining and Mineral Resource Policy Issues in Asia-Pacific: prospects for the 21st century*, proceedings of the conference at the Australian National University, 1–3 November 1995, Division of Pacific and Asian History, Research School of Pacific and Asian Studies, The Australian National University, Canberra:107–109.

Kennedy, Danny, 1996. 'Development or sustainability at Kutubu, Papua New Guinea,' in Richard Howitt with John Connell and Philip Hirsch (eds), *Resources, Nations and Indigenous Peoples: case studies from Australasia, Melanesia and Southeast Asia*, Oxford University Press, Melbourne:236–50.

Kituai, August, 1993. My Gun, My Brother: experiences of Papua New Guinea policemen, 1920–1960, PhD thesis, The Australian National University, Canberrra.

Larmour, Peter, 1991. 'Introduction,' in Peter Larmour (ed.), *Customary Land Tenure: registration and decentralisation in Papua New Guinea*, Monograph 29, Institute of Applied Social and Economic Research, Boroko:1–8.

Merlan, Francesca and Alan Rumsey, 1991. *Ku Waru: language and segmentary politics in the western Nebilyer Valley, Papua New Guinea*, Cambridge University Press, Cambridge.

Munro, William A., 1996. 'Power, peasants and political development: reconsidering state construction in Africa,' *Comparative Studies in Society and History* 38(1):112–48.

Narokobi, Bernard, 1980. *The Melanesian Way*, Institute of Papua New Guinea Studies, Boroko.

——, 1986. 'The old and the new,' in Gernot Fugmann (ed.), *Ethics and Development in Papua New Guinea*, The Melanesian Institute, Goroko:3–16.

Nelson, Hank, 1995. 'Going finish: the ending of Australian rule in Papua New Guinea,' Seminar, Research School of Social Sciences, The Australian National University, Canberra, 20 July 1995, unpublished.

Ortner, Sherry, 1995. 'Resistance and the problem of ethnographic refusal,' *Comparative Studies in Society and History* 37(1):173–93.

Polier, Nicole, 1995. '"When Australia was the big name for Papua New Guinea": the colonial constitution of Faiwolmin subjects', *Journal of Historical Sociology* 8(3):257–77.

Proulx, E. Annie, 1994. *Postcards*, Flamingo, London.

Ramos, Alcida, 1994. 'From Eden to limbo: the construction of indigenism in Brazil,' in George Clement Bond and Angela Gilliam (eds), *Social Construction of the Past: representation as power*, Routledge, London:74–88.

Sack, Peter G., 1969. 'Early land acquisitions in New Guinea: the native version,' *Journal of the Papua New Guinea Society* 3(2):7–16.

——, 1974. 'The triumph of colonialism,' in Peter G. Sack (ed.), *Problem of Choice: land in Papua New Guinea's future*, The Australian National University Press and Robert Brown and Associates, Canberra and Port Moresby:200–208.

Samana, Utula, 1988. *Papua New Guinea: which way?*, Arena Publications, North Carlton.

Simpson, Gary, 1996. '"Get what you can while you can": landowner and government relations in the forest industry of West New Britain, Papua New Guinea,' *Development Bulletin* 37:52–6.

Standish, Bill, 1994. 'Papua New Guinea: the search for security in a weak state,' in Alan Thompson (ed.), *Papua New Guinea: issues for Australian security planners*, Australian Defence Studies Centre, Australian Defence Force Academy, Canberra:51–97.

Strathern, Andrew, 1993. 'Violence and political change in Papua New Guinea,' *Bijdragen Tot de Taal-, Land-, en Volkenkunde* 149(4):718–36.

Ward, Alan, 1983. 'The Commission of Inquiry into Land Matters 1973: choices, constraints and assumptions,' *Melanesian Law Journal* 11:1–13.

Weiner, James F., 1991. 'Colonial engagement in Third World oil extraction: some examples from Papua New Guinea,' *World Energy Council Journal*:69–74.

Wolf, Eric, 1971. *Peasant Wars of the Twentieth Century*, Faber and Faber, London.

Wood, Andrew W., 1984. Land for tomorrow: subsistence agriculture, soil fertility and ecosystem stability in the New Guinea Highlands, PhD thesis, University of Papua New Guinea, Boroko.

4

Customary land tenure and common/ public rights to minerals in Papua New Guinea

Andrew A.L. Lakau

Throughout Papua New Guinea a wide range of natural resources or substances were extracted from land, sea and waters, using a variety of techniques. In coastal areas coral reefs, shells and other marine resources have always had great value. In the highlands, there is widespread evidence of stone quarries and other extraction sites which were worked on for thousands of years. Haynes (1995:33) summarises the evidence on the use of natural resources

> for pre-colonial trade, significant sub-surface substances were extracted for use in the manufacture of items for trade, or for trade in their original form. These included mineral pigments of various kinds, edible earth (a dietary supplement of pigs), various kinds of stone and clay (for pottery and other purposes). Furthermore, water from mineral springs was used to make salt and mineral oil from seepage was used as a cosmetic, medicine and possibly as cooking fuel. Stone was the substance most extensively extracted, being used for many purposes which included cooking stones, hammer and anvil stones, drill points, awls, scrapers, knives, bark cloth beaters, axe blades and prehistoric mortars and pestles and naturally weathered curiously shaped stones were used in magico-religious rituals.

There were also claims to the exploitation and ownership of natural resources. At times, there were conflicting claims asserted by neighbouring groups over these resources or substances. The rights to use particular natural resources were guided by rituals and laws which developed alongside the discovery of these resources. In the postcolonial period, these traditional laws have been subsumed by what could be termed 'Western' law. Peter Sack argues for a distinction between what he terms 'primitive' law and 'Western' law

> Primitive law being an open system, it cannot be argued that no rights to rock outcrops and patches of poor soil exist because the traditional law says nothing about them (as could probably be argued in Western law). Although not yet defined, these rights will be defined when their existence becomes a practical issue. This definition does not create new rights; they existed all the time, only in a latent form (Sack 1973:20).

Both law and custom are subject to constant adjustment in space and time. It is inevitable that custom has changed in reaction to postcolonial settlement and contemporary circumstances with respec to mineral rights.

Minerals, oil and gas can be seen in two ways. First, they are resources of value which naturally occur. In this case, ownership, and the right to use such resources would belong to the landowners. Second, minerals, oil and gas can be perceived as other natural resources such as rivers and lakes—as public or common property. In this case, landowning groups are merely trustee administrators.

From a societal point of view, there is some justification in the state maintaining ownership rights over minerals and other natural resources without traditional value or use. There is a valid argument in the Papua New Guinea situation that resources of immense economic value should not be left to particular individuals or communities. Ownership of such valuable natural resources should be vested in the state, in the same way as ownership of customary land is vested in the clan or kinship group as a whole. Both such authorities exercise their roles on a trustee basis, one (the state) for the whole society and the other (the landowning group), for its members.

Today, the nation–state of Papua New Guinea encompasses all existing tribal groups. The challenge lies in reconciling this modern state and the numerous tribal societies that had previously performed many of roles of a nation–state. However, wholly reinstating such traditional political units would be inconsistent with nation-building and anti-constitutional as well.

I believe that society as a whole has a right to share in whatever socioeconomic advantages flow from the development of mineral resources. Parties in a mining deal should not just be the mining company and the customary landowners. The state as custodian of the public interest must regulate the deal on behalf of society as a whole, as well as derive its own share of benefits. At the same time, it is the state which can guarantee security on an investment, ensuring fair bargaining and benefits to either side.

The best scenario is one where there is maximum benefit flowing from mining development to society as a whole and the customary landowners. Such a scenario must also continue to attract the necessary commitment from foreign investors and mining corporations who have the expertise and capital essential for continued development of mineral resources in Papua New Guinea.

In democratic States, where governments are representative of the whole society, the value of minerals far exceeds individual or sectional interests. To favour the interest of a minority or sectional group would lead to situations similar to that in the Middle East. There, the vast wealth generated from oil and petroleum is siphoned by a few individuals at the expense of the impoverished masses.

The community or individuals in whose land minerals are found can benefit by way of compensation, royalty payments and various forms of income (Lakau 1995, Haynes 1995). Environmental considerations can be part of that compensatory package. These are provided for all small to large-scale mining operations in Papua New Guinea.

To leave the right of ownership of mineral resources entirely to customary landowners is dangerous. Although this may be acceptable in other countries, in Papua New Guinea, it is likely that this would open the floodgates for numerous claims to gain exclusive benefits from commercial mining, leading to disharmony between those who have the happy accident of minerals under their land, and most, who do not. Private landowners, in the name of customary rights, would try to dictate terms to legitimate governments and society as a whole. Private ownership of minerals would also lead to 'veto', where the landowners may refuse development of mineral resources under their land, virtually holding society to ransom.

Customary landowners cannot be 'free-riders' on other benefits they derive from society. It is largely because of the efforts of society as a whole that land has an economic value. Public funding provides the social and economic infrastructure—roads, bridges, public safety or security, markets, and finance—which enables the utilisation of land and mineral resources.

Private and communal landownership confers on sectional groups the right to profit from public actions in which they have played no part. Such private property rights may be argued as constitutional rights. But when rights are concentrated in the hands of sectional and selected groups, this is an abuse of private property. Speculation, manipulation, concentration of wealth and the like are not desirable and were never the dreams of Papua New Guinea's founders.

Individuals and communities within the nation–state cannot enjoy other privileges and subsidiary rights flowing from them, without the state at large safeguarding everyone's interests. Hence, even customary rights are not persuasive in claims to exclusive possession of minerals on or under their land.

Moreover, customary land tenure systems in Papua New Guinea have clearly demarcated reference to individual, community and public or common property rights. Advocacy of exclusive possession carries connotations of greed, and is arguably alien to customary principles of land use and tenure.

Conflicting roles of the state

However, state ownership of minerals is only fine in so far as the state is representative of the common or public interest. What has turned out in practice in Papua New Guinea over the years leaves a lot to be desired and is a prime reason for the lack of development, the breakdown of law and order, and the masses being left out of the fruits of prosperity and nation-building (Dorney 1990, Holzknecht 1995).

The state has become an arena of conflict. Governments are supposed to manage resources such as minerals which belong to the State on a trusteeship basis. In Papua New Guinea, the governments see themselves as the state. Parliamentarians and bureaucrats have been prone to corruption and mismanagement (Dorney 1990, Holzknecht 1995). Individuals and groups who entered the arena of resource management via the parliament or government have made it an established practice to further private interests, either individually and for their factions. They use slogans such as 'the people', 'national interest' and 'privatisation', when in fact the real beneficiaries are those who wield power and control public coffers.

It is in the midst of these conflicting roles, corrupt practices and mismanagement that state ownership of minerals is being challenged.

More often than not, the challenge is not over the logic or the legitimacy of state ownership of minerals—it is over the distribution of benefits flowing from the development of minerals.

Conclusion

On one hand, ownership of minerals is a right of the state. Legal challenges to state ownership of minerals have had no success in Papua New Guinea to date.

On the other hand, Papua New Guinea is a property owning democracy. It follows that customary landowners have unchallenged rights to ownership of their land and the development of resources found therein. However, the pursuit of national economic growth in Papua New Guinea can only be achieved with a pluralistic approach that contains a mixture of private and common property rights. Customary land tenure systems in themselves have connotations of individual, communal and public or common property rights. Any form of development should be for the benefit of people as a whole.

Instances where many are disadvantaged from development must be avoided. State ownership of minerals is part of common property interests. Customary principles do not necessarily conflict with state ownership of minerals. Only when a genuine and developmental state owns minerals will there be a facilitation of societal development. This is not the case in Papua New Guinea, and this is the fundamental but unresolved issue that is largely to be blamed for the lack of development and most of the people being left out of the mainstream of national growth and prosperity in a mineral-rich Papua New Guinea.

References

Crocombe, R.G. (ed.), 1987. *Land Tenure in the Pacific,* University of the South Pacific, Suva.

—— and Hide, R., 1987. 'New Guinea: unity in diversity', in R.G. Crocombe (ed.) *Land Tenure in the Pacific,* University of the South Pacific, Suva:324–67.

——, (ed.), 1995. *Customary Land Tenure and Sustainable Development: complementarity or conflict?*, South Pacific Commission, Noumea and Institute of Pacific Studies, University of South Pacific, Suva.

Dorney, S., 1990. *Papua New Guinea: people, politics and history since 1975,* Random House, Milsons Point.

5

Improving security of access to customary-owned land in Melanesia: mining in Papua New Guinea

Ron Duncan and Rod Duncan

This chapter takes as its starting point that land ownership arrangements in the South Pacific will continue to change very slowly. Therefore, existing forms of customary or communal ownership will remain in place for a long time. This does not necessarily pose the problem for economic development that many perceive: that communal ownership means insecurity of access for potential users of the land, reducing the incentive to invest in the land with adverse consequences for productivity. As, for example, Crocombe (1995) says, the form of ownership of land is not as important for making the most productive use of the land as the security of access to use of the land. Communal ownership of land should not entail inefficient use of the land as long as security of access to use of the land can be guaranteed.

Accepting that the form of ownership is not as important as security of access, the key question is: how can access for use, essentially through leasehold tenure, be made more secure? In particular, we focus on the situation in Papua New Guinea where access for use seems very insecure, with frequent claims for additional compensation arising after the contract between the lessee and the landowners has been signed. The most prominent examples of this behaviour are in mining projects. However, similar situations have arisen in many other forms of land use, such as hotel construction, timber contracts, and the siting of telecommunication facilities. This insecurity of access which results from the post-contract signing claims for additional compensation is very detrimental to investment. As well as reducing the level of investment below what it would be with more secure access, the investment that does take place tends to be of shorter duration. A policy of 'get in and get out quickly' is encouraged. In mining and forestry, for example, this behaviour leads to the best ore grades and the best trees being taken first and with as little attention as possible paid to the resulting environmental effects.[1]

It is a key proposition of this chapter that the solution to the problem of insecurity of access to use of land is to create a contract that is more appropriate to the situation in these countries than contracts presently in use, or to adopt other mechanisms that will lead to fewer disputes or to quicker resolution of disputes over contracts and therefore provide greater security to lessees and greater satisfaction to landowners and the government. The main characteristics of mining in Papua New Guinea which lead to disputes appear to be the following: first, at the time of the contract negotiations there is a high degree of asymmetry in the information available to the mining company on the one hand and to the landowners on the other hand with respect to three very uncertain variables—the size and quality of the ore (or oil or gas) reserves, the expected prices for the mining output, and the environmental damage that may be incurred during the life of the mine. Information about the first and last of these three issues becomes better known during the life of the project, especially to the landowners. Because primary commodity prices basically behave as 'random walk' processes, it is not possible to forecast them. However, a mining company will have a much better understanding of the (usually highly volatile) behaviour of primary commodity prices than will the landowners. Over the life of the project the landowners will see higher and lower prices being paid for the minerals or crude oil but, given the usual form of royalty payments, may not feel that they are sharing fairly in the fortunes of the project—particularly in the windfall gains from high prices.

Second, the history of land leases in Papua New Guinea shows that landowners are prone to take quite dramatic action in support of their complaints and renewed claims for compensation. The forced closure in 1989 of the Panguna mine on Bougainville island in the North Solomons Province of Papua New Guinea and the court case in 1995–1996 over the Ok Tedi mine are the two most prominent examples.

The Mt Kare gold mine site in the Enga Province was subjected to disruption and closure over the period 1991–1992, leading to the mining company CRA Ltd relinquishing its exploration lease in 1993. At a micro level, the electricity and telecommunications bodies, for example, have reported damage being done to their transmitter stations during disputes over landowner claims for additional compensation.

Third, as stated previously, because of the insecurity of tenure, the mining companies (or timber contractors) will, where scope exists, bias their activities towards short-run exploitation of the resource. In addition to the high-grading of ore bodies mentioned, manifestations of this kind of attitude include flying expatriate labour in and out of the mine site rather than constructing permanent living quarters, constructing roads and bridges without long-lasting foundations, minimising on waste disposal facilities, and no longer providing long-term skills training of indigenous labour.

Fourth, in the context of mining in Papua New Guinea, the national government cannot be treated as a neutral agent, simply providing the institutional environment within which contracts are negotiated. At times the government acts as a facilitator of the negotiations between the landowners and the mining companies. It may also form a partnership with landowners in contract negotiations. But the government also acts in competition with landowners over shares in the mining rents (see Gupta 1992 on the history of the BCL mine in Panguna, Bougainville) and has itself made claims for additional compensation (royalties, taxes) and additional equity (as, for example, with the Porgera mine) during the course of agreements. Hence, in the analysis it may be useful at times to treat the government and the landowners as one decision-maker and at other times as competitors. But in looking for ways to improve the security of contracts, it is also useful to examine separate government roles in negotiating contracts with mining companies as well as in holding parties to their agreements.

For purposes of analysis we use a framework drawn from the economic literature on contracts, including the literature relating to labour strikes. Economic analysis of strikes provides a framework which incorporates behaviour closely paralleling those described above. The analysis highlights the major deficiencies of existing forms of mining contracts, given those factors which are seen as leading to disputes, and suggests actions that should reduce disputes over contracts and thereby improve security of access.

The analytical framework

As described above, a major problem with mining contracts in Papua New Guinea has been the tendency for the PNG landowners to demand re-negotiation of a contract during the life of the contract. Such actions adversely affect investment by increasing the insecurity of tenure. We have identified four major areas in which these difficulties may arise under long-term contracts for resource use in Papua New Guinea. These broad areas can be thought in terms of

- asymmetry of information between the landowners/ government and the company over the expected profitability of the mine
- time inconsistency of long-term contracts
- incompleteness of the contracts
- disagreements between the PNG landowners and government over the allocation of benefits of the mining contracts.

Informational asymmetry

Starting with Ashenfelter and Johnson (1969) and surveyed in Kennan (1986), a popular model in the analysis of the economics of labour strikes has incorporated the notion that, lacking as much information about firms' profitability as the firms themselves, unions use strikes to sort out the more profitable firms from the less profitable. It is assumed that the strikers make the firms a decreasing sequence of wage offers, knowing that the more profitable firms will want to resolve the strike sooner than the less profitable firms as the former have more to lose in terms of forgone profits.

This model appears to provide a partial explanation of why it is that the landowners might seek to renegotiate a mining lease. In the absence of full disclosure by the mining company, it seems reasonable to assume that the mining company has much better information about the expected profitability of the mine than the landowners and the government, and thus of the size of possible royalties. Of course, the mining company will have even better information about its expected profitability once it has begun operations. Thus it may be in the interest of the landowners to shut down the mine, or threaten to shut it down, and demand renegotiation of the mining contract once it has begun operation in order to determine better the profitability of the operation.

Such behaviour seems an exceedingly inefficient manner of gaining information on mine profitability. If the company and the landowners/government knew the final result of the negotiations in advance, they could settle the dispute immediately and both be better off than by undergoing a prolonged mine closure. This anomaly is known in the economics of strikes literature as the 'Hicks Paradox', from Hicks (1963). Due to the asymmetry of information between the parties, the settlement cannot be made in advance because the company has an incentive to under-report profits in order to reduce the payment of royalties. The truthful revelation of company profits is only enforced by the actuality or possibility of a closure.

A reinforcing reason for mine disputes may be provided by factors giving rise to what is known as the time inconsistency of contracts.

Time inconsistency of contracts

After the issue was raised by Barro and Gordon (1983) in relation to inflation policy, economists realised how ubiquitous problems with respect to time inconsistency are in economic relations. Most agreements will specify future actions to be taken by each party to the agreement. The problem may arise, however, that even if the actions specified are optimal for a party at the time of the making of the agreement, when the time comes to perform the action, the action may not be optimal. This problem may occur even when all events have been perfectly forecasted.

If a way cannot be found to ensure that each party adheres to the agreement, the optimal agreement is time-inconsistent. The parties may have to resort to a sub-optimal agreement that is time-consistent. We will illustrate the problem using a simple example.

Assume the PNG government grants a mining lease. The contract sets out the royalties and other payments the mining company must pay in return for the right to mine over the period of the lease. The time-inconsistency problem arises in that the government or landowners have an incentive to attempt to renegotiate the contract once the company has installed the mining equipment. The initial negotiations will be over the profit of the mine net of the operating and capital costs. Once the capital is installed, however, the company will keep mining as long as it covers its operating costs. Hence, the nature of the negotiations changes as the value covered by the negotiations switches to profit net only of operating costs. The pie is larger and so, presumably, will be the government's new share.

If the company suspects that the government or landowners will attempt to reopen negotiations once the capital is installed, the company will minimise its installed capital. This will lower the profitability and length of life of the mine and possible royalties, and thus the company, the government and the landowners are worse off than if the government could promise not to renegotiate.

Another way in which time inconsistency may appear in mining contracts is in relation to the insurance role of such contracts. PNG landowners/government should be the more risk-averse party in contract negotiations with a large and diversified mining company which can borrow at prime rates on world capital markets. As such there is scope for the mining company to provide insurance for the PNG government/landowners in the event of a lower than expected mineral price or a poorer ore quality. This difference in risk preference could be accommodated in a mining contract by having a larger portion of the benefits of the contract made in payments that do not depend on the profitability of the mine, such as in lease payments for the land or in infrastructure investment.

If mine profitability turns out to be low, the PNG government/ landowners will be pleased that they took a larger part of the payments from the mine in a manner that was not affected by the low profitability. However, if the mine is more profitable than expected, the PNG landowners/government would have preferred not to have taken the insurance in the first place, but rather to have negotiated a higher share in the equity of the mine. In that case we would expect to see demands for renegotiation of the contract and a larger share of the mine equity on the part of the PNG landowners/government. This is exactly what happened in the case of the Porgera mine.

Knowing that the PNG landowners/government will want to forgo the insurance if the mine is highly profitable, the mining company will be less willing to provide insurance in the 'bad' state. As the provision of insurance in such a contract is to the benefit of both parties, this time inconsistency will mean that both parties are worse off than if demands for renegotiation could be prevented.

The problem of time inconsistency on the part of the government could be circumvented by a device that allows a present government to bind future governments not to renegotiate the mining lease. The sovereign nature of governments and the wide-ranging powers that they wield, however, means that binding future governments is exceedingly difficult. A usually effective restraint on governments reneging on contracts is the adverse impact that such action would have on investment in the country. As was seen following the PNG government's decision in late 1992 to increase unilaterally its share of equity in the Porgera mine (although allowed under the Mining Act), such behaviour can result in considerable loss in investor confidence and in capital flight (see ANUTECH Pty Ltd 1995 for estimates of capital flight from Papua New Guinea in the early 1990s). Once governments learn this lesson, it is easier for existing governments to bind the actions of future governments.

It is more difficult for current generations of landowners to bind the actions of future generations of landowners. The dispute over the Bougainville mine is a case in point. It was triggered by a younger generation disappointed in the benefits that they perceived themselves receiving from the mine on the one hand, and the environmental damage which they saw being inflicted on their land on the other.

Thus the possibility of inter-generational competition among landowners adds further elements of time inconsistency. Not only may the later generations of landowners place different values on environmental factors than the generation negotiating the contract, but the initial generation may place less value on the happiness of later generations and so attempt to bring forward the payments under the mining lease at the expense of later generations. The later generations may thus desire that the earlier generations had made a different contract, and not act under the contract as the earlier generations would have wished them to act. Both of these problems played a role in the Bougainville dispute.

The appearance of a new set of decision-makers with different desires not taken into account under the contract is an example of what is called an incomplete contract, which is another common difficulty of long-term mining contracts in Papua New Guinea.

Incomplete contracts

Incompleteness of contracts arises when an event occurs that was not detailed in the contract, either due to the undue cost of making a complete contract or the inability of one or both of the parties to foresee the event. Typically with mining contracts, such incompleteness arises due to the resource price being much higher or lower than the parties expected or the ore body being richer or poorer than expected. However, unforeseen environmental damage or inter-generational conflicts may also give rise to this problem.

In practice, it would be hard to differentiate disputes arising from this source from the more opportunistic disputes due to the time inconsistency problem. Unless the contract specified bounds for the resource price or ore quantity/quality, a party could claim that some event had occurred for which it was not prepared and ask for a renegotiation.

As detailed in Deaton and Laroque (1992), the distribution of commodity prices over time is highly skewed downwards with a small probability of very high price spikes. They explain the form of the distribution as due to the existence of inventories and the long lead time required to increase production. When demand is very high and new production will take some time to reach the market, the price rises to clear the market at the given stock of inventories. When demand is very low, however, inventory will be accumulated and suppliers will not sell, so the price will have a floor.

The occurrence of upward price spikes, sharply increasing the profit of the mine, has brought about several demands for increased compensation or renegotiation of mining leases in Papua New Guinea. Improved prospects of ore bodies and observation of environmental damage have also led to changes or demands for changes in contract terms. The increase in the government's equity share in the Porgera mine was as a result of the discovery of the ore body being larger than initially believed. The Bougainville dispute was triggered in large part by observation of the large profits being earned by the mining company in a period of high prices, as well as by perceptions of environmental damage from the mine (Gupta 1992). The Ok Tedi dispute arose largely as a result of concerns over environmental damage, particularly outside the mine lease area. The role played by international political groups exerting influence through international media and foreign governments also has to be acknowledged.

While a price spike may merely provide an excuse for renegotiations for the reasons outlined earlier, another rationale is that the price rise has driven the mine profits out of the region anticipated by the PNG landowners/government in the initial negotiations. The PNG landowners/government may then feel that they do not have a fair share of the windfalls from the price rise. The contracts have provided for landowner royalties involving a payments schedule which is linear in the commodity price. It may be the case that outside of the anticipated range of the commodity price, the PNG landowners would prefer a nonlinear payment schedule, gaining more than proportionately for very high prices.

Contracts have indeed provided for this nonlinearity as far as the government is concerned. PNG mining and petroleum contracts include an Additional Profits Tax which takes effect when the rate of return of a project (for a Special Mining Lease only) exceeds a specified level. The rate of return is calculated on the basis of the cash flow of the project up to and including the year of income. The determination of the cash flow includes development and, within certain limits, exploration expenditure. The government's holding of equity also ensures participation in boom prices. There is not a similar provision for landowners to share in extraordinary increases in revenues as a result of increases in prices of mine products or improvements in mine output except where the landowners hold an equity share. The *Mining Act* gives the state an option to take up to 30 per cent equity (on a pro-rata basis) in new projects. Beginning with the Lihir mine, the government decided in 1995 to provide 5 per cent equity to landowners out of the government's equity share. The landowners' equity share will be provided to them free of charge with the cost to be covered by the other equity holders in proportion to their shares. As discussed above, royalty payments and equity are mechanisms for sharing in high profitability situations; however, they do not provide insurance in the event of low profitability situations. Equity shareholding also internalises disputes by creating a link between land ownership interests and company interests and could be one of the most effective means of curbing disputes raised by landowner interests.

Large-scale mining contracts may have environmental impact much worse than that envisaged by the parties at the signing of the contract, or the impact may be of a type that was completely unforeseen. In the case of Ok Tedi it seems fair to say that the mining company did not have a full appreciation of the difficulty of building and maintaining a tailings dam in that mountainous area. Moreover, it may not have been possible for it to have a good appreciation prior to undertaking mine construction. It is certain that the landowners in the Boungainville and Ok Tedi areas would not have had full information about the environmental effects of mining.

Another possibility is that the landowners will change over time, and the new landowners may place different values on environmental factors. Later generations of landowners may be willing to pay for a tailings dam, where earlier generations did not value cleaner water enough to warrant the construction of a dam. If the mining contract has not specified what would happen in such events, conflicts may arise.

Disagreements between PNG landowners and government

It is important to realise that each of the above difficulties can occur at either the level of the PNG landowners or at PNG governmental level or at both levels, although they have been much more frequent on the part of the landowners. One feature of the Bougainville conflict was that while the government was satisfied with the agreement, the Bougainville landowners felt that their share of the profits of the mine was too small.

An example of the interaction of these problems is that of the Additional Profits Tax (APT) put forward in the previous section as a solution to the nonlinearity of desired payments. While the higher profits tax may satisfy the PNG government in its demand for an equitable share, unless the government passes on at least part of the payments from this tax to the PNG landowners, the landowners may feel unfairly treated.

Another reason for this problem being particularly severe in Papua New Guinea is that landowners as a whole do not feel that the government represents their interests, or that certain landowner groups feel that they are left out of consideration in the contract negotiations. It is fair to say that the ownership of below-ground resources is highly contested in Papua New Guinea. While the government is able to appropriate most of the mining rents, its right to do so is hotly disputed. Current mining laws grant the state rights of ownership of below-ground resources but at the same time acknowledge rights of landowners by granting them rights to royalties and equity. This ambiguity is probably one of the greatest sources of insecurity in access rights and needs somehow to be removed. Further, there is not necessarily a single, cohesive landowner group. Landowner groups may exist within the project area with different interests in the mining project wishing the government to pursue their different interest. As well, those landowners living outside the mining site and not sharing directly in the equity and royalty proceeds, can be adversely affected through environmental damage. They may also feel aggrieved at the government for not protecting their interests. The Ok Tedi court case was instigated as a result of such dissatisfaction.

Solutions/recommendations

In this section we address each of the above four difficulties in turn, suggesting means by which the government and the mining companies may alleviate the problems giving rise to disputes. It must be recognised that doing so is in the interest of all parties concerned. If foreign companies perceive the PNG investment climate as uncertain, or even capricious, levels of foreign investment will suffer accordingly.

These recommendations are made on the basis of the following three considerations

- PNG land and mining claims are not secure
- none of the parties involved can be bound absolutely by contract
- up to a point it is cheaper to forestall difficulties than it is to face disputes later.

The problem of asymmetric information can only be solved by increasing the information flow and degree of trust between the mining company and the PNG landowners and the government. It should be recognised by companies operating in this environment that problems of mistrust can only be resolved by ensuring that the PNG government and landowners perceive the companies as being honest. This problem could be addressed by

- regular and timely release of information by the company
- placement of PNG representatives within the structure of the mining company
- use of a third-party auditor to assure the truthfulness of the reports by the company.

Implementation of Development Forums (see McGavin 1993) is a process put in place by the government to assist in imparting knowledge about each projected mining venture to the landowners and provincial and national governments and as a forum for negotiating the mining development contract. McGavin discusses ways in which the Development Forum process could be enhanced to generate stronger commitment to economic development processes. Mining companies have placed PNG nationals within the company structure. But probably more could be done to establish a reputation for honest dealings through regular publication of information on mining operations and independent auditing of that information.

The problem of time inconsistency is hardly unique to Papua New Guinea. The ultimate form of time inconsistency is the nationalisation of foreign company capital, a common experience for mining companies in developing countries in the 1970s. One reason why such activities are not more common is the chilling effect that such actions have on other investments, as experienced in Papua New Guinea following the 1992 decision to increase government equity in the Porgera mine from 10 per cent to 30 per cent. The demand for renegotiations from one mining company can lead other companies to suspect that similar demands will soon be made on them. The fear of loss of reputation will normally be sufficient to guarantee that governments will honour the contracts they sign. However, the emphasis within the political class in Papua New Guinea on distribution of the resource rents rather than on economic growth—with one result being the rapid turnover of politicians at election time and another the instability of political parties—means that such reputation effects are lessened. Hopefully, the important lesson from the Porgera decision has been learned. Mining companies, as well as the PNG population, should be crucially concerned with the development of a stable political framework within Papua New Guinea.

While the stability of PNG governments can only be enhanced by constitutional and social change, reputation effects can be strengthened by creating bodies which will monitor contracts and make public the likely impacts of governmental misbehaviour. The creation of a body reporting to the parliament rather than to the government on the fiscal activities of the government, similar to the German Economic Commission, has been suggested as a means of ensuring sound fiscal behaviour (ANUTECH Pty Ltd 1995). Such a body should restrain government misbehaviour by being in a position to draw public attention to the difficulties it creates for economic development.

For very long-term mining leases the problem of time inconsistency introduced by disputes between generations of landowners becomes especially pronounced. Again it is in the interests of the company and the PNG government to prevent these disputes from occurring. The front-loading of lease payments by current landowners at the expense of later generations can be avoided by the use of a trust fund for landowner benefits.

The PNG government already has a trust fund for holding mining royalties and other government revenues from mining, the Mineral Resources Stabilisation Fund. These funds are basically held in trust for the society as a whole. Mining companies and Landowner Incorporated Groups have also set up trust funds. Ok Tedi Mining Ltd manages a trust fund for future generations of landowners and for villages outside the Ok Tedi mine lease area. The creation of a trust fund with specified draw-down rules for the lease payments to landowners would prevent the current landowners from benefiting at the expense of future landowners. The BCL mine at Panguna (Bougainville) did have a landowners' trust fund in place but its mismanagement was one of the sources of dissatisfaction of the younger generation. Guidelines for ensuring good management and effective draw-down rules for public trust funds are set out in Duncan et al. (1995).

McGavin (1993) advises that lease payments from resource extraction projects be invested in the infrastructure of the same region from which the resources were extracted through Development Trusts. The problems with this course of action are

- restricting investment to particular areas does not necessarily maximise the country's social rate of return
- there is no guarantee that benefits will flow from these projects to later generations
- such investment projects are easily corrupted, producing benefits only for the current generation of landowners and politicians.

The incompleteness of contracts can only be addressed by widening the scope of the original negotiations, specifying the payments that will occur under even quite unlikely levels of ore prices and ore quality and environmental damage. Parties must consider what actions will be taken in such circumstances and cannot claim to have been taken by surprise if such events do occur. It is also important that all parties likely to be affected should be brought into the negotiations.

There is a requirement for a fully public and widely-framed environmental impact statement for any proposed mining project. However, not only should the possibility of widespread environmental effects be taken into account under a proposed mining lease, but also the mining company and the government should ensure that compensation for any damage flows on to those landowners affected. The inability of the government to enforce compensation arrangements, and to change these where necessary, has proven to be a problem. To assist resolution of such disputes at low cost it seems advisable to appoint an independent mediator to rule in environmental disputes. The problems associated with not undertaking this kind of action are illustrated by the adverse impact that the OK Tedi compensation claim had on the mining company involved and the government.

But no contract can specify all possible future events. Accepting this, all contracts should specify a method of arbitration and airing of grievances by all affected parties. This procedure would allow for periodic review of the terms of the contract, given changing economic and other conditions, and hopefully lead to grievances being taken up within the specified arbitration sphere and not against the mining company capital. Such arbitration should include the possibility of changing environmental preferences of the landowners. Of course, this review process is less necessary when the contract is more widely drawn initially.

The Panguna mine contract which was renegotiated in 1974 following Independence provided for renegotiation at seven-year intervals. There was an extended process of review in 1981 and 1982 but, as McGavin (1993) argues, political distractions facing the national and provincial governments allowed the later review period to be bypassed.

Conclusions

This chapter illustrates the problems leading to insecurity of land tenure in mining in Papua New Guinea in terms of asymmetry of information, time-inconsistency of contracts and incompleteness of contracts as well as the areas of conflict between the landowners and the PNG government. These difficulties are not confined to land use in mining. Likely solutions to the insecurity of tenure in mining, which can have such adverse impacts on investment, can be applied to contracts for land use in other activities. Resolution of the difficulties with mining contracts would appear to be assisted by implementation of the following measures.

1. Increasing the information flow between the mining company and the PNG landowners/government and trying to develop a greater degree of trust in the information provided.

2. Widening of the issues covered in the contract and including all parties likely to be affected in the negotiations. The terms of the contract should cover events such as unusually high prices, new discoveries of ore bodies and environmental effects which may be seen to have only a low probability, and agreement reached on what should be done if they do occur. In particular, landowners should share in the windfall gains of high prices just as the PNG government does already. Equity shareholding by landowners in mining ventures is one mechanism for achieving this objective as well as being a means of internalising disputes by aligning land interests and voting interests in the mining company.

Landowner royalty payments could also be enhanced by a similar mechanism to the Additional Profits Tax. Intergenerational competition between landowners should be catered for through adoption of trust funds which would pay an income stream to future generations.

3. Contracts should allow for formal arbitration procedures to handle grievances rather than attempting to resolve these through the courts.

4. Contracts should specify periodic reviews of fees and royalties. However, the wider the terms of the contract are drawn, the less will be the need for reviews.

5. The government should take action to improve its reputation with investors. A body to review fiscal behaviour has much to commend it.

These recommendations may also have application to forms of land use other than mining. It should be stressed, however, that a necessary condition for Papua New Guinea, and other Pacific island countries, to be able to provide greater security of access to use of land is better identification of landownership, which will entail surveys and registration of land. But saying this is not the same as saying that forms of land tenure have to be changed. As we said at the beginning, communal ownership of land does not necessarily mean that access to use of the land is insecure.

Notes

Our thanks to Rohan Pitchford for pointing to the parallels between behaviour over mining contracts in Papua New Guinea and the assumptions underlying the 'strike model' in labour economics and for other comments on the draft. Very useful comments were also made by Satish Chand, Ross Garnaut, Desh Gupta and Ila Temu.

1. Pitchford (1994) finds that Victorian and Tasmanian policies of short forest tenure and small or uncertain size of forest leases in the early years of this century led to inefficiently low levels of capital and high levels of labour, and likely encouraged timber-cutting firms to adopt poor silvicultural practices.

2. In August 1996, vehicles and sheds were burnt near the Porgera mine by villagers claiming compensation in excess of the US$2.4 million agreed for the loss of access to alluvial gold deposits. The incident occurred a few days after the announcement that the mine's gold reserves had been re-estimated at a 35 per cent higher level than previously—an increase worth about US$1 billion.

3. The Mining and Petroleum Working Committee, set up in November 1988 in response to the outbreak of the Bougainville dispute, in fact recommended that the landowners share in APT (Gupta 1992).

References

ANUTECH Pty Ltd, 1995. 'Papua New Guinea: improving the investment climate', International Development Issues 39, AusAID, Canberra.

Ashenfelter, O. and G. Johnson, 1969. 'Bargaining theory, trade unions and industrial strike activity,' *American Economic Review* 59:35–49.

Barro, R.J. and D.B. Gordon, 1983. 'Rules, discretion and reputation in a model of monetary policy,' *Journal of Monetary Economics* 12(1):101–21.

Crocombe, R., 1995. 'Overview' in R. Crocombe (ed.) *Customary Land Tenure and Sustainable Development: complementarity or conflict?* South Pacific Commission, Noumea and The Institute of Pacific Studies, University of the South Pacific, Suva.

Deaton, A.S. and G. Laroque, 1992. 'On the behaviour of commodity prices,' *Review of Economic Studies* 59:1–23, January.

Duncan, R., P. Larmour and C. Hunt, 1995. '"Held in trust": the role of public funds in economic management', *Pacific Economic Bulletin* 10(2):41–7.

Gupta, D., 1992. The Law and Order Crisis in Papua New Guinea: An Economic Explanation, NRI Seminar Paper 1, The National Research Institute, Port Moresby.

Hicks, J.R., 1963. *The Theory of Wages*, Macmillan, London.

Kennan, J., 1986. 'The economics of strikes', in O. Ashenfelter and R. Layard (eds), *Handbook of Labor Economics*, Elsevier Science Publishers, New York:1091–1137.

McGavin, P.A., 1993. 'Economic Security in Melanesia: key issues for managing contract stability and mineral resources development in Papua New Guinea, Solomon Islands, and Vanuatu', Pacific Islands Development Program Research Report Series 16, East–West Centre, Honolulu.

Pitchford, R., 1994. 'Underinvestment and timber rights: an examination of the early Tasmanian and Victorian timber industries', *The Australian Journal of Agricultural Economics* 38(3):251–69.

6

Common property, Maori identity and the Treaty of Waitangi

Sir Hugh Kawharu

In the terms of the Treaty of Waitangi, New Zealand became a British colony and the Maori people, together with their lands and estates, were given Crown protection as well as the rights and privileges of British subjects. In 1975, the New Zealand Parliament, for the first time since 1840, gave statutory recognition to the Treaty by setting up a tribunal to hear claims by Maori people that the Crown had failed to honour its guarantees under the Treaty. Claims lodged since then have been made mostly by kin-based tribal groups. They depend heavily on recitals of history, tradition and relations with Crown authorities since 1840.

In 1983, the Crown, bearing in mind this 1975 statutory recognition of the Treaty, invited the New Zealand Maori Council to suggest principles which could be used to guide much needed amendments to existing Maori land laws. The Council's response has been instrumental in reaffirming customary relations between tribal (kinship) groupings and ancestral Maori land. It is now the philosophic basis for legislation that was passed in 1993. This is the first matter I shall deal with. The second matter involves the issue of compensation.

Up to 1994, events put the spotlight on the tribe (*iwi*) or sub-tribe (*hapu*) as the valid units to engage in dealings between Crown, Maori, and the marketplace. However, at the end of 1994, the Crown in considering how best to deal with Treaty claim settlements, decided to propose a financial limit of NZ$1 billion for all compensation. This led in 1995 to a nationwide Maori rejection of the proposal, and at the same time to a call for a Treaty-based constitution as a precondition for considering any claim settlement policy at all. The Treaty has now become the cause of a search for a post-Treaty definition of Maori identity—one, however, that does not at the same time exclude the traditional Treaty definition based on kinship and land. This development recognises that

- the majority (more than 80 per cent) of Maori people no longer live in tribal communities
- many of these people form non kin-based interest groups where they live
- nevertheless, this has weakened neither a sense of tribal identity nor effective tribal groupings throughout the Maori population at large.

It is a matter in which the National Maori Congress has performed a facilitating role.

Finally, I shall offer a comment on the way these events are changing the meaning of a key Treaty-derived symbol of Maori identity. More broadly, the Treaty of Waitangi has once again become the principal charter for Maori identity in the non-Maori world.

The New Zealand Maori Council proposals

The Crown's invitation to the New Zealand Maori Council to propose amendments to the existing *Maori Affairs Act* might well have been received merely as an invitation to join in the periodic ritual of modifying Maori land legislation, parts of which had remained fundamentally flawed for over a century. In the event, the Council saw much more in it than that. By the time they had held three major meetings in different parts of the country there was evidence enough for them to show that no further amendments to Maori land law could be justified without such amendments first being reconciled to the Treaty of Waitangi. No broadly representative Maori organisation, statutory or otherwise, had ever had such an opportunity to present to government views on the interdependence of ancestral land, cultural identity, and the nation's founding document. They took the opportunity and two years later delivered their discussion paper, the *Kaupapa, Te Wahanga Tuatahi.*

In the beginning, the Council subcommittee delegated to prepare a draft paper engaged in some soul-searching. Certainly the Treaty of Waitangi had at last come on to the statute books in 1975, but neither it nor even the Treaty's three articles could be posted as a heading for their views, with relevance simply left to the imagination. The Treaty had never been designed as a banner for protest or as a basis for grievance claims against the Crown. On the contrary, it had been meant as a contract which, from the perspective of those ancestors who had signed it and now those who had inherited it, stated what ought to have been the constitutional relationship between Maori and the Crown and the basis for the preservation of Maori culture and identity. In the end the Council saw no reason to be equivocal. It said plainly that the Treaty was a *quid pro quo*. It was about the granting of sovereign power and the guaranteeing of *rangatiratanga*. It said

> Each of the two parties to the Treaty invested it with expectations about the exercise of power. The Maori expected his *'rangatiratanga'* to be protected; the Crown expected to gain sovereignty over New Zealand. The purpose of the Treaty, therefore, was to secure an exchange of sovereignty for protection of *rangatiratanga*.

> In the event, the Treaty was drawn up by amateurs on the one side and signed by those on the other side who understood little of its implications. Yet for both it was a symbol of mana, imbued with the spirit of hope that sovereignty, so simply acquired, would solve all problems of ambition: the Maori would retain their *rangatiratanga*, and the Crown would add New Zealand to its empire.

This unique juxtaposition of bicultural concepts triggered the development of the *Kaupapa*'s thesis, one which resulted in a focus on *rangatiratanga* as the primary theme, with the Crown, in the role of the Maori Land Court, providing a counterpoint. Since the constitutional significance of the Treaty had only recently been uncovered (*Treaty of Waitangi Act 1975*) and the meaning of *rangatiratanga* in government circles was virtually unknown, the Council went to some length to discourse on Maori kinship and tribal cultural values. In doing so several concepts of cardinal importance in addition to *rangatiratanga* were introduced, such as *tangata whenua, turangawaewae, whangai* and *ahi ka* which were not in the Treaty, and others which were, such as *whanau* and *hapu*, all being used in ways designed to illuminate their politico-economic significance. Given the Council's brief, the *Kaupapa* had to focus on land. It said

The rights and privileges granted to the Maori people in the Treaty apply in the fullest sense to land. The protection afforded by the Crown—the guarantees—are needed as much today as ever.

Maori land has several cultural connotations for us. It provides us with a sense of identity, belonging and continuity. It is proof of our continued existence not only as a people, but as the tangatawhenua of this country. It is proof of our tribal and kin group ties. Maori land represents turangawaewae.

It is proof of our link with the ancestors of our past, and with the generations yet to come. It is an assurance that we shall forever exist as a people, for as long as the land shall last.

But also land is a resource capable of providing even greater support for our people—to provide employment—to provide us with sites for our dwellings—and to provide an income to help support our people and to maintain our marae and tribal assets.

It concluded by declaring

Our objective is to keep Maori land in the undisturbed possession of its owners; and its occupation, use and administration by them or for their benefit. Laws and policies must emphasise and consolidate Maori land ownership and use by the whanau or kin group.

At the heart of this was the principle of reciprocity—rights and duties between kin, between groups of kin, between these groups and the natural world, and, not least, between them all and their ancestors. Rights and duties were couched, therefore, in terms both of the sacred and the profane. Such a system of beliefs constituted the scope of *rangatiratanga*, compressed by the *Kaupapa* into the concept of trusteeship. Trusts and incorporations, it said, should therefore be assisted to expand and become more flexible, more responsive to market opportunity—but never at the expense of being accountable. Accountability in fact epitomised Article 2 of the Treaty for the Council, for here there was a double trusteeship, a double accountability. On the one hand there was the fiduciary role of the Crown towards the Maori people and their *rangatiratanga*, and on the other *rangatira*'s fiduciary role towards his or her kin group. It is in this sense that sovereignty and *rangatiratanga* might be seen in their reciprocal relationship as defined by the idea of exchange: that between the intent of Article 1 and that of Article 2. In a narrow sense, that is, in particular cases, the superior authority of the Court can act as a benign check on the performance of trustees acting in the interests of their beneficiaries. Equally, the Treaty-prescribed protection of *rangatiratanga*, for example for a *whanau*, *hapu* or perhaps *iwi* to be consulted by the Crown, can serve as check on the latter's legal sovereignty or more simply, on good government.

At all events the Council believed that ancestral land should be seen as a *taonga*, to be retained as such rather than as a personal possession. It was argued that there can be no *rangatiratanga* in respect of land and its *whanau* or *hapu* if they are not all kept together. 'Uneconomic interests', 'multiple interests' and the like were thus terms to be expunged from policy and practice and replaced by *ahi ka* and statutes consolidating ownership by *whanau* and *hapu*. And by this time (1983) the most urgent mode of consolidating *whanau* and *hapu* was *marae*-centred housing. Here again the Council sought a proactive role for the Court in planning and implementing (*papakainga*) housing schemes and subdivisions.

Throughout this remarkable document there is the Council's expectation that the Crown would accept its assertion that 'justice will remain in jeopardy so long as Maori values are not included in that range of values by which the laws of this country are framed and upheld', and accordingly that it would indeed try to come to some understanding of what these values meant. It was an expectation that it was still not too late to put a brake on more than 100 years of individualisation of land and much else besides, and therefore that the emphasis should be returned to those first principles upon which Maori identity was grounded. The Council was to wait exactly ten years for a statute-defined response.

And so it was that in 1993 Parliament passed the *Ture Whenua Maori Act*, and in the preamble to it there is the following

Na te mea i riro na te Tiriti o Waitangi i motuhake ai te noho a te iwi me te Karauna: a, na te mea e tika ana kia whakautia ano te wairua o te wa i riro atu ai te kawanatanga kia riro mai ai te mau tonu o te rangatiratanga e takoto nei i roto i te Tiriti o Waitangi: a, na te mea e tika ana kia marama ko te whenua he taonga tuku iho e tino whakaaro nuitia ana e te iwi Maori, a, na tera he whakahau kia mau tonu taua whenua ki te iwi nona, ki o ratou whanau, hapu hoki, a, he whakamama i te nohotanga, i te whakahaeretanga, i te whakamahitanga o taua whenua hei painga mo te hunga nona, mo o ratou whanau, hapu hoki: a, na te mea e tika ana kia tu tonu he Koti, a, kia whakatakototia he tikanga hei awhina i te iwi Maori kia taea ai enei kaupapa te whakatinana.

Whereas the Treaty of Waitangi established the special relationship between the Maori people and the Crown: And whereas it is desirable that the spirit of the exchange of kawanatanga for the protection of rangatiratanga embodied in the Treaty of Waitangi be reaffirmed: And whereas it is desirable to recognise that land is a taonga tuku iho of special significance to Maori people, and, for that reason, to promote the retention of that land in the hands of its owners, their whanau, and their hapu: and to facilitate the occupation, development, and utilisation of that land for the benefit of its owners, their whanau, and their hapu: And whereas it is desirable to maintain a Court and to establish mechanisms to assist the Maori people to achieve the implementation of these principles:

BE IT THEREFORE ENACTED by the Parliament of New Zealand —

And in a note on the interpretation to be given to the Act is said

(1) It is the intention of Parliament that the provisions of this Act shall be interpreted in a manner that best furthers the principles set out in the Preamble to this Act. Without limiting the generality of subsection (1) of this section, it is the intention of Parliament that powers, duties, and discretions conferred by this Act shall be exercised, as far as possible, in a manner that facilitates and promotes the retention, use, development, and control of Maori land as taonga tuku iho (sacred heritage) by Maori owners, their whanau, their hapu, and their descendants. In the event of any conflict in meaning between the Maori and the English versions of the Preamble, the Maori version shall prevail.

Thus the Preamble of the Act encapsulates precisely both in Maori and in English the *Kaupapa*'s thesis that, in terms of the Treaty of Waitangi, there was a ceding of sovereignty to the Crown in exchange for the latter's protection of *rangatiratanga*. While amendments had been made to the previous Act at regular intervals since it first came into existence 40 years earlier, none had recognised the Treaty, let alone the values inherent in the Maori version signed by 90 per cent of the Maori signatories. Even ignoring the sanctions of the Treaty, no legislative amendment had ever found a place for such concepts as *wairua, taonga tuku iho, tikanga, ahi ka,* and so forth.

It can doubtless be claimed that Maori Land Courts have always been able to exercise, not only their discretion, but also their initiative in helping owners to achieve their stated goals within the law. The Council's hope, however, was for legislative amendments that would provide firm and more explicit guidelines for the Court, grounded for the first time in Treaty guarantees and some cardinal Maori values. In the last analysis the justification for that hope lay less in the diminution in the per capita ratio of land holding among the Maori people than in the sheer scale of land loss since 1840 and with it loss of capacity to exercise *rangatiratanga*. Notwithstanding that justification, however, whether any government would ever divest itself of a measure of its sovereign power and allocate it to some pan-Maori authority in fulfilment of its fiduciary obligations under Article 2 of the Treaty is, in my view, the decisive question that remains at the heart of Maori–Pakeha relations today.

The fiscal envelope

I turn now to the Crown's fiscal cap proposal on compensating successful claimants before the Waitangi Tribunal. The following excerpts from the proposal convey something of the intent

The Treaty of Waitangi is the foundation document of New Zealand.

- It acknowledged the Crown's right to govern in the interests of all our citizens
- It protected Maori interests
- It made us all New Zealanders.

The spirit of the Treaty required the Crown and Maori to act with the utmost good faith to one another.

Many believe the Crown, in various ways, failed to act with the utmost good faith and that as a result Maori were seriously disadvantaged. Over the past 150 years Maori have sought redress to settle these grievances. Attempts to resolve some of them have been made during that time with varying success, but many grievances remain unanswered.

Later it said

Over the past few years, the Government on behalf of the Crown has attempted to approach the claims in a rational, cohesive and constructive way. It has had to work out what it believes can be done, taking into account its responsibilities to all New Zealanders. This has led to the development of some basic principles

- the Crown will explicitly acknowledge historical injustices
- in resolving claims the Crown should not create further injustices
- the Crown has a duty to act in the best interests of all New Zealanders
- as settlements are to be durable they must be fair, achievable and remove the sense of grievance
- the resolution process must be consistent and equitable between claimant groups

- nothing in the settlements will remove, restrict or replace Maori rights under Article III of the Treaty
- the settlements will take into account fiscal and economic constraints and the ability of the Crown to pay compensation.

And finally, the 'money' bit,

> The Crown has many demands to meet and has to carefully assess how much can be put aside to settle claims. The Crown has accordingly decided to set aside a settlement sum of NZ$1 billion to be available of a period of about 10 years. This has become known as the 'Fiscal Envelope' or the 'Settlement Envelope' and confirms the Crown's commitment to settle claims.

At the first of two major meetings in 1995 held under the patronage of Sir Hepi Te Heuheu and with the National Maori Congress acting as facilitator, the Fiscal Envelope proposal was rejected outright. The report of the meeting said

> The proposal is not explicit on how a sum of 1 billion has been calculated but it is justified as a political decision largely on the basis of affordability and acceptability to the wider community. It is also suggested that the amount should be sufficient to redress claimants sense of grievance. There is an assumption that 1 billion dollars is fair and affordable. However, neither the methodology used to calculate the amount, nor the basis for deciding viability has been disclosed. The cap is simply stated as a given even though most claims have not yet received due consideration while others have yet to be filed.

> Several submission made at the first hui considered that without a wider contextual backdrop, Government proposals to settle claims simply foster the impression that Treaty matters have become irksome and that a piecemeal consideration of each article will eventually do away with the Treaty altogether. Hui participants agreed that any mechanism for the settlement of Treaty claims will only make sense if it is premised upon a wider Treaty framework and that settlements which purport to be full and final will never be durable unless they are formulated within that wider context. In this sense the Proposal is premature. It should have been preceded by the careful development of a constitutional covenant regarding the Treaty and the position of Maori as tangatawhenua.

Congress then declared its hand on terminology. First, *rangatiratanga* can be said to be about *mana whenua* and *mana rangatira*, namely, the right of *iwi* and *hapu* to exercise authority in the development and control of resources which they own, or are supposed to own, and to interact with the Crown according to their own needs and inclinations.

Second, and to an increasing extent, *rangatiratanga* has relevance to the right of all Maori, individually and collectively, to determine their own policies, to participate in the development and interpretation of the law, to assume responsibility for their own affairs and to plan for the needs of future generations. Such a right reflects a Maori constitutional element which has assumed increasing importance over the past 155 years and especially since post-1945 urbanisation. It recognises that not all Maori are linked to tribal structures and networks, and also takes into account the fact that there are many policies which impact on all Maori people but which are not appropriate or relevant to tribal authorities. Further, because *hapu* and *iwi* are particularly concerned about their own areas of responsibility, they do not always give high priority to issues of broad regional or national importance.

The establishment of a national body which allowed for both *iwi/hapu* and Maori community representation would go some way to providing a foundation for a more coordinated approach to Maori policy, appropriate to the twenty-first century.

The National Maori Congress thus came to the conclusion that there should be a national focus for Maori people which is capable of providing a structure for Maori representation at a national level in order to advance Maori interests. However, it said, enthusiasm for establishing a national Maori organisation is not shared by all Maori. Many *iwi* see it as an unnecessary and undesirable step. They are concerned that the formation of a national Maori voice could undermine the authority of tribes if it began speaking on behalf of the tribes.

On the other hand, it argued, without a broadly representative national body, it would be difficult to agree on national Maori policies or to formulate strategies or Maori development. Essentially *iwi* are concerned about their own interests rather than national Maori interests. Moreover, in the pursuit of *rangatiratanga* Maori people will remain vulnerable if there is no body politic which can represent all their interests at constitutional and political levels. First, energies will be dissipated in several directions with a lack of coordination and a dilution of resources, including human resources. Second, by default as much as anything else, various independent groups will assume the role of a national body even if they do not have a mandate. And third, in the absence of a national body able to articulate a national Maori voice, the Crown will continue to fill the perceived gap by itself making policy for Maori people.

It then considered a number of models for a national Maori body politic. One which it had earlier supported in principle took the form of a National Maori Assembly of 40 to 80 members representing both *iwi* and Maori community interests. The Maori electoral roll would be a starting point for determining eligibility to vote and a formula for representation, taking into account the size of the population, *iwi*, and existing Maori community structures. It assumed that an Assembly would be supported by an infrastructure and that all Maori policy units in the State sector, including Te Puni Kokiri, would be retained as Assembly staff, at least in the initial years. The main functions of the Assembly would be the development of Maori policy, Maori appointments (for instance, to Te Ohu Kaimoana, the Waitangi Tribunal, the Maori Land Court), monitoring Government policies in terms of best outcomes for the people. This, now, is *rangatiratanga* and the catchword is 'self-determination'.

The 'challenges' in the Treaty?[1]

The challenges in the Treaty are twofold. The first lies in the structural disjunction between centralised government on the one hand and tribal and non-tribal groups on the other. I add in parenthesis here that this disjunction is not between urban and rural categories, notwith-standing the process we call urbanisation.

The second challenge lies in the two-sided question facing the Maori people—is national political unity desirable, and if it is, is it achievable?

In addressing this challenge let us consider to begin with the options offered by Council and Congress. The Council has a good track record of representing Maori interests at a national politico-legal level. Perhaps the initial all-embracing issue it tackled was the Prichard–Waetford Commission's report on Maori land and the consequent Maori Land Amendment Bill of 1967, when it organised a national *hui* on these matters and later acted as a clearing-house for submissions to govern-ment. One of its more recent and dramatic interventions occurred in 1987 where it sought to negate a government ploy to rid itself of the means to compensate successful Treaty claimants. But, as I have said, it is a statutory body, *pakeha* in structure, lacks clear independence from government and cannot itself speak for one or more tribes or sub-tribes. The lack of a local vested interest could, of course, be seen as an advantage in promoting issues at a national level; but while objectivity is one thing, authority is another. Furthermore, while it has a formal nationwide structure in place—its hierarchy of committees—it lacks administrative capacity to make it function.

As to Congress, it seems to me that it is still finding its feet. It has profited greatly from the patronage of one who symbolises a quintessential *rangatiratanga*, Sir Hepi Te Heuheu of *Ngati Tuwharetoa*, one who, without promoting either his own or his tribe's view at the expense of others, has provided Congress with an opportunity to bring into being a unified independence for the Maori people. Congress, however, still has to grapple with the conundrum that if for centuries tribal emulation has been the Maori people's strength in peace and war, will that strength be compromised through unification? What has yet to be found for this is that elusive factor, incentive.

And for both Council and Congress there is the added problem of one or the other making themselves relevant to a burgeoning number of non-tribal groups—committees, trusts, clubs and so on. It may be that here the Maori Womens Welfare League (MWWL) which for the past 45 years has organised itself on the basis of family-centred interests such as education, health, and housing rather than tribal-resource based interests, can serve as a catalyst in producing a unified Maori voice.

However, there may be another dimension in all of this, that of scale. In 1840 when the Treaty was signed the Maori outnumbered the non-Maori by at least 50 to 1. Well within two decades, the populations were equal. Today disparate units of the Maori population comprise a mere 10–15 per cent of the country's total (depending on the statistics you prefer). Against that level of discrepancy in numbers (let alone capital assets) there is, nevertheless, a notion of partnership between Crown and Maori engendered by the Treaty and almost codified by a recent edict of the country's Court of Appeal. 'Partnership' is beguiling. On the one hand it suggests equality, but talk of political equality is idle. Yet, talk about equality before the law between Crown and a particular *hapu* or *iwi* on a Treaty grievance is anything but idle, as a few recent multi-million dollar settlements would indicate.

Accordingly, while a pan-Maori body like a national assembly is a logical goal to consider seriously, it may also be that governments and the Maori people can just as well discuss global issues such as justice, health, and land, by means of an established circuit of *hui*: a circuit that would include all groups of whatever persuasion without any sacrifice of that vital ingredient *mana*. This has been tried a number of times over the past 20 years. While the ineptness of the practice has to a large extent ensured failure of outcome, it has not, in my view, negated the principle.

So much for some options for a unified approach to a sovereign Maori identity. But what more might be said about the *status quo*, over and above Council and Congress? At the moment a small number of tribal and sub-tribal groups are accumulating quite substantial levels of capital assets. This has come about for a variety of reasons: diversification, increasing levels of managerial and entrepreneurial skills, and compensation from the Crown following successful Treaty negotiations, to name a few. And as there are now some 500 Treaty claims waiting to be heard, the present small number may well grow. While individuals in some of these groups have yet to benefit from their group's recently improved economic fortunes, their trustees are understandably protective of their trust estate and loath to risk engaging in enterprises that might threaten their independence. And on the face of it what applies in the economic field also applies in the political. It is not that bilateral or limited regional arrangements cannot work. Rather it is the prospect of total or near total unity that seems remote at this stage. And neither should it be forgotten that many tribes are engaging successfully in joint ventures with non-Maori commercial enterprises thereby adding another imponderable to pan-Maori unification.

Having said that, there are indeed examples of nationwide unity among Maori people—a unity on other than party political, religious, or tribal grounds. I would mention the MWWL and the Kohanga Reo (pre-school Maori language) Movement, both of which operate among tribal as well as non-tribal groups. Another is the ex-28 Maori Battalion Association, a poignant reminder of what might have been. But these fall into a social welfare category where the capital asset is humanity. Unfortunately governments so far have failed to recognise such capital as a fundamental ingredient in the exercise of *rangatiratanga*, and therefore to be seen as a valid potential claim on the Crown in terms of its Treaty obligations. Nevertheless if the tribes were, for that purpose, to set one side their material asset-based enterprises they might well find common cause with one another and with those disengaged from tribal concerns and so force government recognition of a Maori unity. At least all Maori accept the aphorism: What is the most important thing in this world?—I say to you it is people, it is people, it is people. (*He aha te mea nui i tenei ao? Maku e mea atu ki a koutou, he tangata, he tangata, he tangaga.*)

Conclusion

Does the Treaty of Waitangi have relevance for a Maori political identity today? The best answer given by the limited data I have been able to refer to is

- that the key symbol of identity and unity *vis-à-vis* the Crown since 1840 has been *rangatiratanga*
- that its meaning has been, and still is, 'trusteeship'
- that its referent is the *hapu*
- that at present *rangatiratanga* is also being developed as a demand for self-determination, namely, control over government Maori policy and practice
- that its referent is the Maori nation

Whether, finally, a Maori nation will ever receive practical, let alone constitutional, recognition remains to be seen. At the least the Treaty is providing a context for Maori debate—the outcome of which no New Zealander can ignore. And it is this Treaty context that provides opportunity for a considered response to the question of a Maori identity. If the opportunity is taken with due regard to history it will, I think, ensure an identity viable both in the Maori and in the non-Maori worlds that will satisfy those who need it most.

Notes

1. Before turning to the 'challenges' in the Treaty I should add a word of explanation about the two Maori organisations I have been referring to. The New Zealand Maori Council represents several layers of committees beneath it, which themselves ultimately represent a network of electorates into which the country is divided. The latter were brought into existence with the passing of the *Maori Social and Economic Advancement Act* of 1945 and have a non-party, non-sectarian Maori welfare orientation. The apical body, the Council, was formed and recognised by the *Maori Welfare Act* 1962. Initially it had a mandate from the tribes, but largely due to post war urbanisation that mandate has shifted to the Congress. The National Maori Congress, seems to have acquired its early impetus from an *ad hoc* grouping of relatively well-endowed central North Island tribes in the mid-1980s. At all events since land was, and still is, the major source of tribal wealth and identity, the apparent inability of the Council to represent these interests

resulted in the formation of the Congress in 1990. Its constituency are the 30 or more tribes in New Zealand, and in comparison with the Council it has deliberately abstained from seeking parliamentary recognition. While it has an executive committee and holds general meetings it is more in the nature of a forum than a powerful well-organised pressure group.

References

Cox, Lindsay, 1993. *Kotahitanga: the search for Maori political unity*, Oxford University Press, Auckland.

Crown Proposals for the Settlement of Treaty of Waitangi Claims, 1994. Office of Treaty Settlements, Department of Justice, Wellington.

Gardiner, Wira, 1996. *Return to Sender*, Reed, Auckland.

Kawharu, I.H. (ed.), 1989. *Waitangi: Maori and Pakeha perspectives on the Treaty of Waitangi*, Oxford University Press, Auckland.

New Zealand Maori Council, 1983. Kaupapa, Te Wahanga Tuatahi.

New Zealand Maori Council, Wellington.

Renwick, William (ed.), 1991. *Sovereignty and Indigenous Rights*, Victoria University Press, Wellington.

Te Ture Whenua Maori Act, 1993. Wellington.

7

Common property and regional sovereignty: relations between aboriginal peoples and the Crown in Canada

Peter J. Usher

In a world where even nation–states have declining power and authority in the face of global markets, international trade agreements, and harmonised laws and regulations, what does sovereignty mean at the subnational level? And what is the connection between common property and sovereignty at the subnational level? What challenges and opportunities confront minority indigenous populations in these contemporary circumstances? The situation of aboriginal peoples in Canada provides distinctive perspectives on these questions. In our country, new understandings are being reached, new arrangements forged and implemented, but also, new difficulties and challenges are emerging.

Recognition and disregard of aboriginal property and sovereignty

Aboriginal peoples not only used and occupied their territories, they also regulated access to their lands and resources by outsiders and access within them by members. Aboriginal property in lands and resources existed in at least three forms: as a discrete physical space, as a set of relations among the landholding group, and a right in the eyes of others. Property relations are, of course, rules about who has rights to what, and how they can exercise those rights. They are thus a fundamental element of sovereignty or self-government.

In 1763, a Royal Proclamation declared British recognition of aboriginal title and rights in what is now Canada, although the specific content of this recognition, and of Canada's obligations in respect of it, have been much debated politically and in the courts. At the least, we can say that the Proclamation recognised title insofar as it established a lawful process for obtaining aboriginal lands by negotiation and treaty, and that until this process had occurred, aboriginals were to remain unmolested in their use of their land and under the protection of the Crown. It also, by implication at least, recognised aboriginal sovereignty insofar as it acknowledged treaty-making partners capable of acting politically on behalf of landholding groups.

How the recognition of aboriginal title and rights evolved in practice in Canada is a sorry story, which can only be highlighted here.[1] Canadian courts have from time to time acknowledged the existence of aboriginal title, but characterised it merely as usufructuary, or more recently as *sui generis*, which gives the appearance of recognition while at the same time emptying it of practical content and effect. So it came about that in the eyes of the law, aboriginal rights in land and resources (when acknowledged) were not exclusive, provided neither defence nor remedy against nuisance, trespass, or expropriation, and did not bind or encumber third parties granted competing land or resource rights by the Crown.

The treaty-making process, as it evolved for over a century and a half after the Royal Proclamation, was intended by the colonial government and later Canada to clear the way for settlement and development. According to the English language versions as published by Canada, these treaties constituted surrenders of vast territories in exchange for limited hunting rights on unoccupied Crown lands, cash payments for supplies and personal annuities, and reserve lands which typically amounted to no more than one per cent of the ceded territory.

What Indians regarded as their own lands on which they would be self-governing, Canada cast as Dominion lands 'set apart for Indians' (*Indian Act*, s.18(1)), temporarily it hoped, as places of confinement and assimilation. The effect was to set aside property for Indian **use**, but not to recognise Indian **relations** of property, and certainly not their communal nature or its implications.

Further, the division of powers between the Dominion Government and the provinces at Confederation (*British North America Act* 1867) was considered to have fully allocated sovereignty in Canada, leaving no room for the exercise of aboriginal sovereignty, perhaps least of all with respect to the disposition and management of land, water, and natural resources.

Canada's unilateral intepretation of the treaties, its Constitution, and the *Indian Act*, combined to deny completely aboriginal sovereignty and self-government. Two hundred years after the Royal Proclamation, Canada was firmly committed to an assimilationist policy, and regarded the treaties as quaint anachronisms that could and should be disregarded if they stood in the way of the public good (which government regarded as also the aboriginal good). The idea that aboriginal rights might persist and have substance outside of the treaty areas (the substantial part of Canada not yet included in the treaty-making process when it ended in 1930) was simply not considered.

Reclaiming property and sovereignty—two directions

When the movement to reclaim aboriginal and treaty rights gathered momentum in the 1970s, there was a range of approaches based in no small measure on aboriginal peoples' specific historical experience. In the southern, settled areas of Canada, the focus was on the development of self-government on the reserves. There was little interest in (or hope for) the 99 per cent of land that had been lost. Other than exercising hunting and fishing rights, there was little assertion of territorial rights on settled and alienated land. In the far north, where Inuit and Indians had experienced little impact from settlement and development, and where the use of land and water continued largely uninterrupted, the assertion of rights was over the entire territory. In the mid-north, where although use of off-reserve lands continued, there had been progressive encroachment and restriction by development activities, government regulations, and settlers, the assertion of rights was also territorially extensive, but there was much emphasis on seeking remedies for past damages. In the northern treaty areas, Indians saw these incursions and damages as a long history of treaty violations, and signs of a treaty partner no longer to be trusted.[2]

The effect was that in the south, and to a large extent in the mid-north, Indians pursued autonomy and sovereignty, even if over limited territories, whereas in the far north, Inuit and to some extent Indians sought to retain a range of rights over their entire territories but were more prepared to enter into relations of partnership and cooperation. On the one hand, coexistence in separate spheres, on the other, cooperation and participation. This is necessarily an over-simplification, but it provides some insight into different outcomes in the north and south of Canada, and to the successes and limitations of comprehensive claims agreements.

Modern comprehensive claims agreements

As a result of certain political and judicial events in the early 1970s, Canada acknowledged that there were outstanding aboriginal interests in unceded land and that it was prepared to negotiate modern treaties on the basis of them (Chrétien 1973). The Office of Native Claims was given a mandate to negotiate, in exchange for extinguishment, certain land and resource benefits, title to a limited quantum of lands (including subsurface rights to a small proportion thereof), preferential or exclusive access to fish and wildlife, and limited participation in the management of these resources, and monetary compensation. Other benefits not related to lands and resources were also offered, but the overall package did not include self-government (Canada 1981).[3]

The new policy included some significant departures from the old treaty pattern, with respect to lands, resources, and environment. For our purposes, these were

- the land quantum to be negotiated was far greater than what was provided for (although not necessarily greater than what Indian signatories had understood they would get) in the numbered treaties, although much of this would consist of surface title only
- the lands selected would be held in freehold directly by an aboriginal corporate entity, rather than by Canada for the benefit of aboriginal people
- cash compensation for lost lands would be substantial, and would be paid to an aboriginal corporate entity rather than to individuals
- hunting and fishing rights would be exclusive or preferential, and to some extent compensable
- aboriginal people would have some involvement in wildlife and environmental management.

The land, resource, and environment regimes established under the comprehensive claims process provide some measure of protection of land and resources from the adverse effects of development, and also for mitigation and compensation where such effects do occur. These modern treaties thus address problems perhaps not foreseen, and certainly not explicitly dealt with, in the historic treaties. They do so by acknowledging and balancing both aboriginal and non-aboriginal interests throughout the traditional territory. Some incidents of aboriginal title are formally recognised on all lands (except the very limited areas in freehold tenure), more in some categories of land than in others, yet nowhere are they complete.

The modern treaties also provide an institutional framework for the continuing negotiation and mutual accommodation of aboriginal and non-aboriginal interests in the governance of land, resources, and environment. They provide for aboriginal involvement in the management of the entire territory, but not their exclusive governance or sovereignty over any of it. This is a vision of integration and participation, of a continuing and evolving relationship between partners, rather than of separation and coexistence (Usher 1997).

What follows is a description of what happens when aboriginal rights have been recognised and codified, and must then be exercised in a situation where the presence, interests, and rights of others, both within the territory or 'settlement region' and outside of it, must be acknowledged and negotiated. In most of the cases referred to, the primary economic orientation of the aboriginal population is a mixed, subsistence-based economy, based on local-level subsistence and commercial exploitation of fisheries and wildlife, employment, and transfer payments. Industrial employment, where it occurs, is in the minerals, oil and gas sectors. There is no agriculture, and with few exceptions, no forestry or pastoralism.

The provisions for co-management

The principle of co-management is perhaps the most innovative and yet least understood elements of the modern treaties. It applies not only to wildlife and fisheries —the so-called 'traditional' resources— but also to environmental protection and regulation, and land use planning.[4]

The basic structure of co-management consists of boards or committees responsible for specific management areas such as wildlife, fisheries, impact screening and review, land use planning, and water management. Members are usually appointed in equal numbers by governments and beneficiary organisations. Geographically, the jurisdiction of these boards extends to all of the lands within the settlement area, whether in aboriginal, Crown, or private tenure. The boards are technically advisory to the appropriate minister, and do not replace existing government agencies. They are intended to guide the overall direction of policy, and have a range of powers from making binding decisions, approvals, advice, and research direction. Here, for example, is how the role of the Nunavut Wildlife Management Board (NWMB) is described in the Nunavut Land Claims Agreement

> Recognizing that Government retains ultimate responsibility for wildlife management, the NWMB shall be the main instrument of wildlife management in the Nunavut Settlement Area and the main regulator of access to wildlife and have the primary responsibility in relation thereto (Department of Indian Affairs and Northern Development 1993:5.2.33).

Comprehensive claims have not been the only basis for the development of co-management. Some important and enduring examples pre-date many of the claims, and limited forms of co-management have been implemented outside of the comprehensive claims areas. However, the claims-based regimes are the strongest and most enduring, not least because they are constitutionally protected under section 35 of the *Constitution Act*, 1982. They cannot be unilaterally disbanded or ignored by Canada, or by its provinces and territories.

At the time that co-management options were first seriously negotiated in comprehensive claims, the alternative was continued and more comprehensive devolution to the territorial governments. Instead, at least a nominal form of power-sharing was the outcome. Governments were not entirely averse to this compromise, and certainly preferred it to aboriginal self-government with respect to lands and resources. The Supreme Court's Sparrow decision[5] also provided an impetus for co-management—consultation has become one of the key tests of constitutionally acceptable conservation limitations on aboriginal harvesting rights. The co-management boards provide a useful 'single window' for governments to deal with specific resource issues. With respect to wildlife and fisheries, co-management is a means of enlisting harvester cooperation to ensure conservation, as an alternative to deploying draconian and expensive (but often unsuccessful) enforcement measures.

From an aboriginal perspective, co-management establishes a principle completely ignored (if not explicitly rejected) in Canada's interpretation of the historic treaties. It is that aboriginal people retain, as a result of claims settlements, some rights not only of use but of management, and in effect governance, that apply on all Crown lands and in more limited respects on private lands, throughout the traditional territory or 'settlement region'. The modern treaties create an institutional basis for cooperation and coexistence, for problem solving and for the harmonising of mutual interests, with respect to all lands and resources. This is quite different from the traditional denial of all collective aboriginal rights save residual hunting and fishing rights outside of reserve lands. In most cases where it has been implemented it has been a counterweight and buffer to the progressive encroachment and restriction on the use of customary lands and resources, to harvest disruption, and to the loss of social and cultural as well as economic values.

On the other hand, the emerging pattern is not one of self-determination or autonomy. It would certainly appear, based on the structures and mandates established by the comprehensive claims, that the state management system has been retained. The general pattern is that allocation and licensing is delegated to the boards and the local harvester organisations, but management for conservation is reserved to governments, with the boards having only an advisory role (although in practice their decisions are rarely if ever varied or rejected). The boards are technically institutions of public government, on which aboriginals are guaranteed equal representation with governments. The co-management boards thus do not replace existing resource management agencies—at most they provide guidance to them. This is less than what many, and perhaps most, harvesters wanted.

Co-management in practice

Co-management has been implemented in Canada in a variety of situations since the early 1980s. Some of these have been claims-based, others have been cobbled together as *ad hoc* solutions to land and resource management crises. In both cases, there have been notable achievements in conservation through self-regulation, community land use and conservation planning, co-management of national parks, impact screening and review, negotiating interjurisdictional agreements on resource access and management, and in problem solving generally.

Most co-management boards, and especially the claims-based ones, are bilateral arrangements between aboriginal peoples and governments, and hence do not necessarily include all interested parties. That is probably one reason that boards have often been able to achieve consensus over basic management objectives, for example, management for subsistence in the case of the Beverly–Qamanirjuaq Caribou Management Board (BQCMB) (Usher 1993). As well, the boards are mandated to implement the objectives of the claims agreements, which in the case of the Inuvialuit Final Agreement (IFA), for example, clearly link aboriginal harvesting rights with conservation (Staples 1997). However potentially competing interests such as resident sport hunters or the guiding industry are not directly represented on the boards (although governments may choose in some cases to nominate such individuals as their representatives). While this has not been a significant problem in the Northwest Territories (NWT), it accounts for some of the differences in board structures in the Yukon, and for some of the resistance to co-management in the provincial North (see, for example, Brooke 1997, Larcombe 1997, and Penn 1997). Where third party interests are well established, multi-party approaches at the local level as in the Shuswap pilot project in British Columbia (Pinkerton, Moore and Fortier 1997) or the Barriere Lake agreement in Quebec (Notzke 1997) are likely to be essential elements of success.

Some observers have suggested that co-management offers a potential bridge between indigenous and state systems of knowledge and management (Usher 1987, Osherenko 1988). The record of achievement in this regard is mixed, but co-management has provided a forum or venue for continuing negotiation over matters crucial to both aboriginal peoples and governments. Whether the integration or bridging of traditional and scientific knowledge is always an appropriate or achievable objective of co-management remains to be seen. One substantial achievement in most cases has been agreement on research objectives and methods, and the sharing of data. The scientific research on which management is based is undertaken with the knowledge and consent of harvesters (for example the BQCMB) and often the research priorities, design, and budgets are effectively directed by the co-management board and, for example in the IFA, the

Inuvialuit Game Council. In the NWT, the boards have their own secretariats with technical as well as adminis-trative capacity, hence aboriginal representatives have access to expertise outside of the line management agencies. The composition of boards is quite similar in all of the agreements, in particular the provision for equality of representation. What is crucial to the outcome is who in practice appoints (or which set of interests appoints) the members, the effective mandate and accountability of the members, and the actual operating procedures. These factors can either serve to paper over and suppress real differences, or give proper recognition and expression of them.

The experience of most boards shows that consensus often builds over time among board members, and the agencies they represent. As already mentioned, co-management board decisions are rarely if ever varied or rejected by the ministers they advise. However this is not sufficient, at least on the government side, to bind all those whose actions (or inaction) may have an impact on management. For example, support for IFA implementation on the part of local or regional govern-ment agencies is not necessarily sustained at headquarters, and there are some government departments not directly represented on the boards who are indifferent at best, or hostile at worst, to board recommendations (Staples 1997).

The costs of implementation and of effective participation are proving to be substantial: consistent attention, expert research and advice, and extensive travel are required. The final agreements them-selves do not specify what human and financial resources are required to implement their provisions. That has been a matter for subsequent negotiations, and has sometimes proved the source of fundamental disagreement or dissatisfaction between parties and beneficiaries.

There has been a range of responses to co-management initiatives by aboriginal groups. Some have found that their co-management arrangements suit their needs well, and that they can use them to their advantage. Others find co-management at least acceptable in as much as it is a significant improvement over the former closed-door system of management. Still others have no desire to co-manage resources with outsiders but seek exclusive management authority within a limited geographical area. In assessing co-management, it is necessary to consider the diversity of circumstances surrounding its negotiation and implementation.

There is some evidence that co-management is more likely to be preferred where migratory or transboundary populations are involved. In such cases, governments and users from several jurisdictions are brought together in a single forum. Perhaps not surprisingly, those groups (such as the Inuvialuit) most dependent on migratory species such as caribou, waterfowl, whales, and polar bears, are co-management's most convinced advocates. They regard it as the key to resource conservation, and to social and political stability respecting resource harvesting, despite some day-to-day problems and frustrations. By contrast, the Anishinabe of northwestern Ontario historically relied on fish and wildlife resources with quite restricted ranges, or even non-mobile resources such as wild rice. These resources could be and were managed exclusively within a limited area, hence the benefits of co-management are less obvious (Chapeskie 1995). The differences in environmental circumstances between these two aboriginal peoples is compounded by both ideology and historical experience—certainly, in the case of the Anishinabe, of a much more thorough and devastating history of progressive encroachment and restriction (Usher et al. 1992).

There is no one answer to the question of whether co-management has proven an advantage more to governments or to beneficiaries, or for that matter, whether it has been to the equal advantage of both. Nor is it clear whether it is better to have single, comprehensive boards dealing with large areas (such as the NWMB which covers about one-fifth of Canada), or several more specialised boards (as in the case of the IFA boards), or local, community-based boards in which non-aboriginal residents participate (such as the Renewable Resource Councils in the Yukon).

Nonetheless, three features of the claims-based regimes appear to be critical to the successful implementation of co-management (Usher 1995). First, the co-management structures, and their mandate, objectives, and mode of operation, are themselves negotiated. This is very different from inviting people to sit on a body whose mandate and operations have already been determined unilaterally. Second, aboriginal members of claims-based boards are politically accountable appointees of one of the parties to an agreement, not simply 'stake-holders' or 'users', as is the case on the *ad hoc* boards. In some of the latter type of boards, (including the well-known BQCMB), only governments are signatories to the management agreement. The rights and powers of users are specified but not guaranteed; they are granted by governments and do not constitute a recognition of existing rights. Third, only the claims-based arrangements are permanent. The *ad hoc* arrangements are in place only for a limited period, subject to discretionary renewal and funding by government.

Co-management may work best when the parties have similar interests in and objectives regarding the resources in question. Ideally each contributes its own knowledge to achieve a shared objective of sustainability. If objectives are not shared, then knowledge may not be shared and communication will be impaired. This problem is likely to increase as the number of parties to co-management increases.

Benefits of co-management

The key elements of the modern treaties regarding land tenure, resource access, and co-management provide for enforceable rights of property and governance. The resulting security of tenure, access, and management regime provide essential conditions for local economic growth and social development. Typically, where co-management has been implemented, local and regional economies can be characterised as mixed, subsistence-based economies. They are certainly not traditional in the sense of being antiquated or undeveloped, but northern aboriginal communities have quite distinctive social, cultural, and economic objectives and needs that are not fully addressed by the standard models of economic development. The security achieved by the claims agreements is important not so much for capital investment by lending institutions, as for the investment in social capital by aboriginal people themselves in the form of the skills, knowledge, and values required for harvesting. For the most part, such communities are quite prepared to work with outside resource development interests if they can maximise the economic benefits, minimise environmental and social damages, and retain their renewable-resource based harvesting economies for both subsistence and commercial purposes.

Under the modern agreements, not only are aboriginal priorities with respect to harvesting guaranteed, but co-management arrangements provide the tools of cooperative governance necessary to secure both harvesting and marketing in a national and international context. Aboriginal peoples have been involved in international markets for centuries, and have no interest in returning to some imaginary pristine autarky. Yet this market access is now under unprecedented assault from an urban public increasingly divorced from, and sometimes hostile to, the realities of the sustainable use of living resources.

Through implementing co-management regimes, aboriginal people not only continue harvesting but are learning new and quite different skills: negotiating, marketing, finding out how the larger world works and how to operate in it, directing research, setting priorities, and in general defending and advancing their interests in a positive way. In doing so they reinforce their collective sense of the role and importance of their common property arrangements and subsistence systems, and their culturally-based knowledge, values, and skills that are required to make these things work in contemporary conditions. Scientists and administrators also learn how to expand the knowledge inputs required to operationalise modern systems of conservation and development to include traditional environmental knowledge and understanding.

Another feature of the modern agreements is the provision for negotiating impact benefit agreements where third parties seek to exercise their resource rights on aboriginal lands (where aboriginal entities hold surface but not subsurface titles, or where prior Crown grants survive). These agreements may include such matters as project mitigation, environmental monitoring, compensation for loss of use or direct damages to the environment as well as to property, all of which require continuing cooperative arrangements between the parties and which may also be characterised as a form of voluntary co-management.

Such arrangements are increasingly (although by no means universally) accepted by large resource companies as good business sense in that they provide for certainty with respect to development and investment which the state, on its own, is unable to fully guarantee except by the most draconian and publicly unacceptable methods.

One feature of co-management is that it brings people together in a way that they can learn to respect each other and understand their interests, priorities, and perspectives. When this happens, people are more likely to make accommodations, and more likely to see the process as mutually beneficial rather than as a zero–sum game.

The process of co-management is costly, but it is also necessary to look at avoided costs. Direct actions, disruptions, and court challenges are also costly. In the historic treaty areas where these issues remain unresolved, when aboriginal people want to do things they believe they have a right to do, they act. When charged and prosecuted, they defend themselves in court on the basis of their aboriginal or treaty rights. Some of these cases have significantly enlarged both the legal content and the public understanding of these rights, but there have also been some significant losses. Any major case that eventually goes all the way up to the Supreme Court is likely to take years and cost millions of dollars, all of which creates uncertainty for both customary common property holders and potential investors.

On balance, experience suggests that contemporary co-management arrangements between aboriginal peoples and Canadian governments, as well as third parties, meet the tests of conservation, equity, and efficiency, and therefore provide the conditions for sustainable development. Experience also suggests that the principles of co-management can be applied to other spheres, ranging from the international (such as the recently established Arctic Council and its role in environmental protection, and the standing it provides to aboriginal political organisations). They can also be applied to other resource management issues at the regional level such as non-renewable resource development and to program delivery relating to such matters as health and education.

There is a new way of doing business in the Canadian North, and many are recognising its useful and beneficial aspects. Nothing is permanent, however, and the maintenance of effective co-management requires ongoing vigilance and the solution of new problems.

Challenges for co-management

In the long run, co-management arrangements and agreements will only be as good as the parties are prepared to make them. There is a special requirement for vigilance on the part of the weaker party, which is invariably the aboriginal party. Comprehensive claims agreements are protected under section 35 of the *Constitution Act, 1982*, and their provisions are paramount over any other federal, provincial, or territorial legislation which may be inconsistent with them. Nonetheless, governments must constantly be reminded of these facts, especially when drafting new legislation. Although there are arbitration provisions under the claims agreements, there are no enforceable penalties for federal non-compliance.

It is up to the aboriginal party to ensure that the rest of the world complies with their agreements. The costs and complications of effectively administering such large tracts of land bring both problems and opportunities. The slowness of actual demarcation on the ground has been a problem where development pressures are great, as in the case of forestry adjacent to southern Cree lands in Quebec (Penn 1997). Overly prescriptive regimes which cannot evolve and adapt to changing conditions will ultimately fail to address key problems, and the parties will eventually bypass them (Brooke 1997, Wilkinson and Vincelli 1997).

Although the courts in recent years have led the way in reinterpreting the historic treaty provisions in a more liberal and expansive fashion, this cannot be relied on in the case of the modern treaties. Canadian courts already regard these as more equitable contracts in which the aboriginal parties had full capacity to negotiate agreements and to understand the consequences of what they had agreed to.

There has to be political will to implement agreements. The opportunities for slippage in the first few critical years of implementation, when operational patterns are getting established, are substantial. It is the aboriginal party that must seize the initiative and ensure that implementation is effective.

Co-management thus clearly requires mutual respect and equitable political relations. But it also requires substantial resources to implement. Without adequate resources, there can be no effective participation in co-management regimes, which requires (among other things) travel, translation, access to information, and continuity of representation. The seats may be there, but that is not much help if people have neither the money nor the capacity to fill them, or if for these and other reasons they are discouraged from filling them.

The pattern of modern comprehensive claims settlements was set in the 1980s when governments still spent money freely, and took an activist role in land and resource management. Periodic renegotiation of implementation funding (which after initial one-time implementation tasks relates largely to the co-management system) will get tougher. Disputes may now more likely occur not over differing legal interpretations of substantive obligations, but what expenditures are required to meet these obligations. New measures and practices of management effectiveness and efficiency will be required. How to trade off higher costs of doing business, and of conducting research, against reduced enforcement costs, crisis avoidance, and enhanced sustainability? Co-management can become a victim of its own success: to the extent that it reduces conflict, it becomes less noticeable in the eyes of those who ultimately allocate the funds.

Another area future disagreement may be the role of government in land and environmental management. In an era of downsizing and privatisation, what are the implications of government withdrawal? It is hard to continue to implement an agreement when one partner gets up from the table and walks away. Problems may also emerge in the maintenance of the essential character of common property, with the creation of corporate and state-like entities under comprehensive claims, although it is too early to assess actual developments.

Modern treaties have secured a legal base for aboriginal property. The collective title is held by corporate entities, with certain important limits with respect to transfer or alienation to non-beneficiaries. Is there a risk that in the long run collective property can be converted to private tenure? I believe that aboriginal property systems are in principle recognisable by the common law system even if they are different, but it will be a challenge to characterise them in this way without undermining them. There is also the question of whether, under conditions of scarcity or economic difficulty, limited entry and tradeable resource rights could emerge even in the face of fundamental values of universal access. Customary property relations do evolve and change as new conditions arise.

Boundary issues may also be problematic. Traditional use and occupancy are the basis of aboriginal claims in law and policy. What are the implications of using this concept to define the territorial limits of jurisdiction of 'state-like' institutions? The modern treaty process is creating subnational (or sub-territorial) political and administrative units, with mandates and responsibilities organised along state or corporate lines. This is very far from the recognition and entrenchment of traditional aboriginal forms of socio-territorial organisation. By reifying what were formerly fluid and imprecise boundaries according to contemporary requirements of state administration (even if an aboriginal government is in charge), there is a probability of separation of title and use over time, contrary to aboriginal principles and traditions. Some evidence of the social difficulties this poses with particular respect to registered traplines have been reported in the Cree area of Quebec (McDonnell and La Rusic 1987) and the Yukon. The emergence of 'overlap' and boundary disputes among neighbouring claimant groups is also an indication of the effect of creating state-like jurisdictional boundaries.

Finally, there is the question of how far the model can spread. The most successful examples of implementation come, not by coincidence, from the territorial North. The conditions conducive to success there have not held to the same degree in the provincial North, where third parties are more involved, and more numerous and varied resident interests and property rights are at stake. Because aboriginal people are constitutionally a federal responsibility, provincial governments have historically represented settler interests, and still do. Crown land disposition and resource management are provincial responsibilities, south of the 60th parallel, and there is much more resistance to co-management which is seen, perhaps especially in Quebec, as an attack on provincial sovereignty and territorial integrity. Land claims agreements are meeting increasing resistance in the provinces from a growing sector of the public that attacks them as 'race-based privilege', as a form of apartheid, and as contrary to democratic and egalitarian principles.

Conclusion

Where aboriginal groups have embraced co-management, they have embarked on a path of partnership and cooperation with government, sometimes the private sector, and in effect with other Canadian citizens. There is an alternative, but it implies the maintenance of distance, isolation, and to some extent social if not economic autarky.

While aboriginal and historic treaty rights are protected under the constitution, in the absence of negotiated agreements it is still left to the courts to determine what they are. This is a slow, uncertain, and uneven process, and it is possible that the high-water mark has already been reached in Canada, and the tide is ebbing. Waiting to negotiate until formal recognition of certain principles occurs, or until certain processes are in place, is also risky. True equality cannot be achieved by declaration alone, and it cannot be wished into existence. Imbalances of demographic and economic power are facts of life in Canada and will continue to be such for a very long time. None of this is to deny the tremendous symbolic importance of formal acts of recognition, but rights, once acknowleged, have to be exercised in a real world where neither property nor sovereignty are unbounded.

What Canadian aboriginal peoples have achieved through the comprehensive claims process and through the implementation of co-management regimes is far from perfect. In comparison to the situation of indigenous peoples in other countries, however, much has been achieved by at least some Canadian aboriginal peoples to secure rights of tenure, access, and management of their lands, resources, and environment.

Co-management is not autonomy or self-determination. But it is much more than consultation or participation. Property and management rights have not simply been defined and defended by the law of the state, but also by agreements which were negotiated, not unilaterally imposed, and which are constitutionally protected. Co-management is not a separatist or isolationist vision, but one of cooperation and sharing. These are values not to be dismissed in today's world. There will always be hostility and resistance from some quarters. There will always be a need to form alliances to protect one's interests, and co-management can help people to do that. The struggle continues, but on new and higher ground.

Notes

1. This section is a condensation of Usher, Tough, and Galois 1992. For a useful legal interpretation of the process of conversion of Indian lands to Crown lands, see Slattery 1987. For a more expanded discussion, see Canada 1996, especially vol. 2, ch. 2, 'Treaties', and vol. 2, ch. 4, 'Lands and Resources'.
2. Canada also acknowledged limited responsibility for dealing with past failures to honour its treaty obligations under the Specific Claims Policy (Canada 1982), which applied to the treaty areas. However, policy implementation has been unilaterally and narrowly determined by Canada. Loss of use of off-reserve resources, subsistence or non-market resource values, and resource management issues, are all excluded from consideration.
3. Developments in aboriginal self-government are beyond the scope of this paper, but have also taken two directions. One is the creation of public government in territories in which aboriginal peoples are the majority (Nunavut and Nunavik). The other has been to assert an 'inherent right of self-government' whose content would be negotiable or justiciable (which was a part of the unratified Constitutional proposals of 1992). This discussion focuses entirely on the regimes established by comprehensive claims and related processes and does not address the constitutional debates.
4. This and the following sections are based on the results of the Land, Resource, and Environment Regimes Project undertaken for the Royal Commission on Aboriginal Peoples, consisting of eight case studies of contemporary co-management regimes established by the comprehensive claims process and other circumstances, and a synthetic analysis (Usher 1997). The entire set of reports is available on CD-ROM (Royal Commission on Aboriginal Peoples 1997).
5. *R. v. Sparrow*, [1990] 1 S.C.R. 1075.

References

Brooke, L.F., 1997. 'The James Bay and Northern Quebec Agreement: experiences of the Nunavik Inuit with wildlife management,' [CD-ROM], in Royal Commission on Aboriginal Peoples, *For Seven Generations: an information legacy of the Royal Commision for Aboriginal Peoples*, Libraxus, Ottawa.

Canada, 1981. *In All Fairness: a native claims policy*, Supply and Services Canada, Ottawa.

———, 1982. *Outstanding Business: a native claims policy*, Supply and Services Canada, Ottawa.

———, 1996. *Report of the Royal Commission on Aboriginal Peoples*, Canada Communication Group, Ottawa.

Chapeskie, A., 1997. 'Land, Landscape, Culturescape: Aboriginal Relations to Land and the Co-management of Natural Resources,' [CD-ROM], in Royal Commission on Aboriginal Peoples, *For Seven Generations: an information legacy of the Royal Commision for Aboriginal Peoples*, Libraxus, Ottawa.

Chrétien, J., 8 August 1973. *Statement on Indian and Inuit Claims*, Department of Indian Affairs and Northern Development, Ottawa.

Larcombe, P.M., 1997. 'The Northern Flood Agreement: implementation of land, resource and environmental regimes in a treaty area,' [CD-ROM], in Royal Commission on Aboriginal Peoples, *For Seven Generations: an information legacy of the Royal Commision for Aboriginal Peoples*, Libraxus, Ottawa.

McDonnell, R.F., and I.E. La Rusic, October 1987. *Forestry Operations and Hunting Organization Among Waswanipi Cree*, Unpublished report prepared for Cree Regional Authority, HUSO Services Inc., Montreal.

Notzke, C., 1995. 'The Barriere Lake Trilateral Agreement,' [CD-ROM], in Royal Commission on Aboriginal Peoples, *For Seven Generations: an information legacy of the Royal Commision for Aboriginal Peoples*, Libraxus, Ottawa.

Department of Indian Affairs and Northern Development, 1993. *Nunavut Land Claims Agreement*, Department of Indian Affairs and Northern Development, Ottawa.

Osherenko, G., 1988. *Sharing Power with Native Users: co-management regimes for Arctic wildlife*, Canadian Arctic Resources Committee, Ottawa.

Penn, A., 1997. 'The James Bay and Northern Quebec Agreement: natural resources, public lands, and the implementation of a native land claim settlement,' [CD-ROM], in Royal Commission on Aboriginal Peoples, *For Seven Generations: an information legacy of the Royal Commission for Aboriginal Peoples*, Libraxus, Ottawa.

Pinkerton, E.W., D. Moore, and F. Fortier, 1997. 'A Model for First Nation Leadership in Multi-Party Stewardship of Watersheds and their Fisheries,' [CD-ROM], in Royal Commission on Aboriginal Peoples, *For Seven Generations: an information legacy of the Royal Commission for Aboriginal Peoples*, Libraxus, Ottawa.

Royal Commission on Aboriginal Peoples, 1997. *For Seven Generations: an information legacy of the Royal Commission for Aboriginal Peoples* [CD-ROM], Libraxus, Ottawa.

Slattery, B., 1987. 'Understanding aboriginal rights,' *Canadian Bar Review* 66:726–83.

Staples, W.L., 1997. 'The Inuvialuit Final Agreement: implementation of its land, resource and environmental regimes,' [CD-ROM], in Royal Commission on Aboriginal Peoples, *For Seven Generations: an information legacy of the Royal Commission for Aboriginal Peoples*, Libraxus, Ottawa.

Usher, P.J., 1987. 'Indigenous management systems and the conservation of wildlife in the Canadian North,' *Alternatives* 14(1):3–9.

——, 1993. 'The Beverly–Qamanirjuaq Caribou Management Board: an experience in co–management,' in J.T. Inglis (ed.), *Traditional Ecological Knowledge, Concepts and Cases*, International Program on Traditional Ecological Knowledge and International Development Research Centre, Ottawa:111–20.

——, 1995. Co-management of natural resources: some aspects of the Canadian experience, in D.L. Peterson and D.R. Johnson (ed.), *Human Ecology and Climate Change: people and resources in the Far North*, Taylor and Francis, Washington DC:197–206.

——, 1997. 'Contemporary Aboriginal Land, Resource, and Environment Regimes: origins, problems and prospects,' [CD-ROM], in Royal Commission on Aboriginal Peoples, *For Seven Generations: an information legacy of the Royal Commission for Aboriginal Peoples*, Libraxus, Ottawa.

Usher, P.J., P. Cobb, M. Loney, and G. Spafford, 1992. Hydro-electric Development and the English River Anishinabe: Ontario Hydro's Past record and present approaches to treaty and aboriginal rights,

Social Impact Assessment, and Mitigation and Compensation, report prepared for Nishnawbe-Aski Nation, Grand Council Treaty 3, and Teme-Augama Anishnabai, Ottawa, unpublished.

Usher, P.J., F.J. Tough, and R.M. Galois, 1992. 'Reclaiming the land: aboriginal title, treaty rights and land claims in Canada,' *Applied Geography* 12(2):109–132.

Wilkinson, P.F., and M. Vincelli, 1995. 'The James Bay and Northern Quebec Agreement: an evaluation of the implementation of its environmental regimes,' [CD-ROM], in Royal Commission on Aboriginal Peoples, *For Seven Generations: an information legacy of the Royal Commision for Aboriginal Peoples*, Libraxus, Ottawa.

Property, sovereignty and self-determination in Australia

Henry Reynolds

The concept of national sovereignty is under siege in many parts of the world as states lose power from above to global markets and global organisations and are challenged from below by regions, minorities and entrapped nations. Such developments are particularly apparent in Europe with the break-up of the Soviet Union, Yugoslavia and Czechoslovakia, and with the ceding of power within the European Union to the Commission, the Parliament and the Court. At the same time regions are asserting new or rediscovered identities.

John Keane, the British political scientist and biographer of Thomas Paine, has called for a decentring of the institutions of the nation–state and the return to the more complex pattern typical of the late medieval and early modern periods when Europe was divided into 500 or so political units (Keane 1992:10). Two other commentators have recently advanced arguments of more direct relevance to the Australian scene. The French philosopher Paul Ricoeur observed that 'in modern republics, the origin of sovereignty is in the people, but now we recognise we have *many* peoples. And many people mean many centres of sovereignty...' (Ricoeur 1995:35).

The second argument was put forward by the prominent British Conservative politician Geoffrey Howe who wrote

> I believe sovereignty is not some pre-defined absolute, but a flexible, adaptable, organic notion that endures and adjusts with circumstances...In exactly the same way as property rights of an individual, sovereignty may be seen as divisible and exploitable in the interests of the nation (Howe 1990:679).

To date Australia appears to be untroubled by debates about the nature, extent and the exercise of sovereignty. Aboriginal challenges to absolute Crown sovereignty have been summarily dismissed by Australian judges. The traditional view was reaffirmed by the High Court in the *Mabo* case as was the so-called Act of State doctrine which upholds the view that an extension of sovereignty is an act of prerogative power which cannot be questioned by the courts.

Two key assumptions underpin the conventional view about the imposition of British sovereignty over Australia. They relate to sovereignty itself, on the one hand, and to traditional Aboriginal society on the other.

The traditional British view of sovereignty was summed up by William Blackstone in his classic work *Commentaries on the Laws of England*, published just before the first settlement of Australia. Blackstone argued that in any state there must be 'a supreme, irresistible, absolute, uncontrolled authority' (Blackstone 1773, 1:30). It was this view of authority which was brought to Australia where it was commonly believed there was no government, no law and no ownership of land in the sense understood by Europeans. Several things followed from this situation.

- British sovereignty in Australia was original, not derivative
- the Crown was therefore both the first and only sovereign
- sovereignty applied immediately and everywhere in the absence of any competing sovereign.

But how did this concept of the Crown's sovereignty relate to the idea of *terra nullius*? In the *Mabo* case the High Court rejected the idea in relation to property while confirming it in relation to sovereignty. The bench determined that, contrary to previous assumptions, the aboriginal tribes were in possession of their traditional lands. They had a form of customary tenure. When the Crown annexed Australia it acquired the radical title but not the beneficial ownership of the land which remained in the possession of the indigenous people. Much land was lost by extinguishment but it happened in a piecemeal fashion over a long period of time. Native title had survived on Murray Island because nothing the Queensland government had done between 1879 and 1992 had extinguished it. Traditional Murray Island property law survives as part of the common law. It is the local law, the *lex loci* of that place.

What we have now, then, is two stories in conflict. *Terra nullius* applies in respect of sovereignty, but it has been overthrown in relation to property. Can this situation be sustained? Must there be a new jurisprudential story which treats sovereignty in the same way as property? What would that story be like?

1. Before 1788 the Aborigines and Torres Strait Islanders exercised a form of sovereignty, albeit rudimentary, over their traditional territories. The tribal groupings, however defined, were small nations.
2. The original British claim of sovereignty by discovery was a claim of priority against rival European powers. It was a claim for external sovereignty only.
3. Within Australia, sovereignty was asserted very slowly as settlement advanced gradually over the vast land mass.
4. Colonial Australia had many sovereigns and many systems of law although there were far fewer in 1900 than in 1800.
5. Remnant sovereignty survives among those communities which still exercise traditional law.

What we have, in sum, is a typical colonial situation where the common law applied but only as the circumstances of the colony allowed. This brings us back to Geoffrey Howes' view that sovereignty was imposed, in practice in a complex way and that in Australia it changed considerably over the colonial period.

Such a new story would have major implications for Australian law and Australian politics. It would dramatically change the relationship between indigenous Australians and the state. It suggests that like the First Nations of Canada the Aborigines and Islanders have an inherent right to self-government arising from the survival of their original sovereignty.

In seeking to find support for self-determination indigenous Australians will turn not just outward to international law and documents but also inward to our own society and backward to our own historical experience.

References

Blackstone, W., 1773. *Commentaries on the Laws of England*, 4 vols, 5th ed., Clarendon Press, Oxford.

Howe, G., 1990 'Sovereignty and Interdependence: Britain's place in the world', *International Affairs*, 66(4):675–95.

Keane, J., 1992. 'Democracy's Poisonous Fruit', *Times Literary Supplement*, 21 August:10.

Ricoeur, P., 1995. 'Universality and the power of difference', in R. Kearney (ed.), *States of Mind: dialogues with contemporary thinkers*, New York University Press, New York:33–8.

9

Common property regimes in Aboriginal Australia: totemism revisited

Deborah Bird Rose

In the closing years of the twentieth century, debates in Australia
about Indigenous institutions of common property ownership and
management are inseparable from the highly political issues of Native
Title. In this chapter I intend to move beyond debates about the
politics of land tenure and toward an analysis of a dynamic jurisprudence of duty in which responsibilities and rights are considered
together. I will examine totemism as a common property institution for
long-term ecological management. The purpose is to describe and
analyse this Indigenous regime in order to examine some of the
principles which inform it. The implications of this analysis speak to
the sustainability of life on this arid continent.

The fundamental divide in debates about common property has
been whether common property is to be understood as an absence of
institutions for the management of territory and resources, or whether
common property is to be understood as a type of communal management (Berkes and Farvar 1989:7, Eythorsson 1995:7, Maurstad 1995).
Thanks to Hardin's 'tragedy of the commons' article, debates about
common property make a vital link between systems of ownership
and systems of management. It is now established that there are many
forms of common property institutions for management of resources
including those of land and sea. The terms 'resource' and 'regime' can

be used to distinguish between the resource itself and the set of institutions (or absence of institutions) by which it is held and managed (Berkes and Farvar 1989:9). In many parts of the world common property institutions are not officially recognised by formal legal institutions. Several regimes may coexist, and common property regimes may be hidden from or invisible to formal institutions; coexistence may be complementary or contradictory (Maurstad 1995). The coexistence of different property regimes frequently correlates with the coexistence of different forms of production and different productive groups (for example, Berkes et al. 1989, Berkes 1989).

Common property concepts in Australia

Hunter–gatherer peoples, perhaps more than any others, have been until very recently disregarded as land and resource owners and managers. Only within the last fifteen years have questions of land management emerged as a key component of research with Indigenous people in Australia (Williams and Hunn 1982). The long historical silence on these issues is connected with the settler view that Aboriginal people were parasites on nature. Elkin (1954:15) gave the mark of scientific authority to this view in a book first published in 1938

> The food-gathering life is parasitical; the Aborigines are absolutely dependent on what nature produces without any practical assistance on their part.

This view of parasitism was intricately connected to the view of *terra nullius*. The idea that the land was untransformed led directly to the idea that land was unowned. Locke's famous statement on property and ownership could have been written precisely to justify the dispossession of Indigenous peoples in the European settlement of Australia

> Whatsoever then he moves out of the state that Nature hath provided and left it in he hath mixed his labour with and thereby makes it his property (quoted in Shiva 1993:25).

The reversal of the parasite view dates to Rhys Jones's (1969) work on the use of fire as a tool of land management. He called this system fire-stick farming, and his use of the term 'farming' was deliberate (Jones 1995). It was provocative precisely because it hit a cultural/political nerve. It indicates that, like farmers, Aboriginal people intervened in their ecosystems to transform them in predictable, and to them desirable, ways. They consciously managed their ecosystems for long-term objectives that included the long-term productivity of the land and the long-term fertility of resources. There has been a degree of debate about Jones's analysis, and there are still some adherents to the parasite view, but the evidence is quite clear that Aboriginal people managed resources in definable and observable ways in order to produce long-term productivity in their environments (for example, Bowman 1995; Latz 1995b).

The official view that Indigenous people did not own the land at the time of European conquest has been overturned by the High Court's 'Mabo' decision (1992) which gave formal legal recognition to the fact that at the time of conquest Indigenous people did own the land. In theory, Indigenous people continue to exercise rights of ownership—now labelled 'Native Title'—except in areas where conquest and appropriation have formally extinguished those rights. The more recent *Native Title Act* (Commonwealth 1993) provides a legislative framework within which the continuity of Native Title can be asserted, and the High Court's recent 'Wik' decision (1996) provides further articulation of how Native Title can be understood legally to survive. Where Native Title continues to exist, land cannot be alienated from Indigenous use and management without negotiation with the Indigenous title holders. It is likely that cooperative management agreements will increase as the *Native Title Act* begins to have a greater impact.

Issues of Indigenous land tenure have thus acquired a special urgency in Australia. The analysis of common property regimes brings to these issues a vital perspective: that usufructuary rights are embedded within regimes of responsibility, and that regimes of rights and regimes of management are inseparable. Without rights, resources will not be managed; without management, resources will be degraded and depleted, and rights will become meaningless.

If there are Indigenous regimes of common property ownership and management, what institutional forms do they take? How might they be discerned? In what ways can they be understood to be systems that are produced through time, rather than just the fortuitous outcomes of actions performed by individuals? There can be no single answers to these questions, but I believe that an instructive start can be made by considering totemism as an institution for the management of common property resources. In addition, an examination of the history of anthropological and philosophical analysis of totemism also helps explain why serious consideration of common property regimes has been so long delayed.

Land tenure and common property regimes

Aboriginal cultures across Australia (with the possible exception of some urban people who have been severed from their homelands for generations) construct identity, social relations, and spirituality in relation to local place. In Aboriginal English the term is 'country'. Economic, social and cultural development is articulated most profoundly and productively in the context of country. The Australian continent prior to conquest was articulated as a cultural landscape through the conjunction of local countries (for example, see Peterson and Long 1986). Countries related to each other regionally through marriage, trade, ritual relationships (summarised in Rose 1996). Across the continent articulations of countries were accomplished through major trade systems and the extensive 'Dreaming tracks' which are the travels of creative beings, impressed upon the landscape and told, sung, and performed in contexts of ritual (Mulvaney 1976).

Countries were (in most areas still are) associated with social groups in a reflexive relationship of ownership and belonging. The social organisation of landowning groups has been debated with vigour for decades by anthropologists, and in recent years the Aboriginal Land Commissioner has conducted inquiries into traditional ownership under the *Land Rights Act* (NT) 1976 which have enabled Aboriginal people to place their views into the debate. Local land-based groups, recruited though descent, are generally called clans by anthropologists, and the term has moved into Aboriginal and other Australian English vernaculars. Clans are linked into larger clusters, with those sharing a language are often referred to in the non-technical literature as tribes. Clans are also linked through marriage ties, trade relationships, shared responsibilities in religious ceremonies, and alliances for war—terms like community, tribe, and nation have been used by different observers to refer to clusters of clans that interact on a regular basis. In many areas the devastating loss of population brought about by colonisation has resulted in people's primary identity being framed at the level of 'tribe' or 'community' rather than at the level of a fragmented and devastated clan structure.[1]

Debate has focused on the composition of the clan (patrilineal, cognatic, or some other form of recruitment), and about which level of organisation—clan or larger community—is best considered to be a landowning group (Gumbert 1984 provides a useful summary for the non-specialist). The *Land Rights Act* (NT) 1976 defines Aboriginal traditional owners (section 3[1]) as

> a local descent group of Aboriginals who have common spiritual affiliations to a site on the land, being affiliations that place the group under a primary spiritual responsibility for that site and for the land, and who are entitled by Aboriginal tradition to forage over that land.

It thus designates the local group ('clan') as the landowning group, focuses on spiritual responsibilities, and treats foraging (use-rights) almost as an afterthought. And it is something of a blessing that foraging is not central because in twenty years of land claims it has been shown conclusively that rights to forage are not restricted to local groups such as clans. On all the evidence, use-rights in respect of resources are not restricted to, or best articulated through, small groups such as clans (see Ingold 1987 for a pointed discussion of this issue).

In contrast to the Northern Territory legislation, the *Native Title Act* 1993 speaks primarily to the right to forage: 'The expression "native title" or "native title rights and interests" means the communal, group or individual rights and interests of Aboriginal peoples or Torres Strait Islanders in relation to land or waters (233.[1]); and "rights and interests" includes 'hunting, gathering or fishing rights and interests' (233.[2]). Clearly the framers of this Act had usufructuary rights in mind.

Indigenous philosophies assert that social life is most properly directed toward ensuring that the past and present of a people and their country be brought into the future. Continuity is a key value (Stanner 1979). To return, therefore, to my original point about the inseparability of regimes of rights and regimes of responsibilities, my contention is that these Native Title rights and interests are not parasitical—they include not only the right to take resources, but also the responsibility to ensure that resources will be there in the future. Totemism appears to constitute just such a jurisprudence of responsibility and right.

Intellectual history

'Totemism' was one of the cornerstones of emergent social science and related disciplines around the turn of the century. Sir James Frazer's *Totemism and Exogamy* (four volumes, 1910) and Freud's *Totem and*

Taboo (1918) testify to the grasp of 'totemism' on the minds of these key thinkers. Debated regularly from decade to decade, totemism has become a palimpsest of western social theories. I will not linger in the history of thought concerning totemism, but rather will summarise extensively in order to elucidate some of the assumptions that have hindered an understanding of totemism in the material world, and thus have hindered an understanding of Indigenous common property regimes.

Definitions of totemism vary enormously, as I will discuss, but at the core the phenomenon labelled totemism posits a non-random relationship between particular humans and particular non-humans. It is this human/non-human link that exercised the thinking of early theorists such as Frazer (1910) and Freud (1918) (discussed in Levi-Strauss 1963:2–3). I believe that we must consider that this project, of distinguishing civilisation from savagery, and culture from nature, was given special urgency by the pressure placed on key concepts of western thought under the intellectual revolution taking place in conjunction with secularisation and Darwinian theory. A key feature of western thought since the Enlightenment, the disjunction between nature and culture, was powerfully threatened by evolutionary theory, for if humans are descended from animals, where is the boundary between them?

Hayden White (1978) has shown that these boundary questions become urgent when concepts of humanity are threatened. Totemism filled a wonderfully useful role in providing an answer to the question that was not explicitly being asked. The question was that of boundary maintenance. The answer was that if civilisation is marked by separation of culture from nature, it follows that a religious outlook which posited a relationship between culture and nature must be understood as an absence of civilisation, and must therefore constitute an evolutionary stage at which humans were not fully separated from nature. Analysis of totemism could thus confirm the superiority of western civilisation and the inferiority of the savage, defining and ordering their difference, while simultaneously linking them together as moments in a global history of progress. As Stanley Diamond asserts of anthropology

> We study men, that is, we reflect on ourselves studying others, because we must, because man in civilisation is the problem...The questions we bring to history come out of our own need. The task of anthropology is to clarify these questions (Diamond 1974:100).

In 1912 Durkheim wrote that 'the totem is before all a symbol, a material expression of something else. But of what?' He would go on to assert that the totem is a symbol of god and of society, brought together, in his view, in the clan (quoted in Lessa and Voigt 1979:34). Subsequent social scientists did not devote works specifically to totemism, probably as a result of a number of critiques which cast doubt on the view that totemism constituted an analytically discrete phenomenon (discussed in Levi-Strauss 1963). Nevertheless, the question 'a symbol of what?' provided an opportunity for people to inscribe their particular theories of society and culture on the *tabula* of totemism.

Malinowski, for example, accepted the first part of Durkheim's assertion—that a totem is a symbol of something else. In good economic fashion, he found a consumption value: 'the road from the wilderness to the savage's belly and consequently his mind is very short', he wrote in 1948, 'and for him the world is an indiscriminate background against which there stand out the useful, primarily the edible, species of plant and animal' (Malinowski 1948:44). He would go on to characterise Australian Aboriginal totemism as the most 'elementary' form, and would note that totemic cults had as their purpose the provisioning of abundance (Malinowski 1948:46). He was thus able to draw Aboriginal Australians into his general theory of science, magic and religion. Magic, he contended, is a set of techniques used by people to effect control of nature to their own ends when their practical knowledge and technology are inadequate (Malinowski 1948:19, 29). Radcliffe-Brown developed this view in more elegant manner, suggesting it was a common characteristic of hunting peoples to elaborate a major food item. While Radcliffe-Brown would initiate analysis into the logical properties of totems, both he and Malinowski are expressive of the theory, stated so succinctly by Levi-Strauss, that totems are 'good to eat' (1963:62).

Levi-Strauss himself found another meaning in totemism. In his view, totemism answers a universal question of the mind: 'how to make opposition, instead of being an obstacle to integration, serve rather to produce it.' Natural species, he claims, are chosen because they are good to think, not because they are good to eat' (1963:89). Rather than positing a one-to-one correspondence, Levi-Strauss looks to contrasting relationships between totems, and rather than considering that totems index the world, he held that they articulate the mind.

Levi-Strauss's work only makes sense if one accepts as universal a number of dichotomies that have been characteristic of western thought since the Enlightenment, and that have been subjected to a range of excellent critiques (for example, Young 1990).

- *mind vs body* this dichotomy promotes the view that totems can be good to eat or good to think but not good both to eat and to think. Reading this dichotomy back into Malinowski's work, we see that he inscribes savagery in that short distance between the savage belly and the savage mind. The lack of mind/body split is held to be characteristic of savages, and by implication, to differentiate them from civilised man.
- *culture vs nature* this dichotomy promotes the view that culture is more evolved to the extent that it distinguishes itself from nature. Reading this dichotomy back into Malinowski, the distance between the wilderness and the savage is an index of savagery itself, differentiating that state from civilisation.
- *difference is oppositional* Levi-Strauss talks about 'opposition' when he quite clearly means difference, and he takes it as given that difference is oppositional and is in need of transformation. He further presupposes that integration is a desirable social goal in and of itself. Such a view generates its own paradox. On the one hand it seeks to close the distance between savagery and civilisation by claiming universalities of mind. On the other hand, it oppresses those who find that they are socially positioned as different from those who are socially positioned as not-different, for it indicates that they/we are problems to be overcome. As Diamond so succinctly adverts, 'man in civilisation is the problem' (1974:100).

Dreaming ecology

Thus far I have looked at unifying and universalising theories of totemism. I now turn to the Australian context. Data from Aboriginal Australia, especially that compiled by Spencer and Gillen (1899) were drawn on by all the early theorists of totemism and 'primitive' religion. Subsequently, most of the critiques of attempts to generate unified theories of totemism were supported with evidence from Australia. Thus, virtually every major proposition concerning totemism was supported in part by reference to Australian data. At the same time, virtually every critique of attempts to universalise was also supported with reference to Australian data. As Levi-Strauss indicates throughout his study, although not with this intention, every general theory can be both supported by, and contradicted with, evidence from Aboriginal Australia.

Anthropology in Australia has not sought unified global theories, but rather sought to analyse specific instances of totemic organisation, action, and thought. Lloyd Warner's pioneering ethnography of 1939 *A Black Civilisation*, based on research he conducted in the 1920s, signals in its title the author's distance from the oppressive savagery–civilisation dichotomy. Warner stated that the totemic system of northeast Arnhem Land was 'highly elaborated and permeates all the activities of the group and all of its concepts of life in the world about it' (Warner 1969:378). He found it to be a system of ritual relations between clan members and certain species of plants and animals. Totemism in north east Arnhem Land, Warner contended, 'is intelligible only in terms of the social organisation, the relation of the technological system to society generally, and the ideas which surround the society's adjustment to the natural environment' (Warner 1969:234).

In light of Warner's emphasis on both the religious quality of totemism and its pervasive, indeed foundation, relation to religion, society and the environment, it seems odd that decades were to pass before these ideas were reformulated in other parts of the continent.

In the early 1960s Stanner took a phenomenological approach to totemism and religion, emphasising the mystical quality of totemism (1979 [1962]). He also linked totems with clans and with country, asserting that the group has a corporate title that covers not only the country or site, and a mystical relation to the totemic creators, but also non-material property associated with the country (Stanner 1965:13).

Stanner's study was closely followed by T.G.H. Strehlow's study of Aboriginal religion in Central Australia. He documents a totemic landscape in its social, spiritual and geographical complexity. He uses the term 'totems' to refer to the creative beings ('totemic ancestors') who made the world[2]

> Because the whole landscape of Central Australia was studded with a multitude of sacred sites where supernatural beings had lived and moved and gone to rest, and because these sacred sites were in turn linked by an interesting network of mythological trails left behind by these supernatural beings, every tribal subgroup area…was filled with a large number of sacred sites associated with a diversity of totems (Strehlow 1978:26).

Briefly but tantalisingly he proceeded to discuss some of the ritual which ensured the continuance of each totemic species or other existent. Primarily, however, Strehlow was seeking to draw out the religious or spiritual significance of totemic religion and to bring it into dialogue with contemporary spiritual concerns. In a later study, which I discuss shortly, he turned his analysis more closely to resources and land tenure.

In the same time frame Worsley's (1967) study of totemism, derived from his Groote Eylandt research, followed the tradition of Malinowski in seeking to distinguish totemism from logic and science. Like Malinowski, he shows that non-Western people do possess systems of logic, classification, and explanation which can be loosely equated with western science ('proto-scientific' in Worsley's terminology [1967: 154]). Totemism is distinguished from science, he concludes, by its lack of system; it is 'agglomerative, arbitrary and fortuitous' (Worsley 1967:151). Peterson (1972) follows on from Durkheim, Stanner and Strehlow in examining totemism as a link between person, group and country. He found totemism to be a mechanism for ordering sentiment toward home place, and thus to be a key mechanism in territorial spacing (see also Strehlow 1970).

Ted Strehlow's 1970 article 'Geography and the Totemic Landscape in Central Australia' marks a major turning point. His foundational assumption was that while totems can and do represent many things, they also, perhaps centrally, are themselves. Strehlow thus brings the material world into the analysis in a way that previous scholars, with the exception of Warner, had not done. Like others, Strehlow agreed that the totem and the clan are connected to each other and to an area of land (this was Stanner's point too), and he went on to look to the organisation of ritual life oriented toward sustaining the life of the species, and other totems. Each clan, according to Strehlow's analysis of Aranda societies, is associated with a number of totemic beings, with one of which the clan is most intimately associated and for which it bears a central responsibility. Ancestral tracks, or the Dreaming tracks of these beings link groups along the way

> ...each Aranda local group was believed to perform an indispensable economic service not only for itself but for the population around its borders as well. Thus, the Eastern Aranda Purula–Kamara local group of Ujitja was believed to have the responsibility of creating rain for the whole of the surrounding countryside by the performance of the Ujitja rain ceremonies. Other Aranda rain totemic clans…were credited with performing identical services for the populations in their local areas. In

the same way, the members of kangaroo, euro, emu, carpet snake, grass seed, and other totemic clans were regarded as having the power of bringing about the increase of their totemic plants or animals not only within their local group areas, but throughout the adjoining regions as well (Strehlow 1970:102).

The remainder of this pivotal article is devoted to issues of authority (see Rowse 1992). Strehlow laid out the relevant data for ecological analysis, but chose to proceed in another direction. Thus, it was possible for a 1979 textbook on cultural anthropology that took a deliberately ecological approach to assert that 'since, as far as I know, no one has investigated the ecological functions of totemism...it is impossible to assess the ecological relevance of Australian totemism' (Kottak 1979:201).

Newsome's 1980 study of the Dreaming track of the red kangaroo in Central Australia initiated the work of analysing the ecological relevance of Australian totemism. This sacred track traverses some of the toughest desert country in the world, and the sacred sites coincide with the most favoured areas for kangaroos. In particular, there is a strong correlation between Red Kangaroo Dreaming sites, and the permanent waters which are the sources of fresh herbage during drought. The red kangaroo relies on fresh green herbage; after rains the animals forage widely, but in drought they must rely on restricted areas. As the sites are protected, so too are the kangaroos at these sites. These are places to which living things retreat during periods of stress, and from which they expand outward again during periods of plenty. Clearly, opportunistic predation at these sites, especially during periods of stress (when humans, too, are stressed), would have long-term negative effects on red kangaroos and other species.

Aboriginal people in this part of the world approach a sacred sites with a respect that includes forbearing to hunt. Spears are left at a distance, and the caretaking of the site is accomplished without interfering with the red kangaroos whose site and refuge it is. Peter Latz, a botanist who has carried out extensive work in Central Australia, notes that the most sacred/protected places are likely to be places where a number of Dreamings meet up or cross over. He describes them this way

>...there's a lot of dreaming trails which cross over, these are really important places. They are so sacred you can't kill animals or even pick plants. And of course you don't burn them. You might burn around them in order to look after them (Latz 1995a:70).

Not only in Central Australia, but across the whole continent, there are similar structures of restraint, management for long-term productivity, control of sanctuaries, protection of permanent waters, refugia, breeding sites, and of certain plant communities. As well, there is shared responsibility (Rose 1996). Responsibilities appear to lie with the local group in the first instance, but ritual life extends and develops these responsibilities. In land claims held under the *Northern Territory Act*, claimants in ecological zones from desert to semi-arid savannas to coasts and islands assert that they can only fulfil their responsibilities to their country with the help of various categories of kin.

While the right to forage is widespread, the responsibilities that go with that right differ depending on one's relationship to the country: a major difference is whether it is one's father's country or one's mother's country. For example, in parts of Arnhem Land, men cannot visit the sacred/dangerous sites in their father's country without the men for whom it is their mother's country. They have to make gifts to the matrifiliates, and only matrifiliates can take food and water from the area (Peterson 1972:19). In parts of the Victoria River country (NT), to give another example, patrifiliates are responsible for burning the country; matrifiliates are responsible for organising the burning, and if the patrifiliates burn badly or wrongly they are accountable to matrifiliates who will punish them (see also Bradley 1995). Thus, in many areas it is simply not possible for the patrifiliates of a country to fulfil their obligations without the complementary cooperation of other kin, and in many land claims the claimants have asserted that the patrifiliates and the matrifiliates are all owners of the country as Aboriginal law defines 'ownership'.

A system of complementarity is part of a system for organising of difference in the service of producing interdependence. Difference is organised to be complementary rather than oppositional, and thus is constitutive of cultural, social and ecological life rather than, as Levi-Strauss suggests, an obstacle to be overcome. The result is that individuals and groups hold sets of a complementarity of responsibilities at numerous local and regional levels. The broad complex of responsibilities well matches the rights people have of harvesting and consuming resources both locally and regionally.

Responsibilities, like rights, are differentiated in structure but not necessarily in substance. Both are held and exercised across spiritual, social and ecological domains. Indeed, it is a western convention to separate the spiritual, the social, and the ecological. Indigenous people hold these domains as integral parts of the long-term management of life on earth.

Conclusions

It is now possible to begin to look afresh at totemism as a common property institution. To do so we must set aside the oppressive dichotomies that Levi-Strauss's work highlighted. We must, for a start, propose that subsistence activity and intellectual activity are not necessarily dichotomous or opposing activities. We must ask whether difference might not be a desired characteristic rather than a problem to be resolved, and we must learn to consider interdependence. We must start to look at difference played out not only in the local but also in regional frames. Finally, we must not allow the study of ritual to eclipse the analysis of ecological pragmatics.

The questions I have broached in this chapter are points of departure for analysis which I hope will be carried further in numerous contexts. I conclude with highlighting some of the major implications.

Responsibilities are differentiated and complementary. They are held and exercised both locally and regionally. It follows that no country is self-sufficient. The people of each country depend on others for the proper management of the relationships which sustain them all, and each group depends on others for the very pragmatic practices of land management. The burning, the preservation of species, the preservation of permanent waters: these constitute a sample of the responsibilities which are carried out at the local level, but which have regional implications.

Restraint is equally part of this system. There are sanctuaries where people do not hunt or fish or gather, and places where burning is done with extra caution or not at all. There are responsibilities based on totemic relationships: the kangaroo people can forbid others to kill and eat kangaroo, for example. As a general rule, totems are linked to taboos that enforce restraint and that are managed by the appropriate people.

Differentiated and complementary responsibilities sustain regional interdependencies. There are few hard and fast boundaries, but rather strong ecological, social and spiritual links that are reproduced through the generations. Further, as Strehlow said, to promote the well-being of that which is your responsibility is good not just for you but for others in your region. Restraint from hunting, eating, and burning, for example has wide implications. Proper exercise of responsibilities benefits other species as well as broad systems. The use of fire is the best pragmatic example of symbiotic action toward systemic productivity in time and space (see Rose 1996).

What this means to issues of ownership is thus quite different to Hardin's original proposition. While Hardin contended that private ownership would be the key to responsible land management, an analysis of Aboriginal systems suggests that responsible land management is best accomplished through systems of interpenetrating rights and responsibilities. In this type of Aboriginal system, self-interest is constructed to stand in linked and complementary fashion to the self-interest of other people, groups, species, and ecological systems. In this system, living beings truly stand or fall together. Self-interest is thus accomplished through promoting the interests of others as well as one's own.

The High Court's Mabo and Wik decisions, and the *Native Title Act*, all point in this direction—toward coexisting property regimes, including common property regimes. While some sectoral interests hold that regimes of exclusivity are essential to the full maximisation of their purposes, evidence drawn more broadly from ecological and social analysis indicates that co-management is likely to have long-term advantages for the survival of ecosystems and species, including the human species. Native Title thus constitutes a unique opportunity for the Australian nation to develop long-term strategies for the survival of life on this arid continent.

Notes

1. It is impossible to know what Aboriginal Australia was like prior to invasion, although there are numerous techniques for reconstructing models of probability. I am assuming a multi-layered set of identifications among families in these kin-based societies, but it is by no means certain that all Aboriginal people once were organised into clans, or that clans, if they existed, were organised along one model of descent to the exclusion of others.
2. Often referred to as Dreaming or Dreamtime ancestors.

References

Aboriginal Land Rights (NT) Act 1976 (Cwth).

Berkes, F., 1989. 'Cooperation from the Perspective of Human Ecology', in F. Berkes, ed., *Common Property Resources: ecology and community-based sustainable development*, Belhaven Press, London:70–88.

Berkes, F. and M. Farvar, 1989. 'Introduction and Overview', in F. Berkes, ed., *Common Property Resources: ecology and community-based sustainable development*, Belhaven Press, London:1–18.

Berkes, F., D. Feeny, B. McCay and J. Acheson, 1989. 'The benefits of the commons', *Nature* 340:91–3.

Berndt, R. (ed.), 1970. *Australian Aboriginal Anthropology*, University of Western Australia Press, Nedlands.

Bowman, D., 1995. 'Why the skillful use of fire is critical for the management of biodiversity in Northern Australia', in D. Rose (ed.), *Country in Flames: proceedings of the 1994 symposium on biodiversity and fire in North Australia*, Biodiversity Unit, Department of the Environment, Sport and Territories, and the North Australia Research Unit, Canberra and Darwin:103–110.

Bradley, J., 1995. 'Fire: emotion and politics; A Yanyuwa case study' in D. Rose (ed.), *Country in Flames: proceedings of the 1994 symposium on biodiversity and fire in North Australia*, Biodiversity Unit, Department of the Environment, Sport and Territories, and the North Australia Research Unit, Canberra and Darwin:25–31.

Diamond, S., 1974. *In Search of the Primitive: a critique of civilisation*, Transaction Books, New Brunswick, NJ.

Elkin, A., 1954 [1938]. *The Australian Aborigines: how to understand them*, Angus and Robertson, Sydney.

Eythorsson, E., 1995. 'Who should have a voice in management of local marine resources: some comments on the common property debate and the design of co-management institutions for north-Norwegian fjords fisheries', paper prepared for the 5th Common Property Conference of the International Association for the Study of Common Property, May 24–26, Bodo, Norway, unpublished.

Frazer, J., 1910. *Totemism and Exogamy: a treatise on certain early forms of superstition and society*, 4 vols, Macmillan, London.

Freud, S., 1918. *Totem and Taboo: resemblances between the psychic life of savages and neurotics*, Moffat Yard and Co., New York.

Gumbert, M., 1984. *Neither Justice Nor Reason: a legal and anthropological analysis of Aboriginal land rights*, University of Queensland Press, St Lucia.

Ingold, T., 1987. *The appropriation of nature: essays on human ecology and social relations*, Manchester University Press, Manchester.

Jones, R., 1969. 'Fire-stick Farming', *Australian Natural History* 16(7):224–8.

——, 1995. 'Mindjongork: legacy of the firestick,' in D. Rose (ed.), *Country in Flames; Proceedings of the 1994 symposium on biodiversity and fire in North Australia*, Biodiversity Unit, Department of the Environment, Sport and Territories, and the North Australia Research Unit, Canberra and Darwin:11–18.

Kottak, C., 1979. *Cultural Anthropology*, Random House, New York.

Latz, P., 1995a. *Bushfires and Bushtucker: aboriginal plant use in Central Australia*, Institute of Aboriginal Development Press, Alice Springs.

——, 1995b. 'Fire in the desert: increasing biodiversity in the short term, decreasing it in the long term,' in D. Rose (ed.), *Country in Flames; Proceedings of the 1994 symposium on biodiversity and fire in North Australia*, Biodiversity Unit, Department of the Environment, Sport and Territories, and the North Australia Research Unit, Canberra and Darwin:77–86.

Leach, E. (ed.), 1967. *The Structural Study of Myth and Totemism*, Tavistock, London.

Lessa, W. and Voigt, E. 1979. *Reader in Comparative Religion: an anthropological approach*, Harper and Row, Publishers, New York.

Levi-Strauss, C., 1963. *Totemism*, Beacon Press, Boston.

Malinowski, B., 1948. *Magic, Science and Religion, and Other Essays*, Souvenir Press, London.

Maurstad, A., 1995. Customs in court, Paper prepared for the 5th Common Property Conference of the International Association for the Study of Common Property, May 24–26, Bodo, Norway, unpublished.

Mulvaney, D., 1976. "The Chain of Connection": the material evidence' in N. Peterson (ed.), *Tribes and Boundaries in Australia*, Australian Institute for Aboriginal Studies, Canberra:72–94.

Native Title Act 1993 (Cwth).

Newsome, A., 1980. 'The eco-mythology of the Red Kangaroo in Central Australia,' *Mankind* 12(4):327–34.

Peterson, N., 1972. 'Totemism yesterday: sentiment and local organisation among the Australian Aborigines', *Man* 7(1):12–32.

—— and J. Long, 1986. *Australian Territorial Organization*, Oceania Monograph 30, University of Sydney, Sydney.

Rose, D., 1996. *Nourishing Terrains: Australian Aboriginal views of landscape and wilderness*, Australian Heritage Commission, Canberra.

Rowse, T., 1992. 'Strehlow's Strap: functionalism and historicism in colonial ethnography,' in B. Attwood and J. Arnold (eds), *Power, Knowledge and Aborigines*, Journal of Australian Studies, La Trobe University Press, La Trobe:88–103.

Shiva, V., 1993 'Reductionism and Regeneration: a crisis in science' in M. Meis and V. Shiva (eds), *Ecofeminism*, Spinifex Press, Melbourne:22–35.

Spencer, B. and F. Gillen, 1968 [1898]. *The Native Tribes of Central Australia*, Dover Publications, New York.

Stanner, W., 1979. *White Man Got No Dreaming: essays 1938–73*, Australian National University Press, Canberra.

——, 1965. 'Aboriginal territorial organization: estate, range, domain and regime', *Oceania* 36(1):1–26.

Strehlow, T., 1970. 'Geography and the totemic landscape in central Australia: a functional study', in R. Berndt (ed.), *Australian Aboriginal Anthropology*, University of Western Australia Press, Nedlands:92–140.

——, 1978 [1964]. *Central Australian Religion: personal monototemism in a polytotemic community*, Special Studies in Religions, V. 2, Australian Association for the Study of Religions, Bedford Park, SA.

The Wik Peoples v the State of Queensland & Ors.

Warner, L., 1969 [1937]. *A Black Civilisation: a social study of an Australian tribe*, Peter Smith, Gloucester, Mass.

White, Hayden, 1978. *Tropics of Discourse: essays in cultural criticism*, Johns Hopkins University Press, Baltimore.

Williams, N. and E. Hunn, 1982 *Resource Managers: North American and Australian hunter-gatherers*, Australian Institute of Aboriginal Studies, Canberra.

Worsley, P., 1967. 'Groote Eylandt totemism and *Le Totemisme Aujourdhui*, in E. Leach (ed.), *The Structural Study of Myth and Totemism*, Tavistock, London:141–60.

Young, R., 1990. *White Mythologies: writing history and the West*, Routledge, London.

10

Cooperative approaches to marine resource management in the South Pacific

Colin Hunt

New cooperative approaches to the management of marine resources are imperative in the delivery of sustainable incomes and livelihoods in the South Pacific. While recent international agreements have strengthened the sovereignty of states over their adjacent ocean resources, the actual development and implementation of management regimes for tuna, arguably the region's most important renewable resource in terms of income-generating potential, will require a much more concerted approach by Pacific island states. This will need to be matched by a willingness on the part of the non-coastal states that traditionally harvest the bulk of the region's oceanic resources to cooperate in tuna management. The alternative is the eventual depletion of the great tuna stocks.

In the case of inshore resources, there is a new assertiveness being demonstrated by local communities toward customary tenures. In some instances, local tenures are being reinforced by regional and national governments. Such cohesion between governments and communities, in the face of increasing resource exploitation, is enhancing the prospects for sustaining the livelihoods of coastal communities.

In this chapter, common property issues concerning South Pacific marine resources will be divided by location—offshore and inshore—and their use will be categorised as either commercial/industrial or subsistence.

Commercial and subsistence uses

The value of commercial fishing in the South Pacific is in the order of US$2 billion annually, with tuna alone having a total market value of some US$1.5 billion. About half the world's canning tuna comes from this region.

One way of measuring the importance of fishing sectors to Pacific island economies is to express fishing revenue as a proportion of total government revenue. In the case of Kiribati and Tuvalu, the proportion is between 30 and 50 per cent. It is also high in the Federated States of Micronesia and Marshall Islands. This is expected because these countries receive significant licence fees from foreign vessels. Kiribati and Tuvalu also receive significant repatriated revenues from their citizens that crew foreign vessels.

If we measure fishing by share of GDP, we find that it is 9–10 per cent in Solomon Islands, Kiribati and Tuvalu but only 1.5 per cent in Fiji. The latter economy is diversified and fishing is just one of several important sectors. The developed industrial fisheries and export canneries of both Solomon Islands and Fiji mean that formal employment is significant in their fisheries sectors.

The inshore waters of the Pacific islands are relatively abundant. This fact, and the ease of access for vessels, means that coastal waters are the locus of fishing and gathering activity that provides a large proportion of dietary protein. However, most inshore species are vulnerable to overfishing.

The majority of the population in most of these countries are still in a subsistence economy. Despite the increase in fishing for cash, a large proportion of the catch is still consumed by the fishers, or shared, and does not enter markets. Subsistence fishing's importance or dominance means that the true importance to the island states of their marine resources is not reflected in budget estimates or national accounts.

Commercial fishing in inshore waters includes prawns (in Papua New Guinea), reef and deep slope fish, as well as *bêche-de-mer* and molluscs such as trochus and greensnail. There is also a substantial bait fishery in Solomon Islands coastal waters supplying the pole-and-line tuna fleet of canner Solomon Taiyo.

Figure 10.1, by showing estimates of the value of fish taken in the coastal waters of selected Pacific island countries, provides a more comprehensive appreciation than national accounts of the importance of commercial *vis-à-vis* subsistence fishing and also of the relative size of the coastal fisheries by country. It is clear that the value of subsistence fishing is significant in most countries and that in several countries it has a value of many millions of dollars.

Figure 10.1: Coastal fisheries value (mean of 1989–1994)

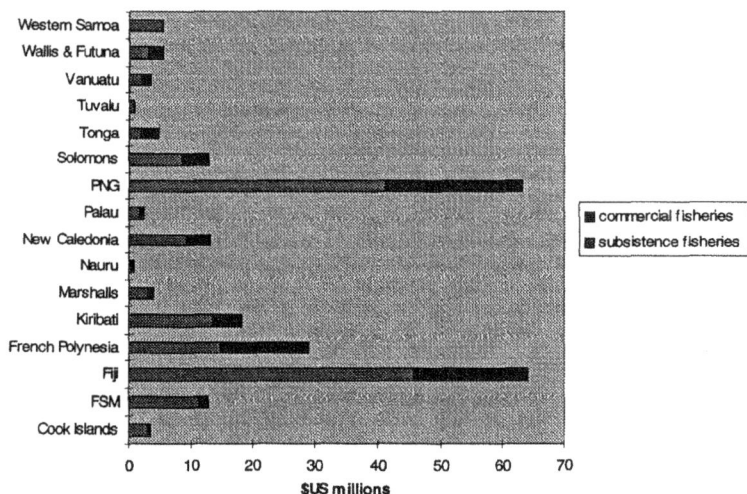

Note: 1. While the source of data for this figure does not provide a definition of 'coastal waters' the term is assumed to be synonymous with territorial seas, ie; within 12 nautical miles of the coast.
2. Details of the method of imputation of the value of subsistence fishing are not given by the source therefore the actual and relative values of subsistence fishing shown in Figure 2 should be used only as guides.
Source: Dalzell, P., Adams, T., and Polunin, N., 1995. 'Coastal fisheries in the South Pacific', paper to the joint FFA/SPC workshop, Management of South Pacific Inshore Fisheries, 26 June–7 July, 1995, South Pacific Commission, Noumea, unpublished:149.

UNCLOS and its provisions

Tenure over, or access rights to, marine resources is crucial to their management. However, 'open access' has characterised the exploitation of all ocean resources outside the 3 nautical mile (nm) territorial limits. Article 2 of the 1958 Geneva Convention on the high seas said that freedom of fishing was one of the established freedoms of the high seas. The implication was that coastal states could not exclusively appropriate or manage marine resources adjacent but outside their territorial waters.

Under open access, marine resource users are unrestrained and competitive, maximising their present harvests to the detriment of the resource, the ecosystem, themselves, society, and future generations. The potential to control open-access fishing was radically enhanced by the UN's adoption of the UN Convention on the Law of the Sea (UNCLOS) on 30 April 1982 (UN 1982). From its adoption to its ratification, in late 1994, the major provisions of the convention have in fact been in force, being interpreted as representing 'customary ocean law'.

The UNCLOS agreement expanded territorial seas to 12 nm and created 200 nm zones (exclusive economic zones, EEZs) around coastal states. The 'sovereign rights' of the coastal state apply to the exploitation and conservation of living and non-living natural resources (UN 1982, Article 55). The extended rights and jurisdictions of several South Pacific coastal states were enhanced by the application of EEZs to islands no matter what their distance from the coast. With the rights go responsibilities, however. Coastal states are required to determine total allowable catches in their exclusive economic zones. They must also implement management measures in cooperation with relevant regional organisations. For their part, fishing states must contribute fishing statistics (UN 1982, Article 61).

All island states have declared extended maritime zones. Table 10.1 sets out the area of EEZs for South Pacific states. It shows the great variation in size of EEZs and in industrial tuna catch. The reluctance of several island states to ratify UNCLOS and to sign the agreement for the implementation of UNCLOS relating to conservation and management of straddling and highly migratory fish stocks, is probably related to the costs of implementation of the laws and agreements.

In the light of total allowable catches and management plans, coastal states that do not have the capacity to harvest the entire total allowable catch shall give other states access to the surplus in their EEZs. In providing access to other states, a coastal state shall consider the significance of the resource to its economy on the one hand, and the needs of nations that have habitually fished in the EEZ on the other. The nationals of other nations must however comply with the conservation measures and other terms and conditions of access (such as licensing and licence fees, provision of catch and effort statistics, port landings and enforcement) established in the laws of the coastal states (UN 1982, Article 62). The access rights of geographically disadvantaged states—coastal states whose position makes them dependent for supplies of fish from resources of the EEZs of other states—are catered for in Article 70.

Table 10.1 Marine sector profiles, South Pacific

States	EEZ or EFZ* area '000 kmsq	Tuna harvest (industrial) 1992, tonnes	Ratified(r) UNCLOS	Signed(s)/ ratified(r) USS & HMS Agreement[b]
Cook Islands	1830	10	r	
FSM	2978	149416		
Fiji	1290	447	r	
Kiribati	3550	113951	r	
Marshall Islands	2131	24959	r	s
Nauru	320	21200	r	
Niue	390	n.a.[c]		s
Palau	629	5317		
PNG	3120	93374		s
Solomon Islands	1340	40689		
Tonga	700	181	r	s, r
Tuvalu	900	5495		
Vanuatu	680	329		
Western Samoa	120	27	r	s
Other		24213		
sub-total	19978	479608		
Dependent Territories				
American Samoa	390	..		US s, r
French Polynesia	5030	..	Fr r	
Guam (US)	218	..		
New Caledonia (Fr)	1740	..		
N. Marianas (US)	1823	..		
Pitcairn Island (UK)	800	..		UK s
Tokelau (NZ)	290	..	NZ r	NZ s
Wallis & Futuna (Fr)	300	..		
sub-total	10569	..		
Total	30569	..		

Notes: ª EFZs, Extended Fishing Zones, are precursors of the EEZs and also have a breadth of 200 nm. ᵇAgreement for the implementation of UNCLOS relating to conservation and management of straddling and highly migratory fish stocks.
Sources: Ron Duncan and Ila Temu, 'Trade, investment and sustainable development of natural resources in the Pacific: the case of fish and timber', paper presented to the Economic and Social Commission for Asia and the Pacific Expert Group Meeting on Enhancing Cooperation in Trade and Investment Between Pacific island Countries and Economies of East and South East Asia in the 1990s, Port Vila, Vanuatu, July, 8–12, 1996, unpublished; United Nations Internet site, http://www.un.org/Depts/los/losg4st.htm; Tsamenyi, B., and Mfodwo, K., 1995. 'South Pacific island states and the new regime of fisheries: issues of law, economy and diplomacy', in J. Crawford and D. Rothwell (eds), *The Law of the Sea in the Asian Pacific region*, Martinus Nijhoff, Dordrecht:121–53, Table 1.

Where the same fish stocks are found in more than one coastal state, the states must cooperate for the conservation and development of the stocks, directly or through regional organisations (UN 1982, Article 63). Where highly migratory species are present, their conservation and optimum utilisation is to be achieved by cooperation between the coastal state, fishing states and appropriate organisations (Article 64). And even in the case of the high seas—areas outside EEZs—states are bound to conserve stocks through cooperation and establishment regional organisations (Article 117).

UNCLOS has formally endowed Pacific island states with extensive marine resources and has formulated internationally recognised frameworks to manage them.

The agreement (UN 1995) governing straddling and highly migratory fish stocks, commonly known as the 'Implementing Agreement', reinforces the Law of the Sea provisions. It has important implications for the Pacific because tuna stocks straddle and migrate through EEZs and the high seas. The agreement charges coastal states and fishing states to agree upon measures for the conservation of stocks and, with respect to migratory species, their optimum utilisation (Article 7). The agreement was signed by 44 countries and at 16 September 1996, it had been ratified by three nations of the thirty required to bring it into force (Table 10.1).

The implications for the regional organisations, the Forum Fisheries Agency (FFA) and the South Pacific Commission (SPC), are that the vehicle for conservation measures is envisaged by the agreement to be regional or sub-regional management organisations. The fishing states are expected either to become a member of the regional organisations or to agree to apply management measures established by such organisations. Moreover, coastal and fishing states should participate in the work of such organisations (Article 8).

The implications for the collection and analysis of data are important given that states are charged with the provision of comprehensive catch and effort data to regional authorities covering both target and non-target species for EEZs and high seas areas (Articles 3 and 5).

Even though some are published by SPC (1994a), data from foreign tuna longline vessels (which account for over half of the total value of the South Pacific tuna fishery) is presently deficient for purposes of management of the stocks of yellowfin, bigeye, albacore and of associated by-catch species. The status of bigeye, albacore and by-catch species is particularly uncertain under heavy fishing pressure (SPC 1994b, SPC 1996). Data is also deficient for EEZs and for the adjacent high seas areas. The latter yield approximately half of the longline catch, but only the Japanese fleet presently provides the SPC with statistics on its high seas catch and this is in aggregated rather than logbook form (personal communication, Dr Antony Lewis, Oceanic Fisheries Coordinator, SPC). The intergovernmental management of tuna is analysed in more detail in Oh's chapter.

Environmental issues

The ratification of UNCLOS also requires countries to adopt, implement, and enforce the rules and standards applying under global treaties governing the marine environment. An example is the International Convention on the Prevention of Pollution from Ships (MARPOL), in place since 1983 and supported by the London Dumping Convention, governing the disposal of ship waste (dumped plastics are particularly dangerous to many marine animals). However, the provisions of this treaty will be effective only if coastal states install shore-based facilities to deal with ship waste. In their absence, ships will pollute the oceans by discharging or incinerating waste at sea.

Land-based pollution is, however, by far the most deleterious to the marine environment, with productive inshore waters bearing the brunt. And, while UNCLOS (Article 207) specifies that such pollution should be prevented or controlled, its provisions are unlikely to be effective for two reasons: the thinness of the recommendations, and the cost and difficulty of pollution control.

Although few countries in the South Pacific are industrialised and populations and densities are relatively low, pollution is serious in some coastal locations, lowering the productivity of resources and causing health problems (Hunt 1996). A regional cooperative approach to deal with coastal pollution is being undertaken by the South Pacific Regional Environment Programme. Problems have been identified through 'state of the environment' reporting and are being addressed through the National Environmental Management Strategies.

But progress in pollution prevention and control in the South Pacific will depend on the application of resources and political will.

> The worst violators are government agencies who, on the one hand, promote government protection but not at the cost of the developing project, such as mining and tourism development (UN, undated, cited by Boer 1995:91).

Inshore management

In the case of the inshore waters of Oceania, the most widespread and important measure for the conservation of marine resources has been controlled access through customary marine tenure arrangements. The rights to fish are controlled by a clan, chief or family. Traditonally, there was no 'ownership' by one group of all rights, but rather a system of allocation of access and use rights. In customary marine tenure, social boundaries are as important as physical boundaries but harder for outsiders to define (Crocombe 1994).

Seasonal closure is one of the measures adopted under customary marine tenure to conserve stocks. The conservation of stocks through such restraints yielded substantial benefits to the right holders (Johannes 1978). However, while acknowledging the management implications of restricting access, Hyndman (1993) argues that tenure systems were probably not developed with conservation *per se* in mind. The purposes were rather to embed aquatic resources in the gift economy and the kinship modes of production, or as Carrier (1987:164, cited by Hyndman 1993) succinctly put it '[customary marine tenure] made it possible to be generous'.

Thus, while customary laws are the basis for decision-making concerning access and the sanctions that might apply in the case of breaches, such laws are flexible in that there are constant negotiations at the community level regarding access and use. And the principles underlying customary marine tenure are subject to continuous interpretation, transformation, and redefinition (Scheffler and Larmour 1987). Indeed, the customary marine tenure of today has very little in common with that of 200 years ago (Crocombe 1994).

Change and erosion of traditional customary marine tenure has occurred largely because of coastal population decreases in the early stages of colonisation, and subsequent population increases (about 3.5 million people now live on the coast in the South Pacific), adoption of technology (fishing power and mobility), the intrusion of the cash economy and a breakdown of chiefly authority (Johannes 1978; Crocombe 1994).

Scientific methods of fisheries management require a knowledge of the biology of target species and the availability of catch and effort data. But, except in a few cases, the data required for scientific fisheries management for inshore waters in the Pacific is not available. Much time-consuming and expensive research is required before

Western-style management can be effected widely, indeed, 'from a management perspective it is unlikely that the Pacific island reef fisheries recruitment processes will ever be sufficiently understood to be incorporated into management initiatives' (Dalzell et al. 1995:80). The task is exacerbated by the archipelagic nature of many Pacific island countries. Moreover, centrally imposed scientific management for inshore fisheries increases the monitoring and regulatory responsibilities of governments. But the fisheries departments in Pacific island countries are typically understaffed and underfunded.

Given the pressing need to manage inshore fisheries and the scarcity of resources, alternative management models have been proposed (Dalzell et al. 1995; Johannes 1994a; 1994b; Petelo et al. 1995). These alternative models strengthen rather than weaken customary marine tenure. Legislative support for local tenure arrangements allows the reintroduction of effective traditional methods, such as temporary closures.

In the alternative models, local knowledge substitutes for, or complements, scientific data, while local planning substitutes for, or complements, fisheries department planning.

The need for inshore management plans is most pressing in some of the smaller islands and atolls where greatly increased fishing effort on fish stocks is jeopardising the supply of essential protein to rapidly growing populations (Dalzell et al. 1995). The harvesting of commercial invertebrates such as trochus and *bêche-de-mer* (which in many cases have been severely depleted) can also come under local management arrangements.

The importance of institutional arrangements

We saw how UNCLOS is fundamental to the management of industrial fisheries in that it has enabled the coastal states to exclude or license foreign fishing and thus control fishing efforts in their EEZs. However, the main species of tuna are common to the South Pacific and are migratory. Therefore, the size of local catches of tuna are determined to some extent by the fishing of the same species in other EEZs. The commonality and the mobility of stocks dictate the need for a regional approach to tuna management.

Fortunately, regional institutions are already in place to give effect to regional planning. The FFA in Honiara acts on behalf of members in generating fishing policy options and providing a regional forum for their discussion, while the SPC in Noumea collects, analyses, and disseminates catch and effort data (for tuna and other species) to its members. These institutions will have an indispensable role to play in maximising the benefits to Pacific island countries of their marine resources and in the development and implementation of regional resource management plans.

It needs to be emphasised, however, that presently there is no regulation of the level of tuna catch by species. The participants in the industrial fisheries have every incentive to maximise their harvests. A regional plan would need to apply not just to EEZs but to high seas where the common regional stocks are found and where fishing effort by industrial distant water fleets is considerable.

At the local (inshore) level, just as in the case of EEZs, tenure and access rights to marine resources should be clearly defined, otherwise there is a tendency for open access to prevail (Hunt 1996). The tenured group can then make access arrangements and exclude unwanted effort

A powerful incentive for local groups to restore and enhance customary marine tenure is the acknowledgment of their jurisdiction by local and central government, and the endorsement of their plans. In some cases the acknowledgment of tenure and plans means that the local group has recourse to the law of the country in upholding local access rules.

International cooperation

While there are significant industrial fishing operations based in Fiji, American Samoa and Solomon Islands, the migratory tuna stocks are mainly exploited by distant water nations supplying markets in the United States and Asia. Through the licensing vessels under these flags Pacific island countries receive about US$70 million from a fishery worth some US$1.5 billion. The dominant fleets are those of the United States, Japan, Taiwan, and the Republic of Korea.

The Pacific island countries have jurisdiction over their EEZs and their collective jurisdiction covers much of the tuna fishing grounds of the central, western and south Pacific, while the FFA and the SPC allow the exercise of collective power. Despite this, there is only one multilateral fishing agreement in place—the one between several Pacific island countries and the US tuna fleet.[2] All other foreign fleet access is through bilateral negotiation between individual island states and the representatives of the various national fleets.

While the FFA has developed harmonised terms and conditions of fishing and effected economies of scale in regional monitoring and surveillance, there is still variation in the level of licence fees as a proportion of value of catch (Maxwell and Owen 1994). The Pacific island countries put themselves in weak negotiating positions in that the distant water nations can threaten to walk away and take their fishing fees elsewhere. They are also particularly vulnerable to persuasion that access fees to tuna should be concessional because of the level of aid being supplied. Japan has consistently rejected multilateral frameworks on this latter ground (Doulman 1989; Tsamenyi and Mfodwo 1995).

A major constraint on the development of a united approach to negotiations with the distant water fleets is the unwillingness of some island states that depend heavily on fishing fees, for example Kiribati and the Federated States of Micronesia (FSM), to adopt the cooperative model. Both have been vocal in their opposition to multilateral agreements (*Pacific Report* 1995, 1996; *Islands Business Pacific* 1994) although they have not ruled out united sub-regional approaches to negotiations by the tuna-rich countries under the Palau Agreement.[3]

The limitation of sub-regional approaches are illustrated by the recent rejection by Taiwan of specific attempts by Pacific island countries to negotiate a sub-regional agreement.[4] If all FFA countries —including FSM and Papua New Guinea, which host considerable Taiwanese fishing efforts (SPC 1994a)—have given weight to the negotiations, there would have been a far greater probability of the conclusion of a beneficial sub-regional longline agreement.

The FSM fears that it could be worse off under multilateral agreements and sees present bilateral arrangements as providing more opportunities for domestic fisheries development. It will confine regional approaches to the setting of umbrella terms and conditions under which bilateral deals are made.

In the face of the difficulty in negotiating increased access fees with distant water nations, the policy adopted by Pacific island countries to achieve greater economic benefits from their tuna stocks is one of trying to develop local fishing operations. The development of domestic tuna industries is taking two forms. First, by the encouragement of local short-trip longlining operations that supply sashimi export markets (short-trip longlining has the potential to confer substantial benefits on Pacific island countries (ESCAP forthcoming; South Pacific Project Facility 1995)). Second, through regional arrangements that encourage purse-seine vessels to base locally, instead of at foreign ports.[5]

The economic benefits of the second thrust of localising purse-seine vessels has not been demonstrated. A preliminary analysis suggests that the fishing rents or profits of distant water vessels would be curtailed by localisation as would their consequent ability to pay fishing royalties.

Local cooperation

As mentioned above, there are several factors which are tending to break down the customary marine tenure that previously enabled the conservation of inshore (as opposed to offshore) marine resources. The introduction of cash benefits in exchange for access by industrial or commercial fisheries is one of these factors: this is evident in Papua New Guinea, Solomon Islands, Marshall Islands and Fiji. Narrow groups or spokespersons, not fully representative of the traditional descent groups, have been able to appropriate rents for their own use (Crocombe 1994, Turner 1994, Hviding 1996).

While acknowledging that customary marine tenure may present impediments to governments undertaking industrial fisheries development, I would argue that strengthening customary marine tenure, rather than weakening it, should often be the preferred policy. The reasons are threefold.

First, in many countries, subsistence fishing dominates and the local communities that are dependent on the resources for their livelihoods should be in a position to manage those resources. Second, the development and resilience of management and conservation plans for commercial resources by governments in cooperation with communities is facilitated by clear access rights. Third, where commercial exploitation of local resources is a possibility, for example in the cases of trochus or *bêche-de-mer*, strengthened customary marine tenure puts the local communities in a more advantageous position in negotiating with traders. In some Pacific island countries, customary marine tenure is already reinforced by central governments. For example, local rights are recognised by the Fiji Fisheries Commission (Cook 1994), and in Solomon Islands (over both land and fisheries) through the *Provincial Government Act* of 1971 (Crocombe 1994, Pulea 1993).

Central governments have been prone to ignore the difficult process of clarifying customary marine tenure and carrying out development or conservation through 'top down' approaches. However, the resilience of any development or conservation arrangements is heavily dependent, in the Pacific, on local people being involved in decision processes and receiving rents from any arrangement.[6]

Cooperative models

The arrangements for intergovernmental cooperation in tuna management are analysed in the following chapter by Oh. Here I simply summmarise the advantages of cooperation. Intergovernmental cooperation

- should generate **higher royalties** by increasing Pacific island countries' negotiating power, and breaking the nexus between fishing access fees and development aid
- facilitates the introduction of **control of fishing effort** on regional tuna stocks by
     input controls (gear and/or vessels numbers), or
     output controls (quotas)
- reduces **transaction costs** to both sides
- makes the content of agreements **transparent**, compared with bilateral arrangements
- facilitates co-management arrangements with **other coastal states** (outside existing forums) in the region that exploit the common tuna stocks
- facilitates co-management arrangements with **distant water fleets** in the region that exploit the common tuna stocks.

For inshore areas, however, the thrust should not be so much in the documentation of customary marine tenure but in its definition and strengthening so that it can be effective in developing local arrangements, and can integrate more effectively with planning and policy, for marine resource management and conservation, of central governments (Hyndman 1993).

A cooperative approach between communities, acting in their local interests, and governments, acting in the national or public interest, has much to offer. Strengthened customary and local resource management arrangements, albeit based of necessity on customary practices rather than scientific fisheries management principles, can assist the central government in its overall policy of conservation of marine resources (as set out, for example, in National Environmental Management Strategies).

An example of where the strengthening of customary marine tenure has assisted the declaration of a protected area is provided by the work of Tacconi under an Australian Council for International Agricultural Research project in Vanuatu.

A very significant step in biodiversity conservation in Vanuatu is the development of provincial legislation, under the national constitution, enabling local groups to strengthen their property rights and hence their ability to protect and to manage their natural resources. This step was the direct result of Tacconi's negotiations with the Attorney General's department and using a draft by-law (obtained from Santa Ysabel province, Solomon Islands) as a model.[8] Such legislation has been adopted in principle by the local government councils of Santo and Malekula, and has been enacted in Efate (Bennett 1996).

In 1994 the local government region of MALAPA, which includes Malekula, was empowered to create protected areas by the passage through the Vanuatu Parliament of the Bill for Decentralisation and Local Government Regions, Act No. 1, of 1994. MALAPA was now able to introduce by-laws that 'outline create and draw up regulations governing the environmental protection zones (natural parks, natural reserves or tourist-attraction areas in the national interest' (Act 1, Section 20[9]).

Tacconi subsequently assisted MALAPA in drawing up a by-law that facilitates planning by local *ni-Vanuatu* (Tacconi 1995a). Features of the by-laws are as follows.

- Areas are protected on the basis of **custom, amenity,** and **livelihood** provision.
- The regional council by-laws (under national legislation) strengthen **customary tenure** by making it an offence to contravene the rules governing a protected area.
- The term of the by-law is specified by the landowners.
- Amendments may be made by landowners to a by-law at any time.
- For every declared protected area a committee of management is set up, representative of both landowner interests and community interests (through chiefly representation).

An important feature of the by-law legislation is that it is distinct from, but complements, the *Vanuatu National Parks Act,* No. 7 of 1993. This latter act is designed to protect unique ecosystems, habitats of threatened species or areas possessing outstanding features. The by-law, in contrast, allows the protection of natural areas that are significant in the support and maintenance of livelihoods (Tacconi 1995a).

An important characteristic of the protected areas that have arisen under by-laws is that they often incorporate several different eco-systems. At the same time they may stipulate degrees of conservation, given that livelihoods must still be derived from the protected areas. For example, in the case of the declared protected area of the Wiawi coastal community on Malekula, the forest is protected but the forest zone also includes plantations and gardens, while protection straddles the coastal zone, conserving turtle as well as reef zone resources (Tacconi 1995b).The eight kilometres of protected coast is currently subject to bans on the collections of trochus and green snail and to closure to fishing on six days a week.

Other conservation arrangements that depend on local jurisdictions exercising their customary rights include that of a Cook Island Council enforcing limited trochus harvesting. The arrangement features individual transferable quotas and inspections upon landing (World Bank 1995). In Solomon Islands, the maintenance of the Arnavon Marine Conservation Area depends on the cooperation, and coordination through the provision of rangers, of three village councils on Choisel and Ysabel, with the support of governments and non-government organisations, to enforce bans on the harvesting of turtle eggs.

Such inshore conservation regimes are most applicable in rural rather than peri-urban areas, where traditional authority is still strong. And the communities must be able to substitute alternative sources of subsistence and cash income during closures (World Bank 1995).

Notes

The author has benefited from the comments of Transform Aqorau but any omissions or errors are the author's sole responsibility.

1. This paper deals generally with the countries served by the SPC and in the case of industrial fishing by the FFA.
   The island member countries of the FFA are: Cook Islands, Federated States of Micronesia, Fiji, Kiribati, Marshall Islands,

Nauru, Niue, Palau, Papua New Guinea, Samoa, Solomon Islands, Tonga, Tuvalu and Vanuatu.

The 22 island members served by the SPC are: American Samoa, Cook Islands, Federated States of Micronesia, Fiji, French Polynesia, Guam, Kiribati, Marshall Islands, Nauru, Niue, New Caledonia, Northern Mariana Islands, Palau, Papua New Guinea, Pitcairn Islands, Samoa, Solomon Islands, Tokelau, Tonga, Tuvalu, Vanuatu, and Wallis and Futuna.

2. The US fee is set at US$18 million for 10 years under the 1993 regional agreement. The US Tuna Boat Association receives a subsidy from the US government of US$14 million and itself contributes US$4 million. The fee of US$18 million implies a rate of payment of 9 to 14 per cent of the value of tuna caught—this is a subsidised rate. Under the multilateral treaty with the United States, US$1.8 million is paid annually into a project development fund administered by the FFA, 15 per cent of the balance is shared equally among the parties, and the remainder is divided between the parties according to the weight of catch taken from their EEZs (FFA 1996).

3. Federated States of Micronesia, Kiribati, Marshall Islands, Nauru, Palau, Papua New Guinea, Solomon Islands and Tuvalu.

4. In 1995 an attempt was made by a group of Pacific countries, Cook Islands, Fiji, Niue, Solomon Islands, Tokelau, Tonga, Vanuatu and Western Samoa, to negotiate a sub-regional agreement with representatives of the Taiwanese fishing interests that operate freezer longline vessels in the Pacific (FFA 1995). The group expressed dissatisfaction with the poor level of compliance in catch reporting and transhipment displayed by Taiwan vessel operators in the region. The resulting suspension of bilateral arrangements by some Pacific island countries in the group had caused part of the Taiwanese fleet to relocate to the eastern Pacific and the Indian Ocean. A sub-regional annual access fee of US$870,000 for 75 vessels, and US$650,000 for 50 or less, was proposed. However, the Taiwanese rejected the proposal out of hand on the grounds that the fee was too high when considered along with the impositions of prohibition of transhipment at sea (which was objected to) and compliance with observer programs and reporting.

5. This latter encouragement is through a cooperative arrangement by Pacific island countries party to the Nauru Agreement and the Palau Arrangement, and takes the form of licensing priorities and concessional access to purse-seine vessels prepared to invest, provision, and employ locally. An additional incentive to achieve the latter is a phased reduction in the number of licences available to foreign vessels while the number of licences available for localised vessels is increased.

6. In the PNG bait fishery the allocation of part of the rents to a trust fund and to the provincial government, rather than to local groups, became a bone of contention (Turner 1994).
7. For every 1 per cent increase in collective access fee, an extra US$15 million would flow to Pacific island countries (given the value of catch by distant water fleets was approximately US$1.5 billion in 1995). If royalties could be increased to a level equivalent to 10 per cent of the value of catch, income to Pacific island countries would double, to some US$150 million.
8. Awareness of the potential for local management of marine resources had already been raised by an education program conducted by the Vanuatu Fisheries Department and the Environment Unit.
9. Personal communication, Chief Timothy Nehapi, Wiawi Community, Malekula, Vanuatu, 20 June 1996.

References

Bennett, J., 1996. Highlights for 1995–96—an update of the 1994–95 Annual Report, Australian Council for International Agricultural Research (ACIAR) Project 9020, ACIAR, Canberra.

Boer, B., 1995. 'Environmental law and the South Pacific: law of the sea issues', in J. Crawford and D. Rothwell (eds), *The Law of the Sea in the Asian Pacific region*, Martinus Nijhoff, Dordrecht: 67–92.

Carrier, J., 1987. 'Marine tenure and conservation in PNG', in B. McCay and J. Acheson (eds), *The question of the commons: the culture and ecology of communal resources*, University of Arizona Press, Tucson:142–67.

Cook, A., 1994. The quoliquoli of Fiji, MSc dissertation, University of Newcastle-Upon-Tyne.

Crawford, J., and D. Rothwell (eds), 1995. *The Law of the Sea in the Asian Pacific region*, Martinus Nijhoff, Dordrecht.

Crocombe, R., (ed.), 1987. *Land Tenure in the Pacific*, University of the South Pacific, Suva.

——, 1994. 'Overview', in R. South, D. Goulet, S. Tuquiri and M. Church (eds), *Proceedings of the international Workshop on Traditional Marine Tenure and Sustainable Management of Marine Resources in Asia and the Pacific*, University of the South Pacific, Suva:291–300.

Dalzell, P., Adams, T., and Polunin, N., 1995. 'Coastal fisheries in the South Pacific', paper to the joint FFA/SPC workshop, Management of South Pacific Inshore Fisheries, 26 June–7 July, 1995, South Pacific Commission, Noumea, unpublished.

Doulman, D., 1989. 'Japanese distant-water fishing in the South Pacific', *Pacific Economic Bulletin* 4 (2):22–8.

Ron Duncan and Ila Temu, 1996. Trade, investment and sustainable development of natural resources in the Pacific: the case of fish and timber, paper presented to the Economic and Social Commission for Asia and the Pacific Expert Group Meeting on Enhancing Cooperation in Trade and Investment Between Pacific island Countries and Economies of East and South East Asia in the 1990s, Port Vila, Vanuatu, July 8–12, 1996, unpublished.

ESCAP, forthcoming. Strengthening seafood export capabilities in the South Pacific, Proceedings of a workshop, ESCAP, Bangkok, 27–29 March, 1996.

Forum Fisheries Agency, 1995. Record of discussion, meeting of Pacific island countries and the Taiwan Deep Sea Tuna Boatowners and Exporters Association to discuss a regional licensing agreement for longline vessels, Brisbane 8–19 May, 1995, Forum Fisheries Agency, Honiara.

—— 1996. Treaty on Fisheries with the USA: seventh licensing period, distribution of the 85 per cent shares, Forum Fisheries Agency, Honiara.

Hunt, C., 1996. 'Tackling environmental threats on Pacific atolls', *Pacific Economic Bulletin* 11(2):58–69.

——, 1996. 'Property rights and environmental management on Pacific atolls', *International Journal of Social Economics* 23:221–34.

Hviding, E., 1996. *Guardians of Marovo Lagoon: practice, place, and politics in maritime Melanesia*, University of Hawaii Press, Honolulu.

Hyndman, D., 1993. 'Sea tenure and the management of living marine resources in PNG', *Pacific Studies* 16 (4):99–114.

Islands Business Pacific, 1994. January:46.

Johannes, R., 1978. 'Traditional marine conservation methods in Oceania and their demise', *Annual Review of Ecological Systems* 9: 349–64.

——, 1994a. 'Design of tropical nearshore fisheries extension work beyond the 1990s', in R. South, D. Goulet, S. Tuquiri and M. Church (eds), *Proceeding of the international workshop on traditional marine tenure and sustainable management of marine resources in Asia and the Pacific*, University of the South Pacific, Suva:162–74.

——, 1994b. 'Government supported village-based management of marine resources in Vanuatu', Forum Fisheries Agency Report 94/7, Forum Fisheries Agency, Honiara.

McCay, B., and J. Acheson (eds), 1987. *The question of the commons: the culture and ecology of communal resources*, University of Arizona Press, Tucson.

Maxwell, J., and Owen, A., 1994. *South Pacific Tuna Fisheries Study*, AusAID, Canberra.

Pacific Report, 1995. 8(18):5.

Pacific Report, 1996. 9(18):3.

Petelo, A., Matoto, S., and Gillett, R., 1995. 'The case for community-based fisheries management in Tonga', Paper to the joint FFA/SPC workshop, Management of South Pacific Inshore Fisheries, 26 June–7 July, South Pacific Commission, Noumea.

Pulea, M., 1993. An overview of constitutional and legal provisions relevant to customary marine tenure and management systems in the South Pacific. FFA Report 93/23. Forum Fisheries Agency, Honiara.

Scheffler, H. and Larmour, P., 1987. 'Solomon Islands: evolving a new custom', in R. Crocombe (ed.), *Land Tenure in the Pacific*, University of the South Pacific, Suva:303–23.

South, R., Goulet, D., Tuquiri, S. and Church, M., (eds), 1994. *Proceedings of the international Workshop on Traditional Marine Tenure and Sustainable Management of Marine Resources in Asia and the Pacific*, University of the South Pacific, Suva.

South Pacific Commission, 1994a. *Tuna Fishery Yearbook*, South Pacific Commission, Noumea.

——, 1994b. By-catch and discards in western Pacific tuna fisheries: a review of SPC data holdings and literature, Oceanic Fisheries Programme Internal Report 28, South Pacific Commission, Noumea.

——, 1995. Work programme review 1994–95 and work plan 1995–96, Oceanic Fisheries Programme, South Pacific Commission, Noumea.

——, 1996. Status of tuna stocks in the western and central Pacific Ocean, Paper to the Forum Fisheries Committee, 13–17 May, Vava'u, Kingdom of Tonga.

South Pacific Project Facility, 1996. *Papua New Guinea Fishing Industry Seminar—tuna longlining*, South Pacific Project Facility, Sydney.

Tacconi, L., 1995a. 'Participatory conservation in Malekula Island, Vanuatu, Research Report 10, University of New South Wales University College, Canberra.

——, 1995b. Proposal for the establishment of the Nagha Mo Pineia Protected Area, Research Report 11, University of New South Wales University College, Canberra.

Tsamenyi, B., and Mfodwo, K., 1995. 'South Pacific island states and the new regime of fisheries: issues of law, economy and diplomacy', in J. Crawford and D. Rothwell (eds), *The Law of the Sea in the Asian Pacific region*, Martinus Nijhoff, Dordrecht:121–53.

Turner, J., 1994. 'Sea change: adapting customary marine tenure to commercial fishing: the case of the Papua New Guinea bait fishery', in R. South, D. Goulet, S. Tuquiri and M. Church (eds), *Proceeding of the international workshop on traditional marine tenure and sustainable management of marine resources in Asia and the Pacific*, University of the South Pacific, Suva:141–54.

United Nations, 1982. *The United Nations Convention on the Law of the Sea*, United Nations General Assembly, New York.

——, 1995. *The United Nations Conference on Straddling Fish Stocks and Highly Migratory Fish Stocks*, United Nations General Assembly, New York.

——, no date. 'Protection of the oceans and all kinds of seas, including semi-enclosed seas and coastal areas and the protection and rational use and development of their living resources', paper jointly prepared by the UN Office for Ocean Affairs and the Law of the Sea, United Nations, New York.

Vanuatu Government, 1993. *Vanuatu National Parks Act, No, 7, of 1993*, Port Vila.

World Bank, 1995. *Pacific Island Economies: building a resilient economic base for the twenty first century*, World Bank, Washington DC.

11

Common property management of highly migratory fish stocks: tuna in the Pacific

Janaline Oh

The purpose of this chapter is to consider possibilities for sustainable management of highly migratory tuna fisheries in the Central and Western Pacific—specifically the area covered by the 200 nautical mile exclusive economic zones (EEZs) of South Pacific Forum member countries and contiguous high seas areas. The chapter adopts a definition of common property as property that is controlled collectively by a defined group of decision-making units, rather than as no property or open access. Sustainability is defined as management that will enable long-term harvesting of the fisheries resources at their maximum sustainable yield. This chapter does not attempt to consider issues of biological diversity nor of the social aspects of sustainable development.

Changes in international law over the past decade have affected the international legal and political environment for fisheries management. I do not enter into the debate over the role of fisheries in economic development for Pacific island countries, other than to acknowledge that the development aspirations of those island countries have a strong bearing on the way in which they are likely to approach fisheries management and access issues. The interactions discussed in the chapter refer to government to government negotiations on international fisheries issues. Although inshore communities are important in decisions relating to fisheries management, for the deep sea tuna fisheries considered in this chapter, it is governments (represented by their officials) who undertake negotiations and reach agreements which must then be implemented domestically. Finally, the chapter concludes that a common property approach is the only feasible way of developing a conservation and management regime for highly migratory fish stocks in the Pacific, and that such an approach entails an essentially political process.

The nature of the fishery: framing the problem

The tuna resources of the Central and Western Pacific, which covers the zones of the independent Pacific island countries, represent one of the few remaining internationally significant tuna fisheries. The principal tuna species are skipjack (*Katsuwonus pelamis*), yellowfin (*Thunnus albacares*), bigeye (*Thunnus obesus*) and albacore (*Thunnus alalunga*). The region supplies over 50 per cent of the world's canning tuna (Maxwell and Owen 1994). These fisheries also provide a significant foreign exchange and government revenue earner for Pacific island countries, particularly the Micronesian countries which have few other resources available for development. The economic benefits to island countries come mainly in the form of licence fees for access from distant water fishing nations under bilateral or multilateral agreements. Some benefits are generated through domestic fisheries and onshore processing and associated activities, or through employment of Pacific island nationals on deep sea tuna boats. Atoll countries, in particular Kiribati, Federated States of Micronesia and Marshall Islands, aspire to develop their domestic fisheries to increase the economic benefits, including in terms of employment, and to reduce reliance on licence fees from distant water fleets. This affects their approach to access to fisheries within their fishing zones, and to regional fisheries management.

The tuna stocks of the South Pacific region are in good health, with scientific assessments indicating that harvesting remains within sustainable levels, although some uncertainty exists for bigeye tuna stocks. This contrasts with a number of significant collapses of fish stocks in other regions of the world, for instance the Grand Banks cod off the coast of Canada. The reasons stem from the low rates of harvesting of tuna in the region, well within the sustainable harvesting range, the rapid growth and strong recruitment for the tropical tuna species (compared with temperate tuna such as southern bluefin tuna—*Thunnus maccoyii*), and the region's relative isolation from major markets, which reduces the rate of return from fishing operations.

The Central and Western Pacific tuna fisheries present an opportunity for coastal states in the region to demonstrate that sustainable management of highly migratory fish stocks is possible. An important factor in the outcome will be the ability of coastal states to cooperate with distant water fishing nations within a management regime.

Property rights: some definitions

Before going further, it would be useful to state some definitions underlying the arguments of this chapter. First, this chapter adopts the view that property rights do not exist objectively, but rely upon a prior social contract whereby others recognise one's right to that property (Bromley 1991:6). Second, it takes Bromley's definition that a 'right' is 'the capacity to call upon the collective to stand behind one's claim to a benefit stream' (1991:15).

In other words, the property is not the object (in this case, the fish), but rather the benefit stream arising from the resource. This is important in the context of tuna fisheries because the coastal state's right to charge foreign fishing vessels to fish in exclusive economic zones was not recognised by distant water fishing nations until a relatively late stage in the negotiations of the United Nations Convention on the Law of the Sea (UNCLOS). The definition of property as a benefit stream is significant to the distribution of benefits from a fishery that spans the fishing zones of several coastal states, and further includes distant water fishing fleets. This is relevant to the Central and Western Pacific where most fishing operators are from distant water fishing nations rather than coastal states in the region.

Bromley identifies four types of property rights within these broad definitions: individual property rights, where one clearly defined entity (a person or a corporation) holds the right; state property rights, where a government or other administrative authority holds the right on behalf of society; common property rights, where a clearly defined group of decision-makers holds the rights and acts collectively in the exercise of those rights; and open access or no property rights (1991:23). Bromley then notes that different types of property rights also entail responsibilities. This is important for fisheries access under UNCLOS which requires coastal states that cannot exploit their fisheries resources to the full total allowable catch to allow others to fish in their zones (United Nations 1983: Article 62)—although this has not been fully applied in practice. It is also relevant to fisheries management when one looks at those parts of UNCLOS that require fishing states (both coastal states and those fishing on the high seas) to undertake measures for the conservation and management of a resource. The Law of the Sea Convention does not itself define property rights explicitly, but Bromley's definitions describe the assumptions of property rights that underlie those parts of the Convention that relate to fisheries exploitation, conservation, and management.

Commercial fisheries management within individual countries has tended to rely on a mixture of state property rights and individual property rights, where states have powers over licensing or total catch quotas, and individuals can hold fishing rights through tradeable licences or individual transferable quotas. Fisheries management involving more than one country, especially where the fishery also operates on the high seas, has tended to bear more relation to a common property regime, where the governments of the countries involved have acted collectively or through negotiation to manage the resource (Tsamenyi and Kaye 1994 review some of the existing international agreements for cooperative fisheries management). In this case, the individual governments behave in a way analogous to community elders managing a village resource: the collective decision-making body (whose membership is clearly defined) exercises control over the resource with respect to individual units (in this case fishing operators). This has been the case in the Central and Western Pacific.

Access and management[1]

At this point it is worth distinguishing between access to fisheries and management of fisheries. A management regime must include controlling effort within a fishery, which may also involve limiting access. Access relates to who is allowed to participate in the fishery, whereas management seeks to ensure that those who are participating behave in a way that is consistent with the long-term sustainability of the resource. Indeed, when one talks about management of the fish resource, one is really talking about management of those who are exploiting that resource: we are not managing the fish, but rather the fishing operators (Bromley 1991:21).

The principal means of controlling access to stocks used by individual countries, or collectively by groups of countries, has been through licensing in domestic fisheries or negotiating fleet access by foreign operators. Access is generally based on: considerations of sustainability (are there enough fish?); distribution of benefits (capturing the resource rent); and allocation of quotas (where necessary). Under the Convention for the Conservation of Southern Bluefin Tuna, for instance, there is a provision for catch quotas to be allocated between the fleets of the Parties, currently Australia, Japan and New Zealand (DFAT 1993: Article 8[3]).

Within the context of a particular management regime, the use of economic instruments has been adopted in some countries to maximise the economic efficiency of the fishery. In particular, the use of individual transferable quotas within a total allowable catch, has been shown to have met general criteria for economic efficiency (Ministry of Fisheries 1996). Duncan and Temu (1996) have proposed the auctioning of tradeable licences in Pacific island countries. There is still some debate within fisheries management circles as to whether output controls such as catch quotas or input controls such as limits on vessel numbers (for instance through licensing) or gear restrictions are more effective in ensuring fisheries management. Input controls seek to control catch level by placing limits on effort, while output controls place limits on catch. Under both systems, limits on effort that compromise biological imperatives are either prescribed or proscribed.

A key part of this debate is the effectiveness of monitoring and enforcement. While some argue that output controls are a more reliable means of controlling stock levels, they also raise significant potential compliance problems, such as high grading (where lower quality or smaller fish are discarded, but nonetheless killed), which can have detrimental effects on the status of the fish stocks. They also require significant resources for monitoring, control and surveillance. Input controls such as limits on vessel numbers (for example, through licensing) are the alternative means of controlling the exploitation of the resource, and can place overall physical constraints on the harvest—without the incentive to high grade, there is a physical limit to the amount of fish that one vessel can catch within a given amount of time. Input controls are, however, vulnerable to changes in technology. More efficient gear or fishing techniques can extend the physical constraints on a vessel's catch per unit of effort.

Management, however, involves considerably more than control of effort. Regardless of whether one opts for input rather than output controls, there remains a requirement for significantly better regional surveillance and compliance enforcement than is currently available. While Forum member countries are exploring the possibility of applying a regional vessel monitoring system, which will enable both location monitoring and the entry of catch and effort data, there are still significant issues to be negotiated, such as the application of the vessel monitoring system on the high seas.

Other issues important for management include the provision by vessels of verifiable catch and effort data, which is essential for stock assessment and thus for an understanding of whether the stocks are being over-fished; the capacity to enforce management measures; and the role of flag states in controlling the activities of their nationals fishing in other countries' fishing zones or on the high seas. Procedures for the peaceful settlement of disputes are also important both for the confidence of fishing operators that their vessels will not be subject to arbitrary harrassment, and for the assurance of coastal states that they can apply legal measures to protect the resource from illegal behaviour on the part of fishing operators.

The international legal environment

Common property management of fisheries in an international context has been developed and codified in international law through the United Nations Conferences on the Law of the Sea, the third of which culminated in 1982 with the adoption of the Law of the Sea Convention. UNCLOS now provides support under international law for coastal state claims to the benefits from fishing zones beyond their territorial seas, and an agreed legal framework for common property management of international fisheries. The Law of the Sea negotiations, which took well over a decade to complete, covered a range of issues from boundaries to innocent passage, and from fisheries management to sea-bed mining, in recognition of their interdependence (United Nations 1983). The focus on conservation and management of fisheries resources acknowledged that countries could not individually manage fish stocks that either straddled fishing zones or the high seas, nor stocks that migrated beyond individual fishing zones (Doulman 1995). UNCLOS did not come into force until 1994, twelve years after its conclusion and opening for signature. Partly because the Convention was adopted by consensus, however, its provisions were recognised internationally well before it came into force, and it has long been established in customary international law.

Two aspects of the Law of the Sea that are pertinent to this chapter are the definition of an exclusive economic zone (EEZ) not more than 200 nautical miles (nm) from a coastal State's territorial sea baseline (United Nations 1983: Articles 55–9), and provisions for the management of ocean resources for conservation and optimum utilisation, both within EEZs (United Nations 1983: Articles 61–7) and on the high seas (United Nations 1983: Articles 116–20). All South Pacific Forum member countries have now declared either exclusive economic zones or fishing zones at 200 nm from their baselines. The combined fishing zones of Forum countries (including eastern Australia) amounts to around 20 million sq km, or around 80 per cent of the area serviced by the FFA, the rest being high seas (Maxwell and Owen 1994:2). All Forum countries except Kiribati and Palau are signatories to UNCLOS (or have acceded) and most have ratified (United Nations 1996).

UNCLOS has two important consequences for the (mostly) newly independent island countries of the Pacific. Firstly, it confers upon coastal states a property right to fisheries resources within their EEZs. UNCLOS provides only qualified fishing rights both within EEZs and on the high seas. Article 56 defines for coastal states 'sovereign rights' (but **not** 'sovereignty') and jurisdiction with regard to installations, marine scientific research and protection of the marine environment, but it also stipulates that

[i]n exercising its rights and performing its duties under this Convention in the exclusive economic zone, the coastal state shall have due regard to the rights and duties of other states and shall act in a manner compatible with the provisions of this Convention (United Nations 1983: Article 56[2]).

Similarly, all states have a right to fish on the high seas, but only subject to 'the rights and duties as well as the interests of coastal states' (United Nations 1983: Article 116).

Secondly, it confers upon coastal states and fishing states the associated responsibility to manage marine resources for conservation and optimum utilisation. UNCLOS sets out detailed requirements for coastal states to conserve fisheries resources through the determination of allowable catch on the basis of the best available scientific advice (Article 61), to allow others to fish in their EEZs if their nationals lack the capacity to harvest the entire allowable catch (Article 62) and to cooperate with others in managing shared and straddling stocks (Article 63) and highly migratory species (Article 64). States fishing on the high seas are moreover required to take measures to conserve fisheries resources (Articles 117 and 119), and to cooperate in the conservation and management of high seas resources (Article 118).

The provisions of UNCLOS, and particularly Articles 63, 64 and 117–19, are important for the Pacific islands region. All four of the major tuna species harvested in the region are listed in Annex I of UNCLOS as highly migratory species. Under UNCLOS and its associated Implementing Agreement (UN 1995) there is an international legal requirement on Parties to cooperate in the conservation and optimum utilisation of the stocks. The Implementing Agreement, which was opened for signature in December 1995, and has been ratified by the United States, Saint Lucia and Tonga, details the application of those Articles of UNCLOS (63, 64 and 117–19) that relate to management of straddling and highly migratory fish stocks, in particular in relation to the respective responsibilities of coastal States and distant water fishing nations (Doulman 1995). It also requires the application of the precautionary principle, where a conservative approach must be taken in the absence of conclusive scientific evidence (United Nations 1995: Article 6).

Many specific measures for fisheries management have been incorporated into the UN Implementing Agreement, which provides for the establishment of limit and target reference points to be applied to catch quotas, according to the best estimates of maximum sustainable yield (Annex II); provision of catch and effort data and verification of that data (Annex I); elaboration of the responsibilities of flag states to control the operations of their fleets on the high seas (Articles 18 and 19); surveillance and enforcement procedures both within EEZs and on the high seas (Articles 19–23); and procedures for the peaceful settlement of disputes between countries (Articles 27–32).

The Implementing Agreement further provides that, where a regional or sub-regional organisation or arrangement has been established for conservation and management of straddling or highly migratory fish stocks

> [o]nly those states which are members of such an organization or participants in such an arrangement, or which agree to apply the conservation and management measures established by such organization or arrangement, shall have access to the fishery resources to which those measures apply (United Nations 1995: Article 8(4)).

The capacity to exclude from fishing those who refuse to apply measures agreed within a regional conservation and management arrangement is a significant step in minimising the possible third state problems in regional fisheries management identified by Tsamenyi and Kaye (1994). It is also significant in further limiting the traditional Grotian notion of the freedom of the seas: while the Law of the Sea Convention limits this by qualifying the right of states to fish on the high seas (Tsamenyi and Kaye 1994), the UN Implementing Agreement further suggests that states can be excluded from fishing in certain high seas areas if they are unwilling to comply with conservation and management measures that others have agreed to apply in those waters. It also raises questions about the application of the Vienna Convention on the Law of Treaties which provides that states are not bound by obligations they have not signed onto (DFAT 1974: Article 34). It is not clear whether a non-Party to the UN Implementing Agreement can be excluded from high seas fisheries for which a conservation and management arrangement has been agreed.

Existing regional arrangements for management

Concerns about the management of the highly migratory fish stocks in the Pacific are not new to the region. South Pacific Forum members[2] have a long history of cooperation in the management of their fisheries resources, based on common property concepts. The Forum Fisheries Agency (FFA), comprising a Committee and Secretariat, was established in 1979 when its Convention was opened for signature at the 1979 South Pacific Forum (OPA 1995: Vol I, 1979 Forum Communiqué). The Committee was 'to promote intra-regional co-ordination and co-operation' in *inter alia* fisheries management policies, interactions with distant water fishing nations, and surveillance and enforcement (FFA 1979: Article V). Since then, FFA member countries have put in place a number of cooperative arrangements affecting regional fisheries management. The Nauru Agreement Concerning Cooperation in the Management of Fisheries of Common Concern was adopted in 1982, and the Parties to the Nauru Agreement[3] have since formed an influential sub-regional grouping within FFA on fisheries access and management issues.

In 1987, the US government signed a treaty with FFA member countries governing fisheries access for the region. This ended a decade-long dispute between the United States and FFA members over fisheries access, where the United States had refused to recognise fishing zones beyond territorial seas (Bergin 1994). The Treaty provides for significant management controls, including the presence of observers, paid for by vessel operators, catch and effort data provision both within fishing zones and on contiguous high seas, and cooperative enforcement procedures. The Treaty also provides for a flat rate access fee and a limit on vessel numbers (FFA 1994: Articles 3–5 and Annex I). The Treaty was seen as a significant step towards regional fisheries management and similar arrangements were subsequently sought with other distant water fishing nations (OPA 1995: Vol II, 1994 Forum Communiqué). Since the Treaty was concluded, however, no multilateral agreement on access has been concluded with another distant water fishing nation, although negotiations are underway between some FFA member countries and the Taiwan Deep Sea Tuna Boatowners' Association over access to the albacore longline fishery (FFA 1996).

Other legal instruments that have been adopted in the region relating to fisheries management include the Palau Arrangement for the Management of the Western Pacific Purse Seine Fishery (1992), which provides for cooperative action on limiting the number of licences for foreign purse seine vessels. Although the licences are then made available for domestic operators, it acts as a limit on total vessel numbers as domestic fishing operators are not in a position to take up the additional licences. Limiting the number of licences available to foreign fishing vessels was also intended to increase competition for those licences to raise the licence fees. The number of licences allowed under the Palau Arrangement is higher than the existing number of operative licences, but the Arrangement's provisions remain generally constraining on foreign fishing effort within member countries' EEZs. The Niue Treaty on Cooperation in Fisheries Surveillance and Law Enforcement in the South Pacific Region provides a head agreement under which member countries can enter into bilateral subsidiary agreements to share surveillance and enforcement assets, such as patrol boats and personnel. Tuvalu and Tonga are the only two countries that have concluded a subsidiary agreement.

A significant development in regional fisheries management was the adoption in 1991 of the Minimum Terms and Conditions for Fisheries Access (MTCs). These provide for the positioning of observers on boats at the expense of vessel operators, catch and effort data provision (including for fishing on the high seas where that was part of a trip that included fishing within EEZs), prohibition of transhipment at sea, and registration on the Regional Register of Fishing Vessels held by the FFA Secretariat. The Regional Register gives status of 'good standing' that can be withdrawn for serious transgressions, whereby a vessel without 'good standing' will not be allowed to fish in the zone of any FFA member country (FFA 1993). FFA members have gradually incorporated the MTCs into bilateral access arrangements. Although they have no separate standing under international law, the MTCs and the Regional Register have contributed to management through regional cooperation. The ban on transhipment at sea, which took effect in mid-1993, led to a significant improvement in catch reporting and compliance, and the risk of losing 'good standing' on the Regional Register has encouraged transgressing vessel operators to settle disputes expeditiously and out of court (Bergin 1994).

Sustainable management for the future?

FFA member countries have acknowledged the need for a cooperative approach to future management arrangements for regional fisheries (FFC 1996). The 27th South Pacific Forum in Majuro agreed to convene in mid-1997 a second High Level Multilateral Consultation on the Conservation and Management of Fisheries Resources of the Central and Western Pacific, involving coastal states and territories in the region and distant water fishing nations (South Pacific Forum 1996). The first High Level Multilateral Conference on South Pacific Tuna Fisheries was held in Honiara in December 1994 (FFC 1996).

The highly migratory nature of the resource and its importance to island countries proscribes consideration of regional fisheries management in isolation from its political and social context. Treatment of Central and Western Pacific tuna fisheries under a system of individual property rights (as separate fishing zones governed by countries acting independently) is unrealistic because of the highly migratory nature of the stocks. Furthermore, the coming into force of the Law of the Sea Convention and the adoption of the UN Implementing Agreement creates an international legal obligation on coastal states in the region to cooperate with each other and other fishing nations in fisheries management. On the other hand, the kind of open-access regime where no property rights are established, such as occurred in international waters (beyond territorial seas) prior to the Law of the Sea, is inimical to the sustainability of the stocks. Although the creation of property rights can assist the exploitation of a terrestrial resource (implying that an absence of property rights can impede exploitation), the experience of fisheries has been that unrestricted access has led to resource depletion. This threat is increasing in the Central and Western Pacific where distant water fleets are expanding rapidly without explicit management constraints. The common property management approach that has been taken to date in the Forum would thus seem to be the only one feasible: indeed, this is why collective management approaches to international fisheries issues have been pursued all over the world.

The island countries of the Forum region are by no means uniform in their fisheries interests. The tiny atoll states of Micronesia, and Tuvalu, have enormous fishing zones but little else in terms of potential foreign exchange earnings and development opportunities. The larger Melanesian countries have significant fisheries resources (from time to time, depending on the migration of the stocks), which are important sources of income, notwithstanding other development options and a better natural resource endowment. In contrast, most of the Polynesian countries do not have substantial pelagic fisheries resources: whereas over 70 per cent of reported catches of the northerly yellowfin and skipjack tuna in the region are caught within EEZs, the more southerly albacore and bigeye fisheries involve a higher proportion of high seas activity. The significant differences in fisheries endowments and the relative importance of fisheries to different island economies has an obvious influence on the approaches that island countries take to regional fisheries management and access arrangements, and will have a bearing on the cohesiveness of their approach to fisheries negotiations with distant water fishing nations.

Despite commitments in the Forum in favour of multilateral access arrangements, the benefits from a US Treaty-style arrangement with other distant water fishing nations are not uniformly distributed between island countries. The US Treaty fees are distributed according to a formula by which all Pacific island parties (including Australia and New Zealand) receive an equal share of 15 per cent of the fee, with the residual (after deduction of administrative costs) divided up between countries according to the proportion of catch taken in their zones. Thus, those countries with little or no catch taken in their zones are in effect subsidised by the others. The resource-rich Parties to the Nauru Agreement countries might then have some justification in feeling that they could negotiate higher fees bilaterally than through a similar arrangement. This is particularly the case for the Asian distant water fishing nations, which have already made clear that, unlike the United States, they will not subsidise their fleets to boost licence fees. On the other hand, the less resource-rich FFA member countries argue with justification that the generous fees obtained through the US Treaty would not have been forthcoming without their cooperation in negotiating the agreement, and that collective bargaining by all FFA member countries has brought concrete dividends in the form of higher fees that have benefited all members, and particularly those with significant catches in their fishing zones.

Notwithstanding their differing fisheries interests, which might affect their individual attitudes towards access arrangements with distant water fishing nations and their aspirations to develop their own domestic fishing industries, Forum island countries have a common interest in the conservation and sustainable management of regional fisheries. The challenge before them now is to find similar common interests with distant water fishing nations and other coastal states that share the fisheries resources, and to negotiate a management regime that ensures the long-term viability of the resource while still meeting their economic needs and development aspirations.

Recent changes in international law, with the conclusion and coming into force of the Law of the Sea Convention and the adoption in December 1995 of the UN Implementing Agreement, lend considerably more support now in international law for collective management between countries of highly migratory resources. Associated with the support afforded in international law comes an increased obligation on Forum island countries to cooperate with distant water fishing nations and non-Forum coastal states and territories in fisheries conservation and management: in effect to negotiate a common property management regime that extends the existing cooperation between coastal states in the region.

Implications for common property

The process that Forum leaders have committed themselves to in calling the second High Level Multilateral Consultation on regional fisheries conservation and management will provide another test of the ability of countries with widely varying interests, endowments, and levels of development to cooperate in the common property management of a resource that is important to all players. It is a classic example of a common property situation, where the decision-making units (the governments of the countries involved) interact at a level of at least nominal equality. The developing coastal states in the region are small and have little international political clout, but have a history of collective action and a right acknowledged in international law to the benefits of the rich fisheries resources within their exclusive economic zones. For some, the resources represent the principal opportunity to achieve their development aspirations. By contrast, the distant water fishing nations include the two largest economies in the world who have considerable international political and economic weight—including the capacity to use their aid funds as leverage—but who nonetheless view the resource as significant to at least certain influential sections of their societies. It is a situation in which significant negotiating power resides with the politically and economically weak island countries in the form of rights to the benefits of their exclusive economic zones. The test lies in the ability of all parties to ensure that the strong interests apparent on all sides in the resource work towards a collective management outcome rather than dissipating into a conflict that could threaten the future of the fisheries.

The advent of the UN Implementing Agreement is also important in altering the boundaries of the resource.[4] Whereas the Law of the Sea Convention is based on the individual property rights created for countries through the declaration of exclusive economic zones, the Implementing Agreement blurs that distinction in its application. The Agreement is to apply to 'the conservation and management of straddling fish stocks and highly migratory fish stocks beyond areas under national jurisdiction' (Article 3), except that the general principles of the Agreement (Article 5), the provisions relating to the application of the precautionary approach (Article 6) and to the compatibility of conservation and management measures (Article 7) are to be applied by coastal states within areas of national jurisdiction.

The provisions for compatibility outlined in Article 7 arose from the recognition by the UN Conference on Straddling Fish Stocks and Highly Migratory Fish Stocks that national and international measures for conservation and management needed to be compatible in order to be effective (Doulman 1995:9). From a common property perspective, however, the effect of this eminently sensible management approach has been to soften the boundaries between the individual property rights exercised within EEZs ('sovereign rights' as characterised in UNCLOS and the Implementing Agreement) and the high seas areas where a common property regime is to apply.

The compatibility provisions have the additional effect of potentially strengthening the position of coastal states in determining common management measures. The first criterion for compatibility required states to

> take into account the conservation and management measures adopted and applied in accordance with article 61 of the (Law of the Sea) Convention in respect of the same stocks by coastal states within areas under national jurisdiction and ensure that measures established in respect of such stocks for the high seas do not undermine the effectiveness of such measures (United Nations 1995: Article 7(2a)).

This implies that, if coastal states apply conservation and management measures in accordance with the relevant provisions of UNCLOS (Article 61), they are in a strong position under international law to require distant water fishing nations to apply compatible measures under a common property regime on the high seas, or at least to apply measures that do not undermine the management regimes that apply within their EEZs. In the Pacific, this could have practical implications for the outcomes of negotiations on regional management measures for tuna stocks.

Conclusion

The capture of economic rent by individual coastal states within the context of an agreed conservation and management regime is within the bounds of those states' sovereign rights to benefit from the resource, and the mechanisms for maximising that benefit can be developed unilaterally. The most difficult task facing coastal states in the South Pacific Forum region is to agree on a management regime whereby distant water fishing nations (and their fleets) bear their share of the responsibilities of conservation, and in which catch allocation and access to the resource is structured in a way that both maximises the benefits to island countries and distributes those benefits in an acceptably equitable way. These issues are not unique to the Pacific, but are being played out in fisheries forums in the Indian Ocean and the Antarctic. The experiences of each set of negotiations will, over time, inform and influence each other in providing precedents and models for common management of common resources.

Notes

The views expressed in this chapter are those of the author and not necessarily those of the Department of Foreign Affairs and Trade, Canberra.

1. I am grateful to Jonathon Barrington of the Commonwealth Department of Primary Industries and Energy, and to Ian Cartwright and Tony Kingston of the Forum Fisheries Agency for elaborating the fisheries management concepts in this section.
2. South Pacific Forum member countries are Australia, Cook Islands, Federated States of Micronesia, Fiji, Kiribati, Marshall Islands, Nauru, New Zealand, Niue, Palau, Papua New Guinea, Solomon Islands, Tonga, Tuvalu, Vanuatu and Western Samoa.
3. Parties to the Nauru Agreement are Federated States of Micronesia, Kiribati, Marshall Islands, Nauru, Palau, Papua New Guinea, Solomon Islands and Tuvalu.
4. I am grateful to Transform Aqorau of the University of Wollongong for alerting me to the implications of these provisions of the UN Implementing Agreement for common property.

References

Bergin, Anthony, 1994. 'Political and Legal Control Over Marine Living Resources—recent developments in South Pacific distant water fishing', *International Journal of Marine and Coastal Law* 9(3): 289–309.

Bromley, Daniel W., 1991. *Environment and Economy: property rights and public policy*, Blackwell, Cambridge, Mass.

Department of Foreign Affairs and Trade (DFAT), 1974. *Vienna Convention on the Law of Treaties 1969*, Australian Treaty Series 1974, 2, DFAT, Canberra.

——, 1993. *Convention for the Conservation of Southern Bluefin Tuna 1993*, DFAT, Canberra.

Doulman, David J., 1995. *Structure and Process of the 1993–1995 United Nations Conference on Straddling Fish Stocks and Highly Migratory Fish Stocks*, FAO Fisheries Circular 898, Food and Agriculture Organization of the United Nations, Rome.

Ron Duncan and Ila Temu, Trade, investment and sustainable development of natural resources in the Pacific: the case of fish and timber, paper presented to the Economic and Social Commission for Asia and the Pacific Expert Group Meeting on Enhancing Cooperation in Trade and Investment Between Pacific island Countries and Economies of East and South East Asia in the 1990s, Port Vila, Vanuatu, July, 8–12, 1996, unpublished.

Forum Fisheries Agency (FFA), 1979. *South Pacific Forum Fisheries Agency Convention*, FFA, Honiara.

——, 1993. *United Nations Conference on Straddling Fish Stocks and Highly Migratory Fish Stocks: New York, 3–20 July 1993*, Forum Fisheries Agency, Honiara, unpublished.

——, 1994. *Treaty on Fisheries Between the Governments of Certain Pacific Island States and the Government of the United States of America* (1994 Edition), Forum Fisheries Agency, Honiara.

——, 1996. *Forum Fisheries Agency: Report of the Director 1996*, Forum Fisheries Agency, Honiara.

Forum Fisheries Committee, 22 February 1996. *Forum Fisheries Committee Meets in Fiji and Appoints New Deputy Director*, press release.

Maxwell, J.G.H. and A.D. Owen, 1994. *South Pacific Tuna Fisheries Study*, AusAID, Canberra.

Ministry of Fisheries, 1996. *OECD Committee for Fisheries: fisheries management techniques: country report: New Zealand*, Wellington.

Office of Pacific Island Affairs (OPA), 1995. *South Pacific Forum Communiqués, Vols 1 (1971–90) and 2 (1991–95)*, DFAT, Canberra.

South Pacific Forum, 5 September 1996. *Twenty-Seventh South Pacific Forum Communique*.

Tsamenyi, Martin and Stephen Kaye, 1994. 'The Southern Bluefin Tuna Convention: the management of highly migratory species and third States', *Maritime Studies* 75:1–13.

United Nations, 1983. *The Law of the Sea: United Nations Convention on the Law of the Sea*, United Nations, New York.

United Nations, 1995. *Agreement for the Implementation of the Provisions of the United Nations Convention on the Law of the Sea of 10 December 1982 relating to the Conservation and Management of Straddling Fish Stocks and Highly Migratory Fish Stocks*, United Nations, New York.

United Nations, 1996. *Information on the Law of the Sea*, Internet site http://www.un.org/Depts, Division for Ocean Affairs and the Law of the Sea, Office of Legal Affairs, New York.

12

Common property conflict and resolution: Aboriginal Australia and Papua New Guinea

Kilyali Kalit and Elspeth Young

It is often assumed that customary concepts of common property must hamper development, and must be eradicated in favour of more individualistic ownership which promotes entrepreneurial approaches and wealth generation. Such assumptions are not new. History presents some strong supporting evidence for their validity, but also raises questions, particularly in relation to equity in resource distribution. In Scotland, for example, the transformation two centuries ago from the communally based run-rig system to the enclosure of the land into individual plots laid the basis for land improvement, agricultural intensification and the introduction of new crops and livestock. Without such changes the population could not have sustained itself, and these new forms of resource management fostered wide-ranging development. However there were also some disadvantages. Many people became landless and were forced either to seek subsistence land elsewhere, usually in ecologically marginal areas, or to migrate to distant lands such as Australia or Canada. More commonly, they moved to the cities to become factory workers in the burgeoning industries of the period. While many of those displaced reaped undoubted economic benefit these changes certainly caused some social dislocation which, although healed by time, must have initally made a significant impact. This agricultural intensification also generated some long-term changes which have been detrimental to the Scottish environment as a whole.

Commitment in today's industrialised world to the positive benefits of individualisation of property is almost universal. However this doctrine also has wider implications. Because resources are traded on a global scale, the interests and ideas of the industrialised world directly impinge on people from other societies where industrialisation is still a relatively recent process. As Baines (1989) points out, there is widespread feeling among agents of economic development that such a process is constrained by traditional systems of land and sea tenure and that customary resource management systems are largely irrelevant. In the Pacific pressures to transform common property resource holdings to more individualistic forms of ownership are strong and are causing concern for indigenous peoples. Key stakeholders in resource use—the state and, through its arrangements with external financial agencies, organisations such as the World Bank or the International Monetary Fund, development companies and other interested non-indigenous people—have been the main instigators of change. In Papua New Guinea, for example, the World Bank in collaboration with the government has worked tirelessly to encourage conversion of customary group tenure into some form of freehold, involving legislation for customary land registration. Although efforts towards conversion of customary land started in the 1950s the process has never been finally resolved. The most recent attempt (in 1996) under the auspices of the Land Mobilisation Program had to be called off even before making it to Parliament, due to outright rejection by the public, demonstrated through violence and loss of life.

Such concerns and conflicts are not restricted to Melanesia, Micronesia, and Polynesia. They are also supremely important in the industrialised Pacific countries of Australia and New Zealand, both of which have indigenous minority populations which have retained a strong commitment to common resource property concepts and whose customary tenure systems have received only limited recognition under the laws of the state.

Key questions concerning the change from common resource property concepts to more individually defined resources include the following

- who would benefit most from these changes—indigenous customary landholders, the developers, or the state?
- would these changes lead to better or worse distribution of development benefits (jobs, income, control over resources) within the customary landholding group?
- is the type of development driving these transformations—

capitalistic/individualistic rather than communally-based with sustenance derived from both monetary and non-monetary activity—ultimately the most sustainable for such Pacific indigenous societies?

- can these concepts of resource property be reconciled so that development is supported? Can viable alternative solutions, recognising both systems, be created?

This chapter focuses primarily on the last of these questions. It refers to local level examples of how indigenous communities have responded to the demands of both communal and individual property definitions, and it examines these within the broader regional frameworks required for people to make these adjustments in ways that promote the future sustainability of their societies. While the two Pacific indigenous groups referred to here (Aboriginal Australians in remote areas and Papua New Guineans) are very different, some common themes can be identified. These relate to the definition of common property resources and traditional ecological knowledge, pressures to change these exerted by commercial resource developments, and the methods devised by indigenous people for coping with the ensuing conflicts.

Relevant common resource property concepts

Concepts of resource property lie on a continuum ranging from unfettered resources, which users may exploit freely for their own benefit with no consideration for others or for longer-term sustainability, to absolute private ownership, in which a single individual exercises complete exclusionary control over the use of the resources (Bromley 1991). Between these two extremes are communally-owned resources (the group uses the resource according to agreed rules designed to sustain all its members and maintain the future viability of the resource), publicly-owned resources (under state or national jurisdictions), and leased resources (individuals or groups hold tenure for an agreed limited period and are subject to certain restrictions on how to use these assets).

For Australian and Pacific indigenous societies communal ownership is the principal form of common resource property holding. This contrasts with the principal forms of tenure recognised in industrialised societies—public, private and leasehold tenures. The latter forms of resource ownership are largely individualistic. Australian and Pacific indigenous societies have not, despite many misconceptions, held their land as a free good, the uncontrolled use of which was seen to lead to the 'tragedy of the commons' (Hardin 1968). Their common property concepts follow distinct rules agreed to within that particular society. Incoming settlers, then largely of European and Anglo-Celtic origins, generally ignored the prior existence of these forms of tenure, a basic failure which has been a common characteristic of colonial occupation over the last five centuries (see, for example, Bromley 1991; Berkes and Farvar 1989, Grima and Berkes 1989, and Ostrom 1990). This failure, a major source of conflict, has had dire consequences.

Colonial settlers in Australia wrongfully assumed that the land was *terra nullius*, a place that belonged to no one and was therefore free to be taken over by any interested settler. For over 200 years the resource rights and beliefs of indigenous Australians have been largely discounted and they have had little opportunity to share in the benefits flowing from resource development. Only in recent decades, following passage of Land Rights legislation in the Northern Territory in 1976, have some Aboriginal people been able to regain control over customary land and negotiate for a share in monetary benefits from development. And it has only been in the 1990s, with the Mabo decision and subsequent passing of the Native Title Legislation, that the fundamental misconception of *terra nullius* has been legally overturned. While this clearly has implications for resource development the practical consequences are still to be clarified, although mineral resources will still be subject to separate claim by the state.

In Papua New Guinea, in contrast, customary property rights, explicitly recognised under the country's legal framework, extend over at least 97 per cent of the country's land area and most of its forest. The remaining area is 'referred to as alienated land because it was bought or taken away from its customary owners' (Clarke et al. 1996:1). Indigenous kinship groups control land use and natural resource management. As in Australia the state also claims interest in mineral rights over both customary and non-customary land. Pressures to suppress the detrimental characteristics of common resource property regimes in favour of more individually-defined systems are strong. Both countries also demonstrate that forms of resource tenure—communal, state and private—can overlap, and reconcilation of the differences between them becomes very difficult. As Berkes and Farvar (1989) suggest, finding satisfactory ways of dealing with such overlap is a key challenge to resolving resource development conflicts.

Underlying all of these questions is the key point of how common property concepts and rights are defined. As far as commercial resource development is concerned, the main issues concern the spatial definition of boundaries between property groups, the determination of membership of the groups, and the characteristics of various mechanisms by which these groups exercise control over their resource. Unless these issues are clearly understood no practical resolutions can be devised.

Boundaries and group membership

The perception that Australian Aborigines did not define their territorial boundaries but were 'aimless wanderers' was, from early European settlement, a remarkably persistent myth. On the contrary, as later anthropological and linguistic studies (such as Tindale 1972, Peterson 1976) have demonstrated, Aboriginal groups held communal responsibility for broad but distinct areas of land and resources and exercised that responsibility through both traditional ecological knowledge and their cultural and spiritual knowledge. Recent land rights recognition and legislation, based primarily on establishment of proof of the customary ownership of claimants (Young 1992b), has brought the issue of spatial definition of these 'countries' into sharp focus. As a result, non-indigenous understanding of Aboriginal boundary parameters has greatly increased. As Sutton's recent exploration of boundary issues reveals (Sutton 1995), researchers have become increasingly convinced both of their overall complexity, and less willing to see them as rigid lines dividing different 'countries' from one another. Similar complexities have emerged in attempts to define group members, commonly called 'traditional owners'. Here, as Hiatt et al. (1984) discuss, the lineage group remains the core of those claiming to hold customary responsibility for a particular 'country'. However, there is, and probably always has been, some fluidity in group membership, reflecting demographic changes in pre-contact times and, more recently, population changes resulting from dispossession and mobility. As with spatial boundaries it is the decision of the group itself which counts in determining who does, or does not, belong.

Papua New Guinean indigenous societies also define their spatial boundaries but, as continuing inter-group conflicts show, areas of contention have always been present and still remain. Systems of land tenure in Papua New Guinea are complex and vary greatly. Highland societies, for example, distinguish between territory and property—'territory is a group resource, whereas occupied or improved land, used for gardens, houses, and other individual or group purposes, is property' (Brown 1978:113). As this implies, while the whole is common resource property, there are degrees of difference in the way that ownership is demonstrated. Through regular use, land—inevitably th' most fertile—can become individual property. This obviously has implications for resource development, whether through cash-cropping, forest logging or claims for mineral development compensation Membership of the extended kin group responsible for the whole region is inextricably linked into such tenure systems through reciprocity and resource sharing. That membership, in terms of rights to land, can be extended beyond the immediate lineage to include other long-term residents who originally were granted only temporar resource rights (Brookfield and Brown 1967). Banks's (1996) recent discussion on compensation and relocation payments for the Porgera gold-mine in Papua New Guinea shows that the incorporation of thes more broadly defined lineage groups into the agreement has posed very difficult questions for the company concerned.

Control

A common characteristic of indigenous regimes in both Papua New Guinea and Aboriginal Australia is the existence of distinct control, both on group activities and on individual use of resources within the group's area. In addition, this control was exercised through internall' upheld rules and behavioural norms with which all responsible member of the group were familiar. As Gibbs and Bromley (1989) comment, such control is essential if common resources are to be properly managed. Transgression against the agreed rules, such as allowing your livestoc to devastate your neighbours' crops (in Papua New Guinea) or visiting spiritual sites from which, for gender or group affiliation reasons, you should be excluded (in Aboriginal Australia) were punishable. Thus control was internally defined and exercised, a situation which, as Ostrom (1990) has stressed, provides much greater group cohesiveness and stability than one in which control is externally imposed, such as from the state.

Common resource property definition and development

Increased recognition of the complexities of boundary and group definitions has been accompanied, somewhat ironically, by increased pressure to make firm decisions on these parameters. Davis and Prescott's (1992) analysis of Australian Aboriginal frontiers and boundaries provides an obvious example of how one resource developer has tried to exert such pressure. This research study, financed by a major mineral development company, set out to map and define contemporary Aboriginal territories, with a view to providing a definitive text which could be used by both present and future developers in determining with whom they must negotiate over shares in resource rights. As Sutton's (1995) detailed éxpose of this study describes, not only did this study include glaring inaccuracies in definition but it also raised ethical problems because it imposed external control over systems which should be internally determined.

Development companies in Papua New Guinea have also been eager to determine rigidly which common resource properties will be affected by their activities (such as from mining), and would prefer that their negotiations with traditional owners be restricted to the members of core groups. This would obviously, as Power (1995) argues, suit them better. He suggests that the rightful landowners should be identified as early as possible, before a project begins. He feels that this would avoid the proliferation of claims of ownership and demand for increased royalty shares once high levels of production are achieved, as has occurred in the Kutubu project. However, rigid definition of affected areas and of those deserving compensation has its pitfalls. It may well cut out people whose claims are well-founded. Subsequent problems arising with compensation from large-scale mining developments such as Ok Tedi or Porgera show that the dangers of such approaches are very real.

Aboriginal Australia: common resource property and development

The history of land tenure change in Australia can be classified, as far as Aborigines are concerned, into two distinct periods. First there was the period of alienation and privatisation, during which large-scale dispossession occurred and direct evidence of Aboriginal common resource property was hidden 'underground'. Second, there was the period of land rights recognition, reinforced by legislation, when Aboriginal concepts of landownership came firmly back into focus. Both of these periods emphasise not only the importance of land tenure transformation in relation to economic use and control over natural resources but also, as Sutton (1995) has recently stressed, the highly political nature of these changes. During the first period, which lasted from first contact until around 1970, state and private forms of property ownership prevailed and indigenous interests in resource development benefits were ignored and went uncompensated. It is the second period, commencing approximately 25 years ago with the adoption by the Federal government of policies supporting Aboriginal land rights, which is of greatest interest in this discussion. This period has seen significant concessions on Aboriginal Land Rights (over 15 per cent of the Australian continent, primarily in remote areas, is now under Aboriginal ownership—Figure 12.1—but also the beginning of processes which have spread resource development benefits more equitably to customary owners. It has also shown how common resource property concepts and more individual forms of ownership might be reconciled. The following discussion focuses on the pastoral sector, with brief references to human settlement, which pervades all resource use.

Figure 12.1 Aboriginal land in Australia

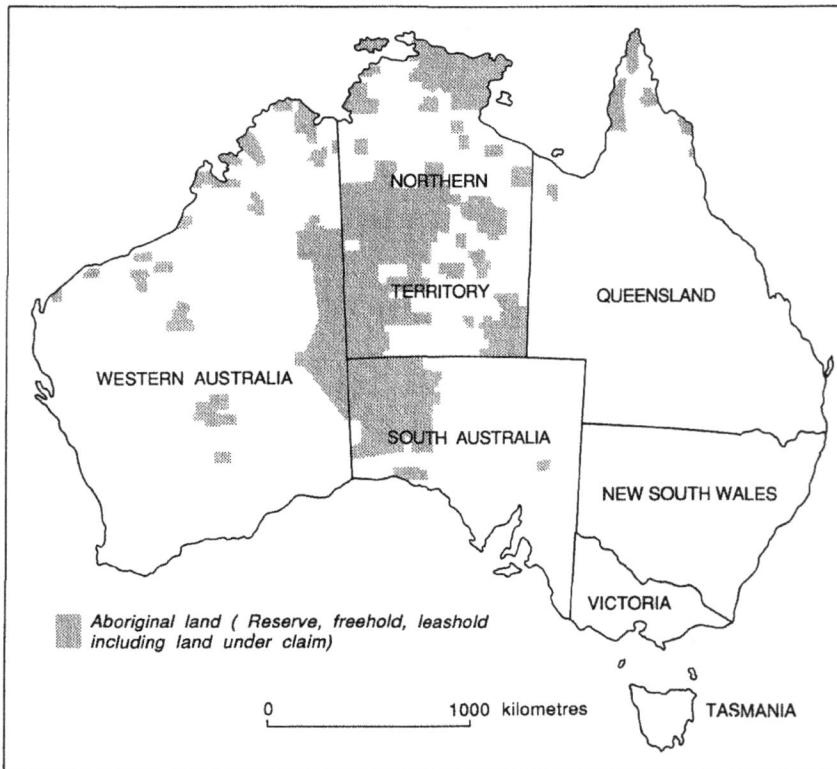

Aboriginal land (Reserve, freehold, leashold including land under claim)

0   1000 kilometres

Settlement

The use of land for settlement is the most basic form of resource use. The last 25 years have seen a marked reoccupation of many of the remotest parts of Australia by Aboriginal groups who have regained legal title to their customary lands which they had earlier been encouraged and sometimes forced to leave (see, for example, Young 1992a; Australia 1987; Cane and Stanley 1985). Centralised administrative settlements, a prime instrument of earlier assimilation policies, have declined as people have returned to the land, establishing well over 200 'outstations' or 'homeland centres' in central Australia alone. As Taylor (1992) has demonstrated for the Northern Territory, this has led to a marked dispersal of population. The locations of these outstations accord as closely as possible with customary human/land linkages. However, because of the need to accommodate to non-indigenous systems of land tenure and to meet modern demands for services, they do not fit completely with these patterns. Thus, for example, people may have been unable to establish their new camps at a chosen waterhole either because that waterhole lay on land now legally alienated to the state or a non-indigenous developer or landholder, or because the water resource was neither large nor predictable enough to support the returning group. Attempts to find alternative ground water supplies were often frustrated because drilling in the chosen site was unsuccessful or the water supplies were non-potable because of their high salt content. The existence of roads and tracks, services such as schools and clinics, permanent houses and the provision of electricity, telecommunications and other increasingly vital attributes of modern lifestyles have also influenced site choice. Administrative pressures for centralisation rather than dispersion have been strong, with persuasion sometimes applied through legal restrictions on land settlement and less directly through introducing user-pays programs for electricity and water at price rates which are beyond the pockets of most Aboriginal outstation dwellers. Many outstation sites are therefore compromises, located on or near customary land but accessible to externally provided services.

The use of the land around outstations also reflects this compromise. Subsistence hunting and foraging is practised as closely as possible to customary norms with particular individuals holding detailed knowledge and responsibilities. But other outstation residents with less obvious traditional claims to these resources are not excluded. Over time, they may well gain most of the basic spiritual and ecological lore already held by the recognised customary landholders. They may even, as traced for the Anmatyerre people to the northwest of Alice Springs (Young 1987) be fully accepted as customary resource owners. And physical access for vehicles, vital to the success of contemporary hunter–foragers, inevitably means that track networks also play a significant role in determining where people go and what they harvest.

These compromises present challenges to the Aboriginal groups concerned, and also to the administrative authorities charged with providing them with basic services. For the people the challenge has been to approximate their chosen customary settlement patterns as closely as possible. For the administrators, it is the need to deal efficently with scattered, highly mobile populations who still have prime needs for services such as power, education, and health to be satisfied (Young and Doohan 1989).

Pastoralism

Government policies fostering Aboriginal development have generally followed the paradigms of the industrialised world, stressing monetary economic gain as the only path to the future. In the pastoral industry commercially-oriented development, in which Aboriginal groups would acquire properties and run them, like their non-indigenous neighbours, as successful money-making ventures has been generally promoted. For many complex reasons—historical, political, environmental, social and cultural—few Aboriginal properties have fulfilled that promise (Young 1995).

Over the last 20 years more than 40 pastoral properties have been acquired by Aboriginal groups, primarily through government land purchase funding. Although encouraged, and sometimes coerced, into managing these properties commercially, many new Aboriginal owners have had different priorities for the use of the land, priorities which demonstrate adaptation between common resource property regimes and more individualised forms of tenure. As recorded in a number of studies conducted in the decade from 1978 (Young 1988a and 1988b), properties in the Northern Territory were able to convert themselves to freehold title through claims lodged through the Northern Territory Aboriginal land rights legislation. Once released from restrictions imposed through leasehold regulations, the people could therefore use the land as they wished. Their earlier common resource property regimes often began to surface. This resulted in the dispersal of extended family groups from centralised homestead settlements, where they had worked for the former non-indigenous owner, to scattered 'outstations' located in the traditional country of each group; the development of multiple small-scale cattle enterprises, ecotourism ventures and arts and craft ventures focusing on these outstations; the re-emergence of subsistence hunting and foraging as a major activity; and the maintenance of cultural activities. In the case of Mt Allan (Fig. 12.2), following a successful land claim the Anmatyerre people split into three major groups, one centred on the existing homestead and the others, associated with honey ant and emu dreaming respectively, in new outstations located within their customary 'countries' and accessible to important cultural sites about which they were concerned. As discussed elsewhere (Young 1987) the Aboriginal interpretation of responsibility for the country within the former Mt Allan pastoral

Figure 12.2 Anmatyerre and non-Aboriginal delineations of property on Mount Allan

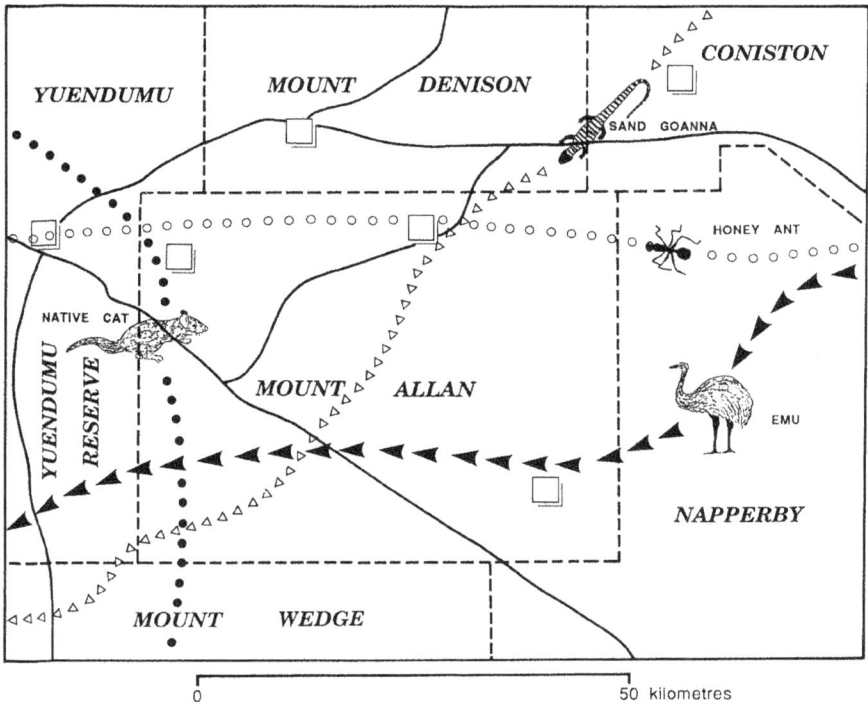

lease focuses on a number of ancestral beings whose activities trace 'tracks' in the landscape. Non-indigenous concepts of land tenure in the same area, in contrast, emphasise introduced boundary and infrastructure definition—fences, roads and substantial permanent buildings.

In some cases, such as the former Utopia cattle station to the northeast of Alice Springs, significant reduction in stocking rates has led to a marked regeneration of natural vegetation and the rehabilitation of wildlife habitats, with a resultant improvement in the potential of the country for subsistence hunting and foraging. Here most of the Alyawerre people abandoned the former centralised settlement in favour of a number of outstations located in the traditional country of each group concerned. Many established reputations as artists both in the national and international scene (NT Department of Primary Production 1983). To many non-indigenous people, including pastoralists and government officials, developments such as those on Mt Allan and Utopia have been wholly negative because they undermine the continuing advancement of commercial pastoralism. However, they have had a positive effect on many Aboriginal families, now living lifestyles which they find much more attractive than their former ones.

Even outside the Northern Territory, where legislation allowing the conversion of these leases to freehold title has not been established, adaptations have occurred. Aboriginal pastoralists in the Kimberley, for example (Davies and Young 1995, 1996), are increasingly exploring land management regimes which combine subsistence hunting and gathering with commercial cattle production and the development of tourist enterprises. Cattle production has become more intensive, emphasising the production of smaller numbers of larger, more valuable animals in the more accessible parts of properties, while the remainder of the land may be spasmodically used for subsistence fishing and wildlife hunting; and tourist expeditions to the spectacular ranges, gorges and waterholes of this remote far northern region.

An interesting prospect for a region such as this is the possibility of actual land redistribution to reflect these changes in use. Where there are adjoining Aboriginal cattle stations, communities might negotiate to remove their lease boundary fences and amalgamate their accessible lands along the road to form an intensive cattle production section. The 'backblocks' could then be devoted to subsistence and other alternative uses (Sullivan 1995). These new multiple use efforts are usually based on Aboriginal concepts of the common resource and the diversification which they have introduced is arguably better for many marginal grazing lands (Young and Ross 1994).

Common property and individual resource tenure: achieving resolution in Aboriginal Australia

Common themes in the above examples suggest some factors essential for the reconcilation of the differing constraints which common property and individualised forms of tenure have imposed on Aboriginal groups. These include

- the determination of the group itself, operating from a grassroots level, to establish its own priorities and select what they want from both systems
- the existence of a political climate which allows for effective decision-making on these issues within the community
- the provision of facilitating mechanisms, including regional supporting organisations, to enable community landholding groups to talk to, and negotiate with, outside stakeholders to ensure that their interests are taken into account
- the provision of funding, both to establish and maintain such buffer organisations and to support the efforts of the local community groups.

In each example, the Aboriginal groups concerned were very highly motivated in their search for re-identification with customary land from which they had been at least partially dislocated. They deliberately sought resource management strategies which would emphasise traditional cultural and economic values, seeing these generally as more important than resource harvesting for economic gain. And these strategies were adopted during the time when the political climate overtly supported Aboriginal self-determination. Moreover these were very coherent communities, strongly linked through kinship and with a clear view of their status and role as customary landholders. Decision-making accorded closely with traditional value systems and pressures to oppose these were relatively weak. Such characteristics foster coherent community decision-making. There is, however, no guarantee that they will continue to be maintained. Contemporary emergence of arguments about who has the right to speak for land, who belongs to the group, and over whether Native Title has survived or been extinguished by subsequent land alientation, suggest that the disruption of such approaches is now much more obvious.

The pastoral and settlement land management strategies adopted by these groups were also supported by a number of outside agencies, both government and non-government. Principal government agencies included federal and state departments of Aboriginal Affairs, in some cases enthusiastic about encouraging outstation development and solving remote-area service delivery problems. More recently, resource management agencies have begun to develop programs designed to assist the specific needs of Aboriginal land managers. The latter have included programs which undoubtedly recognise the importance of strategies which combine common property regimes with more individual forms of tenure—community management of endangered wildlife species, community programs to eradicate feral animals and introduced plant species, and programs to support subsistence-type pastoral projects rather than stressing commercial viability. These developments have been very positive. However, it must be acknowledged that government support for these initiatives has often been quite grudging and there are many key individuals in these agencies who see such efforts as unnecessary pandering to indigenous interests.

Non-government agencies have been principally the Aboriginal land councils. Over the last decade these organisations, funded by government and, where royalty agreements have been negotiated, through the proceeds of resource development on Aboriginal land (normally from mining), have extended their original focus on the conduct of land claims to include land management. Many of these approaches have been quite innovative. The Alice Springs-based Central Land Council, for example, has established a continuing study of how Aboriginal environmental perceptions of the arid zone differ from those commonly held by others (Rose 1995). These include Aboriginal concern over wholesale eradication of feral animals such as rabbits and cats, now often part of their 'bush tucker'; their interest in the short-term effects of seasonal climatic change (such as what plants thrive, and where animals congregate after rain) rather than recognition of the long-term consequences of erosion stemming from overgrazing and other misuse of the environment; their belief that failure to maintain customary use of fire, particularly obvious in areas from which the Aboriginal presence has been discouraged, is responsible for turning the country to 'rubbish'; and, of universal importance, the need to recognise and respect the cultural value of the land, not only at specific 'sacred sites' but also in its entirety. In all of these cases common property resource concepts are paramount.

The Central Land Council has also established a pilot project in culturally and environmentally appropriate land assessment, a move which offers new potential for improving Aboriginal and non-Aboriginal communication on rangeland valuation. This project exemplifies the possibilities arising from blending Aboriginal traditional ecological knowledge with scientific approaches and technologies (Mahney et al. 1996) It also highlights in a practical way the benefits from encouraging collaboration between scientists and Aboriginal resource managers. Both of these efforts have been supported by tapping into government funding resources such as the National Landcare program and the Land and Water Research and Development Corporation. Not all Aboriginal agencies can hope to do this and the struggle to obtain sufficient support to extend such initiatives to other parts of the country remains intense.

Papua New Guinea: custom and the capitalist system

Most of Papua New Guinea's population continue to live in rural communities, not effectively linked to the major urban centres by communication or transport infrastructure. The essential government services are inadequate and in some cases non-existent. This means that most of the people continue to derive their livelihoods from their land and its associated resources. In these communities, custom continues to play a key role in the management of common property resources.

Despite relative isolation, many of these communities are undergoing a massive transition from a subsistence to a monetary economy. Large-scale resource exploitation projects are being established in commercial agriculture, fisheries, forestry, minerals and petroleum. These projects are all having a significant impact on traditional social structures and customary resource management systems. They have been welcomed by rural communities in the hope of development. For a villager in Papua New Guinea, development is seen in terms of employment opportunities, spin-off business opportunities, funding, and the opening up of access roads, aid posts, and primary schools, and hard cash (perhaps from resource royalties). Project agreements signed between the developer and the local landowning clan specify benefit packages. These packages, however, vary between and within sectors, with greater benefits on the whole flowing through some large-scale mining agreements than occur under smaller-scale forestry agreements. Although people know that resource exploitation has had a negative impact on traditional social structures and has irreversibly damaged the environment, their patterns of thinking and subsequent actions in approving projects is very rational. Without these agreements some of these communities would never have the opportunity to see any positive changes at all, or even be able to send their children to school. Thus, as Hayne states, 'they will take those actions which they think will yield them the largest net advantage' (1994:5).

Resolution of the contradictions between customary land tenure and the individualisation of resource property is essential if the problem of providing Papua New Guineans with sustainable livelihoods for the future is to be solved. Attitudes towards this are ambivalent. Legal and official policy statements uphold customary tenure, but consecutive governments in the last twenty years have advocated economic development through the capitalist or free market system. This poses a development dilemma which is crucial for the future of Papua New Guinea (Baines 1989:273).

In some cases appropriate programs for administration, marketing, and credit have been established to promote export-oriented agricultural production on communally-owned land. This has encouraged individualisation of common property resources, especially for the establishment of permanent tree crops such as coffee. Smallholders produce much of Papua New Guinea's pyrethrum and well over 60 per cent of the total volume of coffee.

Forestry provides a different example. Here development is preceded by the Government Forest Authority signing a Forest Management Agreement with a Incorporated Land Group (ILG), incorporated under the *Land Groups Incorporation Act* of 1974. The *Forestry Act* itself sets out a preference for resource owners to form representative groupings in line with this Act. Despite the ILGs being officially recognised as the instruments for utilisation and conservation of natural resources, government assistance in this area is minimal. Landowners have to take responsibility for their own incorporation, and in general they are forced to seek assistance in this process from the developers themselves. This gives the developers a strong hold over the ILGs. The landowners are left vulnerable to outside influences and may be rushed into making decisions that are not mutually beneficial to other members of the community or their tribe. Primary rights may be denied and in most cases secondary right-holders are excluded from participation, involvement, and benefit sharing. In the resultant conflicts, relations between the landowners themselves, with the government, and with investors often deteriorate and are increasingly becoming areas of concern.

Land reform, involving the individual registration of customary land, presents an alternative to the promotion of development under existing customary tenure. This has so far failed and indications are that prospects for Papua New Guinea's development through land resource utilisation seem poor.

The government is caught in a contradictory situation. The Land Mobilisation Program (LMP) was designed to contribute to economic growth through productive use of the land resources throughout the country, whilst promoting equity, employment, participation and social stability (World Bank 1989). This assumes that land resources are now inadequately utilised and that outputs generated from customary land are insufficient. As the dominance of smallholder production in pyrethrum and coffee shows, this is questionable. Papua New Guinean communities have adapted very well in meeting the demands imposed on them by the capitalist system. The other under-lying assumption is that customary tenure is the prime constraint to economic development. Other structural problems that hinder development include availability of credit; provision of appropriate extension services; poor market access; lack of efficient technology; and poor communication and infrastructure. Even if all the customary land were registered, there is no gurantee that rural production would increase. These structural problems would also need to be addressed.

As the outright public rejection of land mobilisation suggests, pursuing this approach is not a realistic option. Instead the government needs to undertake a massive awareness program on the existing legal and policy provisions on customary tenure and explain why the registration of customary land is necessary. By educating landowners on these issues people might make more informed decisions on the conversion of customary land. In other words, working within the existing policy and legal framework, which explicitly recognises customary tenure, is to be preferred (Kalit 1996). This, in turn, will depend upon recognising and dealing with some threats and constraints to the overall sustainability of Papua New Guinea's rural communities. The current *ad hoc* approach to development is a prime example. In most cases it is local leaders and the educated élite who invite the government or introduce potential developers to possible projects. This unplanned and uncontrolled approach, which is already leading to the approval of many projects in Papua New Guinea, is potentially very damaging both to the country's overall sustainability and to the welfare of many of its people.

Sustainable resource management: a new approach

As most of the resources of Papua New Guinea—its land, forests and fisheries—are common property resources owned by kinship groups, any sustainable development effort must focus on assisting the resource owners to manage their resources on a sustainable basis. The customary tenure means that sustainable development is only practicable when it is endorsed by local communities and groups (Redclift and Saga 1994:13). One of Papua New Guinea's National Development Goals states that development should take place primarily through the use of indigenous forms of social, political and economic organisations. In reality, the government has failed to advocate development through this approach. Colonial and independent governments have only paid lip service to resource owner involvement in decision-making, in management and control and in sustainable resource management (Holzknecht 1995:24). While the government's 1994 approval for the development of a National Sustainable Development Strategy offers some hope for the practical implementation of these earlier national goals much needs to be done, particularly in the realm of indigenous involvement in resource management. Recent reforms to the provincial government system, which target greater empowerment, involvement and participation of local people as well as delivery of services, are a positive move. It will take some time for the restructured system to work and even then it is questionable whether it will be efficient. Meanwhile local landowners will continue to pursue their endeavours on an *ad hoc* basis. Innovative systems need to be put in place immediately to assist the landowners to better manage their resources. An approach for promoting sustainable management of forest resources through customary means is discussed below.

A case for a forest resource owner development agency

Forest resources have significant value to the clan groups whose land has always provided materials for housing, decoration, gardening and more recently a means of gaining cash. Papua New Guinea is now facing an era where there is a global interest in the marketing, and at the same time conservation, of its forests.

The demand for forest resources is expected to grow as supplies from the other Southeast Asian and South Pacific countries dwindle and it is hoped that this feature will enhance Papua New Guinea's bargaining power in the future. From 1991 to 1995 the National Forestry and Conservation Plan, under the auspices of the internationally supported Tropical Forest Action Plan, has provided the impetus for reformation of the forestry sector. Now a new policy, legislation and administrative structure for ensuring proper management of these resources is in place.

The 1994 National Forestry and Conservation Plan Review, while acknowledging that the Program had been successful in achieving its objectives at the national government level, found that it was less successful in enhancing resource owner involvement and field operations (UNDP 1994a:5). This review made specific recommendations to assist landowners during its second phase, including

- rationalisation of an accelerated landowner awareness/ mobilisation program
- strengthening local level capacity in forest management
- non-timber forest products, and biodiversity products and service evaluation.

The Landowner Involvement component of the Forest Management and Planning Project (Holzknecht 1995) proposed a range of ways to increase people's participation in, and management of, their forest resources. The key emphasis was on establishing and operating the Incorporated Land Groups. It also focused on mechanisms for advice and information sharing by landowners. The 1994 UNDP Mission Report on Sustainable Development also made recommendations for reformation of policy and institutions to cater for empowerment and active participation by the rural people. One mechanism suggested was the establishment of a Rural Trust to support non-government organisations and local initiatives (UNDP 1994b).

Papua New Guinea's National Forest Authority will have an important extension function in teaching landowners the principles and practice of sustainable forest management. But who will discuss what non-logging options, such as conservation or agricultural development, they have? Who can help them carry out such ventures? And what will happen to the large flows of funds derived from logging, much of which already goes to wrong people or is wasted on immediate consumption or inappropriate investments? Who can advise landowners on how best to invest these revenues in sustainable agriculture or other investments to secure their future needs? (World Bank 1993).

These issues could be dealt with under a forest revenue system through which some of the revenues earned from logging would be distributed to landowners to be spent however they wished, and the remainder deposited in a trust fund to be devoted to longer-term projects. Despite the political sensitivity surrounding this proposal, it seems worth suggesting that the funds be administered for the landowners by an independent organisation.

Such a Trust Fund could only be effectively operated if there were a competent agency to help landowners prepare and appraise project proposals. There is a strong argument for setting up an independent and visibly landowner-oriented statutory corporation, with its trust fund, which would clearly be divorced from the regulatory and enforcement activities of the National Forest Authority (World Bank n.d.).

The proposed agency might have four components.

1. A development Trust Fund, which would primarily be financed from logging revenues, but could also be readily used to channel funds, as matching grants, from any other sources (such as external donors). The Trust Fund would be administered as a single fund, although a separate account would be established for each ILG, which would maintain exclusive ownership of such funds.

2. An executive board (with suitable representation from Government, private sector, non-government organisations and landowners) to approve the use of these funds.

3. A technical secretariat, whose functions would be to help landowners incorporate new Land Groups; negotiate project agreements; prepare suitable projects and to present them to the board for approval. The secretariat would act as a catalyst, helping landowners to mobilise technical support from government line agencies and private consultants. But it would also require core in-house expertise.

4. A trust fund administrator (probably an international accounting firm) of sufficient repute to be acceptable to both landowners and donors.

It is envisaged that the agency would have the capacity to offer technical advice to ILGs on a full range of options on how best to use their logging revenues. These might include: reafforestation, agriculture development, community services (health, education and water supply), fisheries development and infrastructure development (roads and bridges).

The corporation would have an assured source of funds, if the suggestion for withholding a portion of forest revenue is accepted. If not, it is possible that landowners might voluntarily entrust a portion of their revenues to such a fund, particularly if some kind of matching grant were available to supplement their own funds. In either case, the agency would need to perform well to maintain landowners support.

The lack of a mechanism for helping landowners to manage their resources is also recognised as a constraint in other sectors such as agriculture and mining (Holzknecht 1995, Samana 1993). Landowners need incentives to conserve areas of biological interest. These incentives could be in the form of

- alternative income opportunities
- social services tied to conservation covenants
- direct compensation (rent) payments for maintaining conservation areas.

Similar needs occur in mining, petroleum, fisheries and agriculture, where there are no agencies competent to assist landowners in managing their resources on a sustainable basis. It would nevertheless, be sensible to pilot the proposal in the forestry sector first before trying to expand it to other sectors.

Lessons from comparison

Comparison between the initiatives described in Aboriginal Australia and the options currently open to customary landholding groups in Papua New Guinea show the following to be of prime importance.

First, landowner awareness is now well established for many remote Aboriginal groups but still requires substantial effort in Papua New Guinea. Landowners need to know all the development options they have, the reasons behind any major changes in these options, and all the existing facilities and mechanisms for encouraging sustainable resource management.

Second, governments should accept their role in assisting land and resource management in culturally appropriate ways which incorporate common property resource concepts. They should demonstrate this commitment by allocating more technical and financial resources. The government in Papua New Guinea has yet to move in this direction. In Australia, while some positive initiatives have been taken to support the efforts of Aboriginal Australians, the framework, particularly in current climate of government cutbacks and economic rationalism, is very fragile.

Lastly, there is a need to establish and fund 'buffer' organisations which can stand legally between people, governments and developers, with responsibility to all stakeholders and with the expertise to give advice as required. An innovative development approach like that proposed above for Papua New Guinea gives serious attention to landowner participation. Aboriginal organisations in Australia, particularly the Land Councils in the Northern Territory and Trust Fund organisations provide some interesting models.

Although the contrast between the operation of such organisations in an industrialised country like Australia and a country with limited industrialisation like Papua New Guinea is marked, many of the principles remain the same. The developers and the government should transmit significant amounts of the profits from resource exploitation not only directly to the affected landowners, but also to organisations designed to assist those landowners to make informed decisions about their future.

References

Australia, House of Representatives Standing Committee on Aboriginal Affairs, 1987. *Return to Country: the Aboriginal Homelands movement in Australia*, Final Report, Australian Government Publishing Service, Canberra.

Baines, K., 1989. 'Traditional resource management in the Melanesian South Pacific: a development dilemma', in F. Berkes (ed.), *Common Property Resources: ecology and community-based sustainable development*, Belhaven Press, London:273–95.

Banks, G., 1996. 'Compensation for mining: benefit or time-bomb? The Porgera gold mine', in R. Howitt, J. Connell and P. Hirsch (eds), *Resources, Nations and Indigenous Peoples: case studies from Australasia, Melanesia and southeast Asia*, Oxford University Press, Melbourne.

Berkes, F. and Farvar, M.T., 1989. 'Introduction and Overview,' in F. Berkes (ed.), *Common Property Resources*, Belhaven Press, London.

Bromley, D., 1991. *Environment and Economy: property rights and public policy*, Blackwell, Cambridge, Mass.

Brookfield, H. and Brown, P., 1967. *Struggle for Land*, Oxford University Press, Melbourne.

Brown, P., 1978. *Highland Peoples of Papua New Guinea*, Cambridge University Press, Cambridge.

Cane, S. and Stanley, O., 1985. *Land Use and Resources in Desert Homelands*, North Australia Research Unit, Australian National University, Darwin.

Clarke, B., Crocombe, R., Lakau, A., Larmour, P., and Macintyre, M., 1995. *Customary Land Tenure Systems in PNG*, AusAID, Canberra.

Davies, S.J. and Young, E., 1995. 'Sustainability, development and rural Aboriginal communities', *Australian Geographer* 26(2):150–155.

——, 1996. 'Taking centre stage: Aboriginal strategies for redressing marginalisation', in R. Howitt, J. Connell and P. Hirsch, (eds), *Resources, Nations and Indigenous Peoples: case studies from Australasia, Asia and the southwest Pacific*, Oxford University Press, Melbourne.

Davis, S. and Prescott, J.R.V., 1992. *Aboriginal Frontiers and Boundaries in Australia*, Melbourne University Press, Melbourne.

Denoon, D., Ballard, C., Banks, G. and Hancock., P, (eds), 1995. *Mining and Mineral Resource Policy Issues in Asia-Pacific: prospects for the 21st century*, proceedings of the conference at the Australian National University, 1–3 November 1995, Division of Pacific and Asian

Gibbs, C.J.N. and Bromley, D., 1989. 'Institutional Arrangements for Management of Rural Resources: common property regimes', in F. Berkes (ed.), *Common Property Resource*, Belhaven Press, London.

Grima, A.P.L. and Berkes, F., 1989. 'Natural resources: access, rights-to-use and management', in *Common Property Resources*, F. Berkes, (ed.), Belhaven Press, London.

Hardin, G., 1968. 'The Tragedy of the Commons', *Science* 162:1243–8.

Hayne, P. (ed.), 1994. *The Economic Way of Thinking*, Macmillan, New York.

Heathcote, R.L. and Mabbutt, J.A. (eds), 1988. *Land, Water and People: geographical essays in Australian resource management*, Allen and Unwin, Sydney.

Hiatt, L. (ed.), 1984. *Aboriginal Landowners*, Oceania Monograph 27, University of Sydney, Sydney.

Holzknecht, H.A., 1995. 'Forest Management and Planning Project,' Working Papers Produced as part of the Landowner Involvement Component 1993 to 1995, PNG Forest Authority, World Bank and Groome Poyry Ltd.

Howitt, R., Connell, J. and Hirsch, P. (eds), 1996. *Resources, Nations and Indigenous Peoples: case studies from Australasia, Melanesia and southeast Asia*, Oxford University Press, Melbourne.

Kalit, K., 1996. A sustainable development approach for Papua New Guinea: the landowner support imperative, National Centre for Development Studies, The Australian National University, unpublished.

Mahney, T., Gambold, N., Walsh, F. and Winstanley, D., 1996. 'Looking at country two ways—land resource assessment on Aboriginal lands in Central Australia', *Australian Collaborative Land Evaluation Program Bulletin* 1:2–5.

Northern Territory Department of Primary Production, 1983. *Utopia Land Resources, their Condition, Utilization and Management*, Department of Primary Production, Alice Springs.

Ostrom, E., 1990. *Governing the Commons*, Cambridge University Press, Cambridge.

Papua New Guinea, 1991. *Forestry Act 1991*, Forest Authority, Hohola.

Peterson, N., (ed.), 1976. *Tribes and Boundaries in Australia*, Australian Institute of Aboriginal Studies, Canberra.
History, Research School of Pacific and Asian Studies, The Australian National University, Canberra.
206 | The governance of common property in the Pacific region

Power, A.P., 1995. 'Mining and petroleum development under customary land tenure: the Papua New Guinea experience', in Donald Denoon, Chris Ballard, Glenn Banks and Peter Hancock (eds), *Mining and Mineral Resource Policy Issues in Asia-Pacific: prospects for the 21st century*, proceedings of the conference at the Australian National University, 1–3 November 1995, Division of Pacific and Asian History, Research School of Pacific and Asian Studies, The Australian National University, Canberra.

Redclift, M., and Saga, C., (eds), 1994. *Strategies for Sustainable Development: local agendas for the southern hemisphere*, John Wiley and Sons, Chichester, New York, Brisbane, Toronto, Singapore.

Rose, B., 1995. *Land management Issues: attitudes and perceptions amongst Aboriginal people in central Australia*, Central Land Council, Alice Springs.

Samana, U., 1988. *Papua New Guinea: which way?*, Arena Publications Association, Victoria.

Sullivan, P., 1995. *Beyond native title: multiple use agreements and Aboriginal governance in the Kimberley*, Discussion paper 89/1995, Centre for Aboriginal Economic Policy Research, The Australian National University, Canberra.

Sutton, P., 1995. *Country: Aboriginal boundaries and land ownership in Australia*, Aboriginal History Monograph 3, The Australian National University, Canberra.

Taylor, J., 1992. 'Geographic location and Aboriginal economic status: a census-based analysis of outstations in the Northern Territory', *Australian Geographical Studies* 30 (2):163–84.

Tindale, N., 1974. *Aboriginal Tribes of Australia: their terrain, environmental controls, distribution, limits and proper names*, University of California Press, Berkeley.

UNDP, 1994a. *Review of the National Forest and Conservation Action Program (NFCAP)*, Port Moresby.

——, 1994b. *Yumi Wankain: report of the United Nations joint inter-agency mission to Papua New Guinea on sustainable development*, Port Moresby.

World Bank, 1989. *Staff Appraisal Report: Papua New Guinea land mobilization project*, World Bank, Washington DC.

——, 1993. *Papua New Guinea, Jobs, Economic Growth and International Competitiveness*, Agriculture Operations Division, World Bank, Washington DC.

———, no date. Landowner Resources Development Agency, unpublished.

Young, E., 1987. 'Resettlement and Caring for Country', *Aboriginal History* 11:156–70.

———, 1988a. 'Land use and Resources: a black and white dichotomy', in R.L. Heathcote and J.A. Mabbutt (eds), *Land, Water and People: geographical essays in Australian resource management*, Allen and Unwin, Sydney.

———, 1988b. *Aboriginal Cattle Stations in the East Kimberley: communities or enterprises?*, EKIAP Working Paper 21, CRES, The Australian National University, Canberra.

———, 1992a. 'Aboriginal land rights in Australia: expectations, achievements and implications', *Applied Geography* 12:146–61.

———, 1992b. 'Hunter-gatherer concepts of land and its ownership', in K. Anderson and F. Gale (eds), *Inventing Places*, Longmans, Melbourne.

———, 1995. *Third World in the First: development and indigenous peoples*, Routledge, London.

Young, E. and Doohan, K., 1989. *Mobility for Survival: a process analysis of Aboriginal population movement in central Australia*, North Australia Research Unit, Darwin, and The Australian National University, Canberra.

Young, E. and Ross, H., 1994. 'Using the Aboriginal rangelands: 'insider' and 'outsider' perceptions', *The Rangeland Journal* 16(2): 184–97.

Author index

A

Acheson, J.M. 3, 16, 17, 30, 31,
  141, 161, 162
Adams, T. 161
Aleck, Jonathan 63
Allen, Bryant 60, 62
Anderson, E. 9, 16
Aqorau, Transform 159
Ashenfelter, O. 76, 88
Atwood, D. 7, 16

B

Baines, K. 184, 198, 204
Ballard, Brigid 61
Ballard, C. 10, 14, 47, 48, 50, 53,
  60, 62
Banks, G. 62, 204
Barro, R.J. 77, 88
Bates, R.H. 6, 16, 46
Bennett, J. 158, 161
Bergin, Anthony 174, 175, 180

Berkes, F. 127, 128, 140, 141, 186,
  204, 205
Binswanger, H.P. 42, 45
Blackstone, W. 124, 126
Boer, B. 151, 161
Bond, G.C. 65
Boserup, E. 38, 39, 46
Bowman, D. 129, 141
Bradley, J. 138
Bromley, D.W. 1,
  2, 8, 13, 16, 167, 168, 180,
  185, 186, 188, 204, 205
Brooke, L.F. 110, 116, 120
Brookfield, H. 188, 204
Brown, P. 188, 204, 205
Buege, Douglas J. 62

C

Cane, S. 191, 205
Carrier, J.G. 21, 31, 152, 161
Cavill, James 61
Cernea, M. 1, 8, 16

Chand, S. 10, 13, 14, 44, 46, 53, 87
Chapagain, D. 16
Chapeskie, A. 112, 120
Chatterton, P. 28, 31
Chrétien, J. 106, 120
Church, M. 161, 162
Clanchy, John 61
Clarke, B. 59, 186, 205
Clarke, William C. 62
Clunies Ross, A. 46
Coase, R. 6, 16
Cobb, P. 122
Connell, John 64, 205
Cook, A. 161
Cooter, Robert 58, 61, 62
Cox, Lindsay 102
Crawford, J. 149, 161
Crocombe, R.G. 8, 16, 19, 25,
    31, 39, 45, 46, 71, 73,
    88, 152, 156, 161, 163, 205
Cumberland, K. B. 32

D

Dalzell, P. 153, 161
Davies, S.J. 194, 205
Davis, S. 188, 205
Deaton, A.S. 80, 88
Deininger, K. 45
Demsetz, H. 4, 16
Denoon, Donald 62
Diamond, Stanley 132, 134, 141
Donigi, Peter 55, 62
Doohan, K. 192, 207
Dorney, S. 70, 71
Doulman, D.J. 155, 161,
    170, 172, 178, 180
Dove, J. 49, 62
Duncan, Rod 11, 13, 14, 73
Duncan, Ron 10, 11, 14, 53,
    73, 85, 88, 149, 161, 169, 180
Durkheim, Emile 133, 136
Dwyer, Peter D. 59, 62

E

Elkin, A. 128, 141
Elvin, J.M. 28, 31
Eythorsson, E. 127, 141

F

Farvar, M.T. 127, 128, 186, 141,
    204
Feder, G. 45
Feeny, D. 3, 16, 39, 41, 46, 141
Filer, Colin 54, 55, 61, 62, 63
Fingleton, Jim 57, 63
Fortier, F. 110, 121
Fox, J.W. 32
France, P. 24, 31
Frazer, J. 131, 132, 141
Freud, S. 131, 132, 141
Fugmann, Gernot 64

G

Galois, R.M. 119, 122
Gambold, N. 205
Gardiner, Wira 102
Garnaut, Ross 45, 46, 87
Gerritsen, Rolf 54, 55, 63
Gibbs, C.J.N. 188, 205
Gillen, F. 134, 143
Gillett, R. 163
Gilliam, Angela 65
Gordon, D.B. 77, 88
Goulet, D. 161, 162
Grima, A.P.L. 186, 205
Gulugu, Hebe 51
Gumbert, M. 130, 141
Gupta, D. 75, 80, 87, 88

H

Haley, Nicole 56
Hamidan-Rad, P. 46
Hancock, Peter 62
Hanna, S. 3, 16

McEvoy, A. 3, 16
McGavin, P.A. 83, 85, 86, 88
Merlan, Francesca 61, 64
Mfodwo, K. 149, 155, 163
Minchin, E. 32
Miriung, Theodore 49, 61, 62
Moaina, R. 46
Moore, D. 110, 121
Mulina, R. 46
Mulvaney, D. 130, 142
Munro, William A. 48, 49, 64

N

Narokobi, Bernard 50, 53, 61, 64
Nehapi, Timothy 161
Nelson, Hank 53, 64
Newsome, A. 142
North, D. 4, 17
Notzke, C. 110, 120

O

Oh, Janaline 13, 14, 15, 61, 165
O'Meara, J.T. 24, 26, 32
Ortner, Sherry 60, 64
Osherenko, G. 110, 121
Ostrom, E. 2, 3, 5, 8,
    9, 16, 17, 186, 188, 206
Owen, A.D. 155, 162, 166, 171,
    181

P

Paine, Thomas 123
Penn, A. 110, 116, 121
Petelo, A. 153, 163
Peterson, N. 130, 138, 142, 187, 206
Pinkerton, E.W. 110, 121
Pitchford, R. 87, 88
Polier, Nicole 53, 64, 161
Power, A.P. 189, 206
Powles, C.G. 26, 32
Prasad, B. 41, 45, 46

Prescott, J.R.V. 188, 205
Proulx, E. Annie 47, 64
Pulea, M. 156, 163

R

Radcliffe-Brown 133
Ramos, Alcida 60, 65
Rannells, Jackson 63
Redclift, M. 200, 206
Renwick, William 102
Reynolds, Henry 12, 15, 123
Ricoeur, Paul 123, 126
Rodman, M. 26, 29, 32
Rose, Deborah B. 12, 127,
    130, 138, 140, 141, 142, 196,
    206
Ross, H. 195, 207
Rothwell, D. 149, 161
Rowse, T. 137, 142
Rumsey, Alan 61, 64

S

Sack, P. G. 31, 32, 54, 62, 65, 68, 72
Saga, C. 200, 206
Samana, Utula 50, 65, 203, 206
Scheffler, H. 152, 163
Shiva, V. 128, 143
Simpson, Gary 61, 65
Simpson, S.R. 17
Singleton, Sara 5, 17
Slattery, B. 119, 121
Spafford, G. 122
Spencer, B. 134, 143
Standish, Bill 53, 65
Stanley, O. 191, 205
Stanner, W. 131, 135, 136, 143
Staples, W.L. 110, 111, 121
Strathern, Andrew 53, 65
Strehlow, T.G.H. 135, 136, 137,
    139, 143
South, R. 161, 162

Sullivan, P. 194, 206
Sutherland, W.M. 41, 46
Sutton, P. 187, 189, 206

T

Tacconi, L. 158, 159, 163
Taylor, J. 5, 191, 206
Taylor, Michael 5, 17
Temu, Ila 46, 87, 149, 161, 169, 180
Tetiarahi, G. 25, 32
Tindale, N. 187, 206
Tisdell, C. 41, 45, 46
Togolo, Mel 49, 61, 62
Tough, F.J. 119, 122
Trebilcock, M. 72
Trosper, R. 4, 5, 17
Tsamenyi, B.M. 149, 155, 163, 168, 173, 181
Tuquiri, S. 161, 162
Turner, J. 156, 160, 164
Turner, Lulu 63

U

Usher, P.J., 11, 15, 103, 107, 110, 112, 119, 121, 122

V

Vincelli, M. 116, 122
Voigt, E. 133, 142
Volavola, Ratu M. 41, 46
Vousden, Neil 45

W

Wade, R. 9, 17
Walsh, F. 205
Ward, Alan 25, 32, 56, 65
Ward, R.G. 10, 13, 14, 15, 17, 19, 24, 25, 28, 29, 31, 32,
Warner, Lloyd 135, 143
Weber, Max 10

Weiner, James F. 60, 65
White, Hayden 132, 143
Wilkinson, P.F. 116, 122
Williams, N. 128, 143
Williamson, O. 4, 17
Wills, I. 16
Winstanley, D. 205
Wolf, Eric 52, 65
Wood, Andrew W. 60, 65
Worsley, P. 136, 143

Y

Young, Elspeth 13, 14, 15, 57, 183, 187, 191, 192, 194, 195, 205, 207
Young, R. 143

www.ingramcontent.com/pod-product-compliance
Lightning Source LLC
Chambersburg PA
CBHW040152270326
41927CB00034B/3419